CHEMICAL SOLDIERS

CHEMICAL SOLDIERS

British Gas Warfare
in World War I

Donald Richter

 UNIVERSITY PRESS OF KANSAS

© 1992 by the University Press of Kansas

Published by the University Press of Kansas (Lawrence, Kansas 66049), which was organized by the Kansas Board of Regents and is operated and funded by Emporia State University, Fort Hays State University, Kansas State University, Pittsburg State University, the University of Kansas, and Wichita State University

Library of Congress Cataloging-in-Publication Data

Richter, Donald C., 1934–
    Chemical soldiers : British gas warfare in World War I / Donald
    Richter.
      p.   cm. — (Modern war studies)
    Includes bibliographical references and index.
    ISBN 0-7006-0544-4 (hardcover)
    1. World War, 1914–1918—Chemical warfare. 2. Gases, Asphyxiating
and poisonous—Great Britain—War use—History—20th century.
3. Great Britain. Army. Royal Engineers. Special Brigade—
History. 4. World War, 1914–1918—Regimental histories—Great
Britain. I. Title. II. Series.
    UG447.R498 1992
    358′.344′0941—dc20   92-12329

British Library Cataloguing in Publication Data is available.

Printed in the United States of America
10 9 8 7 6 5 4 3 2 1

The paper used in this publication meets the minimum requirements of the American National Standard for Permanence of Paper for Printed Library Materials Z39.48-1984.

Dedicated to Janie
my best friend
who happens also to be my wife

Contents

Illustrations, Maps, and Tables

MAPS

TABLES

Acknowledgments

I would like to thank the following people for various permissions and assistance in research for this work: Sir Christopher Hartley for permission to examine the Hartley Papers at Churchill College, Cambridge; Maj. J. T. Hancock and his staff for assistance at the Royal Engineers Library; in particular Simon Jones at the Royal Engineers Museum for helpfulness beyond the call of duty; the very capable and helpful staffs at the Public Record Office at Kew, the Imperial War Museum in Lambeth, the National Army Museum in Chelsea, and the Churchill College Archives in Cambridge. Thanks also to Patricia Methven and Kate O'Brien for their professional counsel at the Liddell Hart Centre for Military Archives at King's College London. I would like to single out for particular thanks Peter and Louise Liddle for their kindness and hospitality as well as for access to the rich archives of the Liddle Collection (formerly Personal Experience Archives) at Leeds University, and Nick Gander for capable help in portering heavy boxes to and from the vaults to the reading room and for other research services. I wish to thank Professors Tim Travers at the University of Calgary and David Woodward at Marshall University for responding to particular queries and Col. Rodney Cron for providing valuable advice and suggestions at a preliminary stage in the preparation of the manuscript.

At my own Ohio University, the Department of History, the College of Arts and Sciences, and the Institute for Research and Graduate Studies all provided extremely welcome financial assistance for travel expenses. E. A. Slates prepared the maps in our Graphics Department and Professor Marvin Fletcher provided unflinching software and hardware computer assistance with characteristic forbearance. My wife, Janie, collaborated with me at every stage in the project, from deciphering soldiers' diaries in the Imperial War Museum to bravely criticizing each successive draft of the manuscript. She deserves not only thanks but also recognition as a full partner in every sense of the word.

Introduction

Poison gas. The very thought alarms. The words evoke horror, revulsion, panic. The stereotypical perception of World War I chemical warfare visualizes a thick greenish cloud gliding relentlessly across the trenches. Sinister and deadly, it seeks out ditches and shell holes with hideous and diabolical thoroughness. It wreaks havoc on every living thing in its path. The ultimate destroyer of individuality, more indiscriminate than a machine gun, it renders bravery superfluous, subjecting its victims to the most excruciating agonies of suffocation.

Perpetuated over the years by inflammatory harangues of pacifists, novelists, and misinformed sentimentalists and distorted by legend and sensationalism, the gas myth has obfuscated more than enlightened. Half-truths continue to abound, permeated with emotionally charged sophistries and supported by sensationalizing photographs of selected victims. A curious "coexistence" of fact and legend lingers. Like so many myths, the reality was quite different.

Had World War I gas warfare been even remotely as effective and devastating as the myth suggests, the war might well have ended with its first use. In reality, gas warfare was anything but reliable or effective, except in the most unusual circumstances, and a defensive capability developed very rapidly. Proponents and detractors both tended to overstate gas casualties. Gas was never decisive. This fact, however, did not lessen the agonies of those soldiers victimized by lethal doses or the panic of those initial companies caught unprepared by the German chlorine cloud of 22 April 1915.

Contemporary news reports denounced the Germans' first use of gas as an atrocity. To the British especially, poison gas seemed less chivalrous, less sporting, less gentlemanly than any other weapon in history and adjectives like "dastardly" and "heinous" found new currency. But it did not take long for the Allies to retaliate in kind. "Paying the Hun back in his own coin" was the metaphor one officer used.[1] Moral reservations and ethical compunctions evaporated speedily because the

I

Germans "had done it first." "It is a vile method of warfare," wrote one soldier, "but the Bosches have brought it on themselves."[2]

The task of British "retaliation" fell to a special unit, hastily recruited and trained in the weeks following Second Ypres, a unit composed at first largely of chemists. In the beginning its members were grouped in only two Special Companies, which were expanded to four for the Battle of Loos. What would ultimately be called the Special Brigade eventually reached a strength of just under 6,000. The Special Companies carried out the first British cloud gas attack at Loos in September 1915, then went on to master capability in flame-throwers, smoke screens, gas projectors, and massed train discharges, adapting both to static trench warfare and the mobile battlefield that dominated the last eight months of the war. Except for the gas shells lobbed by the artillery, it was this relatively small unit that managed the entire spectrum of British gas retaliation. Unceremoniously disbanded in 1919, the country subsequently acknowledged as little as possible about the unit's activities.

This is the story of that unique unit—a story largely forgotten, its clandestine details and operations hidden from view in the darkened corridors of closed archives. In this book, for the first time, based on the soldiers' own diaries, letters, and memoirs, the lot of the gas soldier comes to life. The soldiers' own phrases re-create their wartime toil, their exigencies and dangers, their sometimes horrifying experiences in the bumbling use of this new killer weapon. The tale resounds with the richness of authentic human drama while detailing the humble scenes of the troops involved.

Like any other military weapon, poison gas was admittedly not kind to its victims. Yet no matter how repugnant their weapon, the soldiers slogging through the trenches with gas cylinders differed not a whit from other members of the "poor bloody infantry." They shared the same variegated discomforts of the trenches, endured the same wretched food, heat and cold, mud and lice, boredom and danger. In common with all soldiers, gas troops nourished similar hopes of daily survival and eventual victory. They wrote the same letters to parents, wives, and sweethearts, complaining of the same military frustrations and hoping for the same early respite. Although no soldier remained entirely immune to occasional bouts of pondering the morality of war in general, the gas diaries betray no sense that the writers believed they were engaged in anything but a completely honorable contribution to the war effort.

The wartime personal diaries of chemical soldiers provide a rich vein of source material for life in the gas trenches. Although keeping a diary was forbidden for security reasons, the prohibition was rarely enforced, and there were few soldiers who did not keep some sort of personal diary. In many cases written within hours of traumatic events by soldiers still in the trenches and often by the light of a candle, the penciled scribblings exude a raw, honest authenticity that is both moving and compelling. Like the soldiers' personal letters, the field diaries are remarkably articulate and informative, redolent with earthy idioms, poignantly expressive in clarity and freshness. Many are rich in allusion, metaphor, and simile. Occasional passages border on eloquence. As source material for this book, I have endeavored as much as possible to avoid published memoirs in favor of these more authentic original letters and diaries.

Also instructive, but in a somewhat more detached way, are the voluminous official war diaries presently housed at the Public Record Office in Kew. They exist for company, battalion, and headquarters, but the value of descriptive information depends wholly on the personality of the adjutant writing the diary reports each evening. Some entries are bland and spartan, recording routine leaves, unit movements, casualties, honors, and visits by dignitaries. Others include charts, diagrams, and a lengthy and descriptive commentary, though never on as vernacular a level as the personal field diaries. The many reminiscences preserved in the volumes of the Special Brigade's newsletters amplify yet more fully the personal story of the unit's members. Although sometimes tinged by fading memory and glossed by nostalgia, the recollections of aging veterans retain a persuasively genuine sense of pride and authenticity. In one of the last of the brigade's newsletters, distributed in 1979, the secretary wrote, "It is not beyond the bounds of possibility that some researcher of the Great War will read this tribute to the Special Brigade."[3]

Only one "unit history" of the brigade has ever been published, *Gas! The Story of the Special Brigade* (1934). The author was its commander, Charles Howard Foulkes, and he was far too closely associated with the brigade to make the necessary critical judgments. His account is pervasively immodest, self-justifying, and self-serving, and the tone strongly reminiscent of Julius Caesar's Gallic memoirs. Of course, Foulkes was not a trained historian, and although writing with the admitted benefit of first-hand experience, he was not able to view the accomplishments of his brigade in an unbiased and objective light.[4] His most frequently quoted sources are sanguine official transcripts, selective captured enemy statements, and selected operational reports by officers. Foulkes scarcely ever mentions the individual soldier in his gas companies, focusing rather on the larger strategic and organizational aspects of the gas operation. His added responsibilities as head of the defensive branch in

1917 further removed him from the day-to-day operations of the Special Companies in the field.

The wider subject of chemical weapons has generated an extraordinarily extensive literature, both popular and scholarly. Of the latter, a great number of first-hand accounts appeared shortly after the war,[5] and a spate of inferior books dotted the landscape after World War II, based overwhelmingly on published material and mostly recycling information and conclusions reached by earlier researchers. Most of the "surveys" utilized the World War I experience only for introductory or comparative purposes.[6] Since the gradual opening of official files beginning in the 1960s and 1970s (for example, the key Hartley Report was closed until 1976),[7] a number of first-rate specialized studies have appeared, based on a reexamination of the older documentary sources as well as newly available materials. Guy Hartcup's *War of Invention* (1988) contains a strong chapter on chemical weapons, and Edward M. Spiers's *Chemical Warfare* (1986) is both authoritative and comprehensive. Like most other similar books, however, these are comprehensive transnational surveys of gas warfare in its widest sense. *Gas Attack!* (1987) by William Moore, a popularized account lacking scholarly paraphernalia, narrows the focus somewhat. *The Poisonous Cloud* (1986) by L. F. Haber, son of Fritz Haber, is now the definitive study of the industrial, technical, and strategic aspects of World War I gas warfare and the first scholarly account to restrict itself to the Great War. Haber's exhaustive work, although thorough and scrupulously documented in its announced purposes, is similarly transnational and emphasizes policy rather than experience. None of the books focuses specifically on the British use of gas warfare, or on its human dimension. There has been no dedicated reexamination of the mission, structure, and experience of the Special Brigade since Foulkes's unsatisfactory account of 1934.

The terms "chemical warfare" and "gas warfare" are used interchangeably in this book because the chemists in the trenches themselves used the terms indistinguishably. The purist may consider chemical to be the more precise term because most of the "gases" used during World War I were actually pressurized liquids. Vaporization took place only at the instant of discharge when the poison hissed forth as a gas, for the most part clinging to the ground, and was carried on the wind.

In sympathy with John Keegan's appeal for a greater emphasis in Great War scholarship on the individual experiences and emotions of soldiers in battle, this book is about one small band of soldiers in a unique unit and seeks to present the truth of gas warfare as waged by the common British soldier in the Great War.[8] The present study is therefore intended to be more than simply a new unit history of the Special Brigade, as much as that alone is needed. I have tried to recapture also the personal everyday story of the men of that brigade, their humor and their tragedy, and tell as much of that story as possible in their own words.

I

The Germans Do It First

I shall never forget the sights I saw up by Ypres after the first gas attack. Men lying all along the side of the road between Poperinghe and Ypres, exhausted, gasping, frothing yellow mucus from their mouths, their faces blue and distressed. It was dreadful and so little could be done for them. One came away from seeing or treating them longing to be able to go straight away at the Germans and to throttle them, to pay them out in some sort of way for their devilishness. Better for a sudden death than this awful agony.[1]

During 1915 and again after the war German propagandists sought to muddy the waters regarding the initial use of gas by claiming first use by the Allies. They pointed to French employment of a primitive lachrymatory grenade in 1912 at Choisy-le-Roi, but that was a police not a wartime use and remained an isolated incident. After the war, Fritz Haber, the father of German chemical warfare, told of hearing reports in 1914 of British and French use of gas shells.[2] The French at that time did use an explosive charge, called Turpenite, that created a smell the German soldiers mistook for poison gas. Early in 1915 Haber visited the front to investigate alleged British use of gas shells, but he concluded that the peculiar odor resulted from the residual of high explosive shells or traces of picric acid from badly detonated shells. Although scientists on both sides conducted chemical experiments before and during the war, doubt no longer exists that it was German troops who first used the weapon in combat.[3]

The German decision to employ poison gas was the result of long deliberation. Although Haber, together with other prominent chemists, began investigations at the Kaiser Wilhelm Institute in Berlin at the very beginning of the war, it was not then a foregone conclusion that Germany would use gas weapons. Sir Harold Hartley, for a time the head of the British antigas organization during the war and a leading expert in the years following, concluded that the Germans had no defi-

6

nite plans to employ gas before the setback at the Marne in September 1914.[4]

The Hague treaties, to which Germany subscribed, posed the greatest diplomatic obstacle to a use of gas, though the prohibition was obscure. The first Hague treaty (1899) proscribed "the use of all projectiles the sole object of which is the diffusion of asphyxiating or deleterious gases," and the second (1907) added "poison or poisoned weapons" as well as weapons causing "unnecessary suffering." Although cloud gas may not have constituted a technical violation under the ambiguous wording of the treaties, the clear intent of the Hague conferees was to prohibit the kind of gas warfare that Germany initiated and with which the Allies reciprocated.

The Germans were naturally concerned about protection of their own troops, and there was as yet no substantive evidence that gas would be effective against the enemy. Erich von Falkenhayn, successor to Helmut von Moltke as chief of the German general staff, remained skeptical about gas in any form. His son won a wager, a case of champagne, by remaining unprotected in a cloud of dianisidine chlorosulphonate for several minutes.[5] But Falkenhayn, convinced that in the long run the war was lost without a decisive breakthrough on the Western Front, concluded that only new or different methods might achieve this. The chemists at the institute favored the surprise use of gas as "a bid to end the stalemate."[6] Still, there remained the understandable reluctance to provoke almost certain Allied retaliation in kind, a retaliation especially formidable because of prevailing winds favorable to the Allies. Haber, however, contended that the Allies would be unable to retaliate in time to prevent a German breakthrough.[7]

The initial experiments of Haber and his fellow scientists were frustrating and dangerous, and early tests both at the institute and in the field proved disappointing. At Neuve Chapelle on 27 October 1914, Haber's chemists fired several hundred ordinary 105-mm howitzer shells embedded with a tear gas, but the effect was negligible and the French never realized gas had been used.[8] In mid-December 1914, during experiments with cacodyl chloride at Dahlem, an explosion killed one of Haber's assistants, Dr. Otto Sackur. Haber's wife, also a scientist, pleaded desperately with her husband to abandon gas experiments, but to no avail. On the eve of his departure for further discharges on the Russian front, she committed suicide. At Bolimov, on 31 January 1915, Haber's troops fired shells filled with liquid benzyl bromide, a tear gas suggested by Hans Tappan, another chemist, but at the extremely cold temperatures the liquid failed to vaporize. Again the enemy remained unaware it had been the target of a chemical weapon.

The shortage of suitable shells and the limitations of tear gases led

Haber to suggest, instead, the release of chlorine in a gas cloud. During some preliminary trial releases at Hasselt on 2 April 1915, both Haber and Maj. Max Bauer, an experienced staff officer who headed the technical section at GHQ (general headquarters), tested the effects of the chlorine cloud by riding through it on horseback. Mildly gassed and hospitalized for a few days, they suffered no lingering effects. The test was considered successful.[9] Haber contended that gas incapacitated rather than killed, a view his personal experience seemed to substantiate.

To discharge the gas, Haber had formed a special gas unit called the 35th Pioneer Regiment, commanded by a Major von Zingler and including in its composition some leading chemists such as Otto Hahn, Wilhelm Westphal, Erwin Madelung, James Franck, and Gustav Hartz—the latter two, along with Haber himself, future Nobel Prize winners. Although not having much faith in the gas potential, the German high command, without enthusiasm, finally granted Haber a green light to stage a large gas operation on the Western Front. Haber issued his gas soldiers only minimal protection, cotton pads soaked in a solution of sodium thiosulfate and potassium bicarbonate, but no protection was offered the infantry. The whole operation exuded the air of an experiment rather than a serious attempt at breakthrough.[10]

By 11 April 1915, Haber's unit had dug in at Langemarck on the Ypres front to await a favorable wind. Not for another eleven days did the winds cooperate, and during this period the British, in particular, received ample indications of what the Germans were up to.[11] Although captured German prisoners furnished detailed descriptions to British officers of the pipes and cylinders in place in the front lines around Ypres, British intelligence remained skeptical, and no warning reached the men in the trenches. At 5:30 P.M. on 22 April, after waiting in the trenches the entire day for a favorable wind, the German chemists of the 35th Pioneer Regiment at last opened the valves of their thousands of cylinders. Gas hissed fiercely out of the nozzles and drifted westward in a thickening ominous cloud. The era of modern chemical warfare had begun.

For the French and British soldiers in the front-line trenches the appearance of the yellowish-green cloud was a complete surprise, and the effect was devastating. Directly in the path of the advancing cloud, many of the French colonial troops of the 45th (Algerian) Division panicked and fled pell-mell, joined shortly by many from the 87th, a Territorial division. There was no stopping them. "A lot of the fellows—at that time there were no gas masks—had sort of started to scoot away from the gas; in fact doing the very thing they shouldn't have because the gas was drifting with them and the result was that

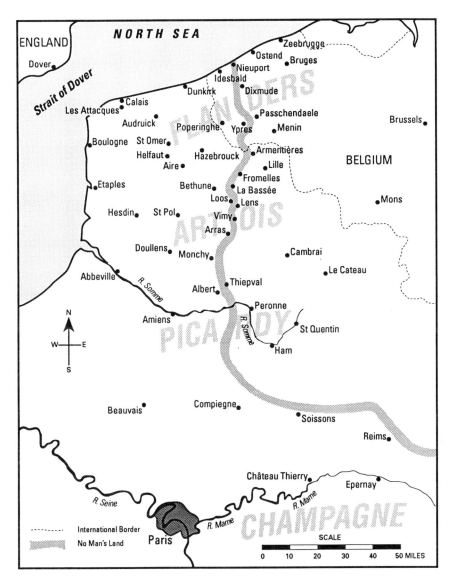

Map 1.1. The British section of the Western Front

you found them dead and lying all over the place." [12] Only truly heroic action on the part of neighboring troops, in particular the 1st Canadian Division, prevented a much wider rupture of the defensive position.[13] In any event, the German high command, not anticipating significant success, had laid no plans to exploit the advantage. The Allied line held.

The initial outrage felt by the British infantryman in the field at the time is illustrated by a soldier of the Dorsetshire regiment, one of the relieving units. "Clean killing is at least comprehensive but this murder by slow agony absolutely knocks me. The whole civilized world ought to rise up and exterminate those swine across the hill."[14] The reaction of the British high command, similarly scandalized but less immoderately expressed, was more purposeful. Sir John French wrote, "I strongly urge that immediate steps be taken to supply similar means of most effective kind," and Lord Kitchener replied, "Before we . . . fall to the level of the degraded Germans, I must submit the matter to the Government."[15] Defense, however, demanded priority, and here there was no delay whatever. Kitchener turned first to the academic community for help both in identifying the German gas and in suggesting an appropriate defensive response. The three research chemists most closely associated with this undertaking in the opening stages were J. S. Haldane of Oxford and H. B. Baker and Jocelyn Thorpe of the Imperial College of Science and Technology in South Kensington. Haldane and Baker rushed to France and quickly corroborated preliminary reports that the gas in question was indeed chlorine. Baker and Thorpe set up a chemical lab at Imperial College. Thorpe was to become one of the leading experts on the offensive use of gas, with Baker on the defensive side. Thorpe gave up all outside employment for the duration of the war, and neither he nor Baker accepted remuneration for their gas research. The British Academy of Sciences shortly offered its services, the Royal Society established a Chemical Defence Committee, and from that time on, the government enjoyed ample expert advice.

The highest priority was an immediate stopgap trench remedy more palatable than the improvised advice of soldier chemists to "piss on your handkerchiefs and tie them over your faces."[16] The initial suggestions of Haldane and Baker were not much better: use "any loose fabric such as a sock, sandbag, woolen scarf . . . soaked in urine, wrung out, sufficient to allow free breathing through it, and tied tightly over the nose and mouth." Haldane also suggested "a sock half-filled with loose earth well broken up and tied over the nose and mouth" and later in May another easily improvised remedy—socks soaked in bicarbonate of soda.[17]

Kitchener simultaneously appealed through the press for homemade

First respirator of cotton waste, 1915. (Courtesy of Royal Engineers Museum)

respirator pads of the most simplified design. The response was both immediate and overwhelming. A plea in the *Daily Mail* of 28 April 1915 resulted in 30,000 cotton wool pads in the first thirty-six hours and within a matter of days, the Red Cross and the Royal Army Medical Corps had distributed these homemade mask-pads to virtually every soldier in France. An infantry sergeant later described them as ''simply pieces of curtaining—you know, the ordinary curtain—which were wrapped round some cotton wool and then we could tie them on the back of our heads, and you had to keep that cotton wool moist."[18] Chemically untreated and apt to dry out too rapidly, these hastily made masks proved of no use whatever and had to be recalled. Another home-made variety came to be called the veil respirator, described by James Davidson Pratt as "a woman's veil filled with cotton waste impreg-nated with hyposulphate." The hyposulphate absorbed chlorine, but again the benefit was negligible if the cotton waste dried out, which it quickly did. Pratt concluded that the veil respirators were "about as much use as a sick headache."[19] In the trenches soldiers desperately sought improvised protection of any sort. An artillery captain in early May was using a ladies' sanitary towel soaked in soda—"*really* the best thing."[20]

An infantryman in the London Rifle Brigade, H. G. R. Williams, re-called his first gas attack at Ypres in May 1915:

We had recently received an issue of make-shift "anti-gas respira-tors" consisting of small pieces of cloth—rather like tailor's pat-terns of Gents' Suitings, with tapes sewn on. These were to be tied on, so as to cover the wearer's mouth and nostrils. Presumably they had been treated in some way, as the instructions were that they must be moistened with water, or failing that, they must be urinated upon, either by oneself or by someone else! Soon we were to have an opportunity of testing these respirators. This opportu-nity came on May 2. We noticed clouds of a greenish-yellow vapour rolling towards us from the enemy trenches. Hastily we "moist-ened" and donned the respirators. Not wishing to use the precious water in my bottle, I used the alternative advised, which, luckily, I was able to provide for myself![21]

Repeated alerts might tax the soldier's physiological system, as the comical account of another infantryman illustrates:

When the alert went off you had to urinate on the cotton waste, tear pieces off to plug your nostrils, shove the rest in your mouth and tie the lot on with the strip of lace curtain. Everyone obliged, but the gas was away to our left and we had the all-clear. However, about 15 minutes later the alert went again and as the lads had made such a good effort in the first instance nothing was forthcom-ing at such short notice and it was really funny to see us all making desperate efforts.[22]

Training and discipline to curb the natural urge to flee proved as es-sential as the improvements in protective masks.

It has been clearly proved that men who remain in their trenches during gas attacks do not suffer so severely as men who leave them. Should gas appear men will remain quiet, but not lie down—the least movement the less the men will suffer. It has been decided by the G.O.C. that all men who leave their trenches during gas attacks will be tried by Field General Court Martial.[23]

Within the month, several men of this regiment faced court martial for violation of the directive. Though the German gas discharges continued intermittently through May as winds permitted, they proved increasingly less incapacitating as Allied discipline and improved masks began to provide genuine protection.[24]

The next order of priority in the new gas warfare involved recruiting a cadre of chemists to advise field units concerning chemical defense. For its initial group, the War Office turned to the universities for recommendations of chemistry students and graduates. The rector of Imperial College and director-general of the Royal Army Medical Corps, Sir Alfred Keogh, selected the first group of twenty-one graduates in chemistry, all already serving in the military and ranking from captain to private. "The Original Special Service Party" list included among the "other ranks" the prolific diarists Richard C. Gale and Donald Grantham. Following a rudimentary orientation at Chatham, headquarters of the Royal Engineers located between Rochester and Gillingham about twenty-three miles east of London on the south side of the Thames, this small party of chemists left Waterloo Station for Southampton and the first leg of their journey to the Continent. Told very little at this point about the mission, Gale wrote that "we all felt that we were on the eve of great events, no one having any idea of our work or ultimate destination." Steaming out of Southampton in the 3:30 A.M. darkness of 14 May on the SS *Normania*, Gale quite prophetically described the group as "a little band of pioneers, who were destined to be the nucleus of a new unit in the British Army, and to put our knowledge of science to strange uses."[25]

On arrival in France, the small band joined in the effort already under way to identify chemicals other than chlorine that the Germans might be using.[26] Professors W. Watson and B. Mouat Jones provided lectures and demonstrations on the effects of gas at the hastily organized central laboratory at GHQ. The chemists-turned-soldiers also tested primitive gas protection devices. In one demonstration they tested respirators by passing through a chamber containing 0.05 percent chlorine. "We were at first rather skeptical as to their efficiency, but the test proved this to us and gave us a great deal of confidence."[27] They also familiarized themselves with the new Vermorel sprayers, similar to insect sprayers, which contained a solution of thio to absorb chlorine. Worn on the back like a knapsack, the sprayer proved capable of decontaminating dugouts and trenches in a remarkably short time.

In late May what had come to be designated the Special Service Party split up into bands of itinerant lecturers, joining others already so engaged as defensive gas advisors to the British units in the field.[28] Grantham thought little of the attempt to indoctrinate through academic "Schools of Chemistry."[29] "It is no use trying to ram chemistry down the throat of the average man, he merely goes away wondering 'what the _____ that _____ officer was _____ well talking about.' "[30] Actual hands-on demonstrations of sprayers and respirators proved far more useful. Primitive demonstrations of the lethal effects of certain gases sometimes failed abysmally: "The 'top brass' party was 5 generals and 15 other officers. Sheep were tied in trenches and treated to SO_2 and cayenne. The same evening the sheep were grazing peacefully outside my tent, with an occasional cough, but eating vigorously. The officers did not think much of our gas bombs."[31] Another of the early gas lecturers, Lt. Col. L. J. Barley of the Scottish Cameronians, "got gassed nearly every day" while giving demonstrations.[32]

The chemists of the Special Service Party constituted as yet no independent unit of any kind but served whatever infantry unit to which they were attached, at times being called upon for routine engineering jobs at the front such as digging trenches or carrying timber. Grantham, tagged by some "the new stink-bomb lance corporal," spent a great deal of time hiking, bird-watching, and catching flies and mice for a pet mole.[33] The Special Service Party constituted only the vanguard of what was to become the Special Companies and, later, the Special Brigade. The immediate defensive organization thus set in motion, it was time to organize retaliation.

2
The Decision to Retaliate

Science of the ages, the highest arts of man,
Degraded and prostituted, that Might should take the van,
Whilst Empire, Justice, Freedom slumbered.
Then chemist, student, artisan answered Duty's call;
Our arms, our arts, our poison fumes
Gained Liberty for all.[1]

In Britain the father of modern chemical warfare was Lord Thomas Cochrane, later tenth earl of Dundonald (1775–1860). A capable but somewhat unpredictable young naval officer during the Napoleonic Wars, he worked out a chemical offensive involving sulfur and presented it to the Prince Regent. After perfunctory study a scientific committee rejected "Arcanum," and the "secret plan" was filed away, its existence known only to a select few. Dismissed from the navy for reasons having nothing to do with his gas suggestions, the indomitable Cochrane became a free-lance admiral for freedom, hiring himself out to Greece and several South American independence movements. After considerable foreign success, Cochrane rejoined the British Navy, gained the rank of admiral, and from time to time urged the adoption of his secret plan to all who would listen. In the late 1840s, Michael Faraday studied Cochrane's proposal but concluded that the wind problem was insurmountable, and authorities again pigeon-holed the secret plan. By the 1850s, Cochrane, now Lord Dundonald and still enterprising, had become something of an eccentric. During the Crimean War, he urged on the Cabinet yet another chemical strategy: to burn 400 to 500 tons of sulfur over 2,000 tons of coke to guarantee the reduction of Kronstadt and Sevastopol within four hours. Palmerston and Panmure (the secretary of state for war) lent tentative approval, but the war ended before Dundonald's plan could be implemented.[2] As for the tenth earl, his body lies under the central aisle of Westminster Abbey, near the very center of the nave in front of the high altar, only a few feet from Livingstone. Part of the large engraved and silvered plaque reads:

Admiral of the Fleet
who by the confidence which
His genius, his science and extraordinary daring inspired
by his heroic exertions in the cause of freedom
and his splendid services alike to his own country,
Greece, Brazil, Chile, and Peru
achieved a name illustrious throughout the world
for courage patriotism and chivalry.

No doubt few of the abbey's visitors realize that the man so honored and laudably described was the first serious British proponent of chemical warfare.

But Dundonald was not the only chemical warfare enthusiast. Both before and after the Hague pronouncements a variety of Britain's most renowned scientists continued the search for a militarily effective yet morally acceptable chemical weapon, and the outbreak of the war naturally accelerated these efforts.[3] Col. Lucius Jackson, a Royal Engineer officer, at the time attached to the War Office in the Department of Fortifications and Works, played a central role, and he later figured prominently as head of the Trench Warfare Department of the Ministry of Munitions. Experiments were carried out at South Kensington, as in France, on a variety of chemical substances. In the search for a gas that was incapacitating and disagreeable, yet not "deleterious," the best that the South Kensington chemists came up with was an eye irritant, a lachrymator called ethyl-iodoacetate, subsequently called SK (for South Kensington) and first demonstrated for representatives of the War Office in January 1915. Following tests at Chatham, the Royal Engineers placed orders for production of the tear gas with Cassel Cyanide Works at Glasgow.

Early in 1915, the twelfth earl of Dundonald, remembering his ancestor's secret plan, brought "Arcanum" to the attention of Winston Churchill, who at that time rejected it because "we were confined to a limited sphere of International Law till Germany forced us to take reprisals in the matter of poisonous gas."[4] Despite numerous claims that gas would be a humane method of warfare, a protector of civilization, a means of shortening wars, or merely an anesthetic, the Government decided against any first use of gas because such use would be seen as violating the spirit if not the letter of the Hague treaties.[5] Moreover, if not technically outlawed, gas was felt to be downright unsporting.

The German gas attack of 22 April 1915 removed all such qualms at a stroke. Not to retaliate would be "suicidal." The unprecedented act demanded retaliation, the term the British invariably employed in reference to their own use of what they had characterized as a dastardly and uncivilized weapon. The term effectively conveyed the notion that the noble and fair-minded British people would never have countenanced resort to such a diabolical weapon except in response to enemy first use. Once having made the decision to employ gas, however, the British, and the French, for that matter, as well as the Americans far later, dedicated themselves quite enthusiastically to the challenge of gas warfare. Maurice Hankey, secretary to the Committee of Imperial Defence, wrote that "we ought to beat them at their own game" because prevailing winds favored the Allied positions.[6] For a full week after 22 April, the newspapers printed nothing of the gas attack, but when the story broke, the press decried the German action in the most florid terms.[7] The *Times* charged Germany with "deliberate resort to this atrocious method of warfare," a "diabolical contrivance," this "enormity," etc.[8] Public outrage as well as military necessity demanded quick retaliation. Actual military deployment, of course, had to await official political sanction, and Herbert Asquith's Cabinet hesitated. The natural impulse of most citizens was to reject British use of what was widely thought to be a barbarous and unnecessarily cruel weapon, and the Hague prohibition made no distinction between first use or retaliatory use. The politicians' delay irritated many military planners. "Grey was no doubt making his peace with the Almighty at our expense," grumbled Sir Henry Wilson at GHQ.[9]

While awaiting the Government's decision, Kitchener took a variety of preliminary steps. At home an enclosed portion of Clapham Common provided three practice ranges for various types of explosive grenades, including gas, and Lord Salisbury converted his Hatfield estate into a gas grenade officers' school.[10] On 3 May, Kitchener asked Colonel Jackson to take charge of the prospective gas retaliation, and he promptly left the War Office to do so.[11] "At the very beginning, when walking back from lunch with Baker and Thorpe, it occurred to me that we could not handle these new materials without the aid of specialists in the trenches. The idea was approved . . . and we got lists of suitable students from all the Universities while the Army was combed for Chemists."[12] The War Office also initiated its own recruitment campaign for suitable officers and men, and on 11 May, a letter from the War Office went out to the principals of fifty universities and colleges soliciting names of chemists.[13]

The response yielded about 520 suitable names, from which the Army Council solicited volunteers. By 30 July, 400 chemists had enlisted for the gas companies, 126 through transfer, 274 by special enlistment, and the Army Council expressed hope for another 300 by mid-August. The officers and men of the Special Service Party already in France were withdrawn from the field to St. Omer, where they formed a unit briefly called 250th Company, Royal Engineers, and served temporarily as an indoctrination staff for the new recruits. In this way the defensive Special Service Party became the nucleus of what later developed into the offensive Special Companies and still later the Special Brigade, but these expansions were far in the future.

For the initial retaliatory weapon Jackson suggested gas hand grenades.[14] Chlorine and phosgene were widely recognized even at this early stage as the chemicals of choice, but there was no ready British source of production. Therefore Jackson selected a mixture of capsicine (a sternutator) and either liquid sulfur dioxide (an asphyxiant) or carbon bisulfide (an incendiary and asphyxiant). Without waiting for adequate experimental testing Jackson ordered the manufacture of thousands of these gas grenades, and by mid-May several members of the Special Service Party were experimenting with them.[15] By the end of the month, 1,250 were reaching the troops weekly, with 10,000 being the weekly target. However, because of bitter complaints from the infantry of widespread leakage in attempting to employ them in the continuing fight for Festubert and Aubers Ridge, the factory orders were cancelled, and remaining stocks destroyed.[16]

In spite of his early involvement on the offensive side, Jackson was not destined to lead the forces of British gas retaliation in the field and instead remained throughout the war in charge of the experimental activity in London. An impatient Sir John French had meanwhile decided to appoint his own gas director from the ranks of the Royal Engineers. The unusual requirements of the job seemed to demand a man of extraordinary initiative and resourcefulness, and French turned to his chief of staff, William ("Wully") Robertson, for a recommendation. Robertson recalled an encounter with just such an individual while serving in Sierra Leone ten years previously, a young officer with the Royal Engineers. The aspiring engineer, during personal leave and entirely on his own initiative, had visited a fortress, sketched its fortifications, taken telescopic photographs, and presented these to headquarters upon his return. Though a mere major in 1915, he had clearly demonstrated initiative and resourcefulness beyond the call of duty.

The candidate Robertson recommended and French appointed to direct the new chemical initiative was Charles Howard Foulkes. Born in 1875 in Bangalore, India, Charles was the fifth of seven sons and one daughter. His father, Rev. Thomas Foulkes, was senior chaplain in the Madras government service and a distinguished Tamil and Sanskrit scholar. Little of that religious family background seems to have

Photo of Charles H. Foulkes taken by K Company in 1917. (Courtesy of Liddell Hart Centre for Military Archives)

rubbed off on young Charles, however, and in later life he made quite disparaging remarks about missionaries and cast aspersions on fundamental Christian beliefs. "Faith," he wrote, "is believing things you know ain't so."[17] His father shipped him off to England at the age of seven to Lord Weymouth's School at Warminster. Following several years at Bedford Modern School he went straight into the army at the age of seventeen. After two years at "the shop" (Chatham), he received his commission into the Royal Engineers in 1894.

Cadet Foulkes, physically strong and sinewy, was a natural athlete. He won the single sculls competition at Maidstone in 1895 and later the open singles tennis competition at Chatham. The corps' rugby team for which he played won the Kent Cup in 1896; he played soccer (fullback) in Scotland for a first-division team, Heart of Midlothian; and he was invited to play professional soccer for Gillingham. At Chatham he excelled at an astonishing variety of sports—billiards, gymnastics, distance running, cycling, speed-skating, rowing, cricket, and weight-lifting.[18] At the age of thirty he took up hockey, played at right half position for the army as well as for Scotland and captained the Scottish international hockey team during the 1908/09 season. Foulkes always considered his competitor's plaque won in the Olympic games of 1908 as his best trophy. The Scottish team beat Germany but lost to England, and Foulkes played in both games.

Foulkes's stamina was remarkable, and he was generous with tales of his exploits. On one occasion in 1909 in Ceylon, at the age of thirty-four, he "played tournament tennis all day, beginning as soon as it was light, knocked off for a soccer match at about 5 P.M., and then sat up all night playing poker." He took up squash for the first time at age forty-seven and was still playing tennis at the age of seventy.

A remarkably versatile individual, Foulkes claimed Cowper's motto as his own: "Variety's the spice of life that gives it all its flavour." An expert photographer, he won prizes for his pictures of Ceylonese children, and he was a skilled wood-worker as well, finishing several pieces of domestic cabinetry, though his specialty was cigarette boxes featuring secret compartments. He was a frequent contributor to journals and newspapers, wrote several books, and spoke French fluently. He was as well a fervent cat-lover and an avid stamp collector.

At the outbreak of the South African (Boer) War in 1899, Foulkes applied to lead a photo reconnaissance team to Africa, where he was to spend almost six years, mostly in Sierra Leone, the Gold Coast, and the Niger. In 1902 Foulkes joined a commission to investigate a boundary dispute between Britain and France in the Niger, but his formal position as commission astronomer did not in any way curtail his naturally adventurous turn of mind. Ever the man of action, upon hearing of the flight of Emir Eliya of Kanu, one of the primary figures in the dispute, Foulkes, on his own initiative and with no authority, pursued him on horseback. After a three-day ride, he intercepted the emir, took him prisoner, and successfully brought him back. Though congratulated by the high commissioner, Foulkes barely escaped the embarrassment of being sent home by the head of the boundary commission.[19] It was about this time that Foulkes made the favorable impression on Robertson. Further assignments took him to the West Indies, the Gambia, South Africa, and Ceylon. In Africa he became enthused about big game hunting: "I shot a leopard, three sloth bears, a water buffalo, two wild boar, a bison and a tiger."[20]

In 1904 Charles Foulkes married Dorothy Oakey, a marriage that would last for sixty-three years, until her death in 1967. They had three sons and one daughter. Although a family man, he never complained of the long absences his military profession demanded.

At the outbreak of the war Foulkes was serving in Chatham, and he reached the front in early November in command of the 11th Field Company, Royal Engineers, during First Ypres. Characteristically restless in the relative quiet and safety of the rear, he reconnoitered frequently in no man's land, spent a considerable amount of time in exposed positions, and experienced several near misses. On one occasion he and his party lost the way and wandered through what they assumed to be French trenches. Not until later did they realize they had instead strayed into German trenches.[21] For rescuing a wounded man under heavy fire Foulkes earned the Distinguished Service Order and, from the French, the prestigious Croix de Guerre with Palm.

Foulkes, a man who thrived on combat and danger, believed that "given a certain temperament a man can cultivate the absolute conviction that nothing can harm him." He vehemently repudiated the characterization of the Western Front as "a nightmare of blood and horror, of depression and morbid self-pity." It was to him, he claimed, an adventure in which resolute men faced danger with exaltation, "a joke and a smile." That such a man did not take kindly to malingerers is not surprising. He displayed open contempt for soldiers anxious for the "Blighty" wound—a wound that would allow escape from the front lines.[22]

Upon learning that the Germans had resorted to poison gas, Foulkes reacted with much the same outrage and retaliatory impulse as most fellow soldiers. He openly ridiculed both the Cabinet's delay in ordering retaliation and its initial proviso to use no chemical more lethal than that employed by the Germans.[23] To him, no weapon seemed inappropriate in the quest for victory. Foulkes liked to quote the Duke of Marlborough: "In the long run the pursuit of victory without slaughter is likely to eventuate in slaughter without victory." And General Sherman: "Every attempt to make war easy and safe will result in humiliation and disaster." And even Clausewitz: "Let us not hear of generals who conquer without bloodshed."[24] Foulkes was a tough man in a tough profession, and he thrived on its toughness. At the end of the war he declared that he honestly had enjoyed every minute of it.[25]

Nevertheless, Foulkes was in several ways a strange choice to direct the British gas offensive. He was only a major at the time of his appointment in 1915, and more to the point, he freely confessed that he knew nothing about either chemistry or gas warfare. Such considerations, however, did not deter him from accepting the assignment with characteristic confidence and enthusiasm.

3
Corporals All

Corporals all, sitting on the firestep,
Corporals all, with their spanners in their hands,
Corporals all, lying on their bellies,
Gassing back the Germans to the Fatherland.[1]

Foulkes took over his post on 26 May 1915. Not the kind of man to waste time wondering why the army had selected him for this assignment, he immediately set about learning as fast as possible the practical basics of gas warfare. Within a week he had made contact with Jackson (who became a close friend), arranged to meet both Sir John French and Robertson, selected a base camp in France, attended chemical experiments at Crewe in northern England, and made another trip to France. He maintained this frenetic pace for several weeks, interviewing chemical experts in Paris and London, politicians (Lloyd George), and Generals Douglas Haig, Julian Byng, Herbert Plumer, William Pulteney, and visiting chemical factories in France and throughout England.

The most pressing decisions involved the organization of the offensive force and the specific form of British chemical retaliation. At this point the British high command had made no irrevocable decisions on these matters—not the form of gas retaliation, the manpower units required, the gases to be used, or the delivery systems—and no prewar gas doctrine existed on which Foulkes might build. In the wake of the disappointing experience with Jackson's gas grenades, no dearth of alternative schemes existed. The British might merely copy the German cylinder scheme, in spite of Jackson's objections that cylinders would require too much preparation and would be dependent entirely on the weather.[2] Sir John French favored dropping gas bombs from planes.[3] The army proposed the delivery of gas to the front lines through underground pipes from a central supply depot.[4] Foulkes, from the first, viewed gas as a possible means to win the war, not merely as an ancillary weapon. Accordingly, he argued persuasively for a massive cylinder discharge that would in a spectacular way clear the path for advancing infantry, and his view eventually prevailed. The question remained, What gas should fill the cylinders? Jackson had argued for a gas that would be "lethal without unnecessary cruelty," but Foulkes urged the use of "the deadliest gases procurable."[5] The latter not being then available, he settled for chlorine, with the intention to switch to phosgene and other more lethal gasses as experience and availability dictated.

Within six days of his appointment, Foulkes, who had hitherto known nothing about gas or chemical warfare, had acquainted himself so thoroughly with the subject and its attendant problems that he was able to prepare a report which laid out a reasonably comprehensive plan for both the organization and the operations of offensive gas warfare. This memorandum, sent to Robertson on 31 May, recommended that a single unit be responsible for both defensive and offensive gas capability. The unit should be housed within the Engineers, have a permanent depot near GHQ in France, and be composed of a high proportion of professional chemists. Subsequent experience showed in large measure this preliminary recommendation to be surprisingly close to the target. Regarding tactics, Foulkes recommended trench discharge by gas cylinder as the primary method, diplomatically adding French's airplane discharge as supplementary, though the latter method was never employed. As to manpower requirements, Foulkes initially estimated that twenty-five officers and about five hundred men would be sufficient, but when told to plan on a gas frontage of 5,000 yards, Foulkes subsequently recalculated the manpower requirements to two companies of ten sections each, thirty-two men to a section. In early June he attended the first large-scale chlorine experiments at the Castner-Kellner factory at Runcorn, near Liverpool. After observing test discharges from various types of cylinders, Foulkes selected a three-foot-long cylinder with an empty weight of about 100 pounds and a full weight of up to 160 pounds.[6] The Castner-Kellner firm eventually obtained the contract to supply the gas-filled cylinders.

French incorporated most of Foulkes's recommendations (including his own preference for aircraft dispersal) in his own recommendation to the Army Council dated 16 June. A significant departure from Foulkes's scheme, however, was the separation of gas defense and gas offense, which continued until October 1917. French cautiously specified a "provisional" establishment of two companies, "sufficient experience not having been gained as to form an opinion."[7] While waiting for official army approval, Foulkes pressed on with a whirlwind of talks and consultations in France and England. Another nine days passed. French could wait no longer. He telegraphed the War Office on the morning of

25 June: "When may reply be expected to my letter 16 June Subject Formation of Special Companies?" Later that same afternoon approval for
the first two companies (186 and 187) came through, giving a total of 670
men. Approval for a third company (188) came in July and a 10 percent
reserve grew into a fourth (189) in early September.[8] As identifying arm-
band colors, Foulkes chose the colors of Italy—red, white, and dark
green—presumably because Italy had joined the Allies on the same day
he took over his new duties, 26 May 1915.

Foulkes considered that the rank of pioneer, equivalent in the Engineers to the rank of private in the infantry, and the corresponding daily
base pay of one shilling nine pence would hardly attract the class of
men desired for his purposes. French, too, had urged a higher rank and
rate of pay on the grounds that many chemists already serving in
skilled positions in the army, especially those in the electrical units,
would already be receiving higher rates of pay than pioneers.[9] Accordingly, the Army Council stipulated a rate of pay of three shillings a day
and an entering rank of corporal.[10]

In late May, Foulkes drew up a poster advertising for volunteers:
"Men with training in Chemistry are required for service in the Royal
Engineers overseas." The poster promised immediate promotion to
corporal, beginning pay of three shillings a day, and a term of service
not to exceed the duration of the war. Usual standards of height and
chest measurement were to be waived as long as the volunteer was "or-
ganically sound and fit for service in the field." Furthermore, the eye-
sight examination might be passed with the aid of eyeglasses.[11] Foulkes
suggested that recruiters also disregard the upper age limit of forty-five,
on the assumption that the chemists would not be called upon to do
anything physically more strenuous than turn gas valves on and off.
One would-be recruit, rejected out of hand by all other units because of
a severe foot deformity and short-sightedness, found an easy entrance
to the Special Companies.[12] Martin Sidney Fox, one of the early recruits, described the initial selection as "almost willy-nilly."[13] Nor was
there a single Regular Army officer in the entire unit except Foulkes.
Until the formation of the enlarged Special Brigade in 1916, all the officers were carried on the army's General List, a miscellaneous category
of officers not permanently assigned to a particular unit.

Foulkes continued the recruitment drive initiated earlier by the War
Office among the universities and colleges to identify graduates and advanced students with chemical knowledge. One such volunteer later
jocularly maintained that he had been "taken in, in more senses than
one,"—that he had been asked about chemistry but not about ability to
perform heavy porterage.[14] "They wanted chemists," a youngster later
recalled, "so I looked up the formula for water and told them it was

H_2O, and I was in."[15] Another soldier remembers being asked only one question at the recruiting office: "What does H_2SO_4 stand for?"[16] The Chatham "examination," as many later came to realize, was the utmost farce, and the examining officer was primed to admit as many acceptable and marginally acceptable applicants and transfers as possible.

Foulkes also circulated notices seeking qualified chemists among the ranks already in service in France, characteristically assuming that his needs would be accorded high priority and that his requests for transfers to the Special Companies would be made expeditiously. L. Hague, a gunner with the Royal Field Artillery, remembers being sent by his adjutant in August 1915 to Chatham where a Royal Engineers recruiter interviewed him: "He reminded me that the Germans had used gas at Ypres. They might use a new type of gas in the future. If so, could I take a motorcycle and a vacuum flask to the front, take a sample of the new gas, return to base and analyze it?" Hague was given a four-day leave and told to visit his chemistry professor and learn what he could about gas analysis. "So, almost overnight, I changed from Gunner to Corporal R.E. (pay 3/- per day) almost unbelievable wealth."[17]

Foulkes's transfer requests, however urgent, did not always meet with such swift accommodation. Actually the notices elicited considerable resistance from commanders asked to release their men. When a Lt. James Pratt saw the notice, he immediately sought out his commanding officer: " 'As regards chemists,' I said, 'I'm a trained chemist myself and I've got at least half a dozen more in the company. Do you want me to submit their names?' He said 'I don't want my men to go into these God-damned cushy jobs. You'll render a nil return.' "[18] Foulkes sought support from the War Office in overcoming such resistance. Occasionally the War Office simply ordered such transfers despite objections from commanding officers and not always with the consent of the individual soldier. Lt. Jack Sewell, a bicyclist with the 28th Division, was repairing telephone connections in the Ypres area when in mid-1915 "a mysterious wire" arrived at divisional headquarters ordering him to report for special duty. Sewell's wording suggests the transfer came as a total surprise. "For some obscure reason the Staff had insisted on the use of trained or half-trained chemists, with a leavening of chemical labourers combed from the P.B.I. [poor bloody infantry], to let off gas in the front line. Little Tin Gods move in a mysterious way their wonders to perform." Sewell thereupon joined the Company 186.[19] A pharmacist maintained he was plucked out of the infantry because his recruiting officer had not been able to spell pharmacist, and so had written chemist instead. Since the Guards unit to which he had belonged suffered severe losses shortly afterward, he considered he owed his life to his fluke transfer to the Special Companies.[20]

Roughly one-third of the gas personnel came from special enlistments, one-third from new army units in training, and the other third from units already in France.

The decision to award each new recruit two stripes created one of the most unusual units in the British Army. Entire companies composed of corporals and no pioneers evoked considerable surprise, derision, and understandable resentment from outsiders. A variety of jokes circulated about the "comical chemical corporals," who became known to other regiments as Fred Karno's Army.[21] Marching through French villages, R. H. Atkinson, another early recruit, recalls hearing the comment *Voilà, ils sont caporaux!*[22] This anomaly created other problems as well, not the least of which was the absence of pioneers for menial tasks such as guard duty, ordinarily beneath the dignity of corporals. Infantrymen expressed considerable astonishment at "the sight of a full-blown Corporal on guard with a walking stick and pipe!!"[23] When, early in 1916, one of them lost his second stripe because of some military offense, the ritualistic ceremony of "reduction to the ranks" took on a curious significance, for the errant ex-corporal became the first pioneer in the Special Companies.[24]

Opinions differed on what to call the new establishment. The army at first employed a variety of names for the gas units—Chemist Companies, Chemical Companies, Special (chemical) Companies, or merely Companies, Royal Engineers—but Foulkes soon settled on the cryptic designation Special Companies. The French likewise disguised their gas units as *Compagnies Z*.

Like the earlier Special Service Party, the new chemical recruits at first knew little of their mission. Few of the men destined for the Special Companies had any idea where they were headed or what they were to do. Some believed they were merely to conduct chemical analyses to determine what kinds of gasses the Germans were using, and Charles Ashley, a twenty-year-old student from the University of Birmingham, recalled a widely held opinion that "our function would be to test the water in wells as the army advanced." Ashley found it hard to imagine "what need the engineers had of our service: it all sounded so improbable. Speculation on our task continued for we were told only that we were a Special Company of the Royal Engineers. . . . The only thing we could discover that we had in common was a knowledge of chemistry."[25] Some of the men thought they were headed for laboratories in France.[26]

Despite almost total ignorance as to their destination or employment, the prospect of being involved in something darkly mysterious and different conferred upon the mission an ambience of adventure. Ashley's transfer from the infantry to the Royal Engineers "filled me with joy." Richard Gale, an electrician by trade, "was very surprised and pleased, it seemed almost too good to be true." Luther Gordon Mitchell, a cavalry officer in the Essex Yeomanry, transferred in mid-August to the Royal Engineers: "Great Scott! Whoever would have thought it! . . . I am now a full corporal in the R.E.s and shall be drawing 20/ instead of 9/ per week—Gee Whizz. It seems that I know a bit of Chemistry and am going to France to analyze gasses."[27] The sense of enthusiasm was unmistakable. L. W. White had noticed a newspaper article titled "Mobilize the Chemists":

> It offered promotion to Corporal on enlistment, pay at three shillings a day and very early posting overseas. I enlisted in the Royal Engineers at St. Mary's Barracks Chatham on Friday 13th of August and joined a party of about fifty, some special enlistments but mostly transfers from other regiments. One morning two or three weeks later we paraded with full equipment and were issued with a meat pie and a ten shilling note before marching to Chatham station, preceded by a drum and fife band, all of us sporting corporal's stripes and armed with revolvers instead of rifle.[28]

At least two factors accounted for Foulkes's decision to arm the Specials with revolvers instead of rifles. The revolvers reinforced the authority of the rank of corporal when it came time for giving orders to the infantry, and the gas soldiers would not be going "over the top," when rifles would be essential, but would be operating in congested trenches, where rifles would be a hindrance.[29]

The new recruits assembled at Chatham and received inoculations, medical examinations, heavy .45-calibur Webley revolvers, and the usual assortment of military uniforms and equipment. Depending on the timing of arrival at Chatham and the schedule of group departures for France, the men remained at Chatham as little as forty-eight hours to as long as two or three weeks. In spite of the decree of secrecy, Fox recalls one Engineer sergeant sending a group of the new corporal recruits off to Southampton with the words, "Well, good luck, and gas every b_____ mother's son of them."[30] They were on their way to France—and the unknown.

4
Putting the Hell into Helfaut

Dear Mary, I joined the R.E.'s last July,
And they sent me to France, shure I didn't know why.
I expected to work in a lab at a bench,
But my work was at Helfaut, my lab was a trench.
We dug all the day in the blazing hot sun,
When we weren't humping Rogers, which weighed half a ton,
Shure Mary, me darlint, did I long to be,
Where the mountains of Mourne sweep down to the sea.[1]

Foulkes thought it desirable to locate the training depot and base camp of his new unit off the main roadways yet in reasonable proximity to British GHQ at St. Omer. After hiking about the environs, he selected the small hilltop village of Helfaut, located only about six miles almost due south of St. Omer. The picturesque village offered a flat central common, quite serviceable for a practice ground. A windmill stood in one corner of the common. The nearby villages of Bilques and Blendecques to the east and Wizernes, Hallines, and Wisques to the west afforded convenient billeting areas. The Aa River and a flooded quarry provided convenient swimming facilities. Foulkes set up headquarters in a school, the Mairie, on the high street bordering the common.

Foulkes placed Gordon Monier-Williams of the Special Service Party in charge of the Helfaut establishment with the title of technical advisor and deputy. This thirty-four-year-old, one of the most experienced and capable of the personnel at Foulkes's disposal, possessed an Oxford master's degree and a Ph.D. from Freiburg, and also had practical experience as a research chemist in industry and as assistant inspector of foods at the Local Government Board. The unpretentious "Ammonia Bill," as he was affectionately known, became both well-liked and highly respected and was to remain in charge of the base camp until his appointment as a Chemical Advisor in 1917.

Other members of the original Special Service Party, already in France, were summoned to Helfaut in early July to constitute the ad-

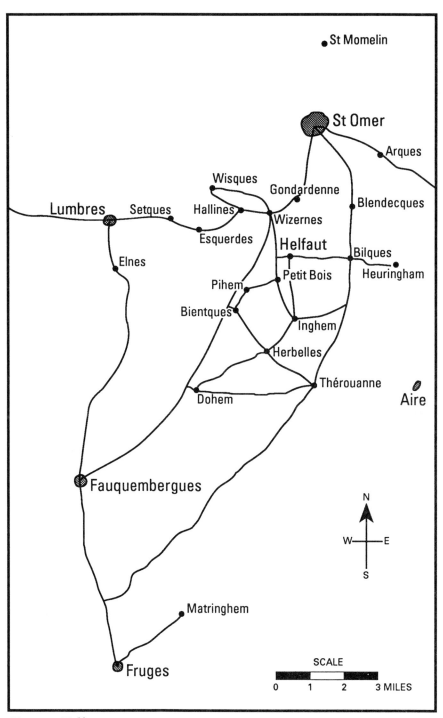

Map 4.1. Helfaut area

vance nucleus of the new unit. On the morning of 18 July the first draft of eighty-two new recruits arrived at Helfaut in London motorbuses painted black, and a second contingent of 105 followed three days later. Foulkes interviewed the men and "got rid of three."[2] Continuing arrivals would eventually allow Foulkes to construct four companies, numbered 186 through 189.[3]

Among those early groups of new recruits was G. O. Mitchell, a twenty-one-year-old transfer from a West Yorkshire regiment who arrived with a group of about fifty, mostly from the London Electrical Engineers. Mitchell's initial appraisal of the operation at Helfaut as "a potty little place" was less than complimentary: "The whole business seemed to be in a very embryonic condition, nobody knowing exactly what was going to happen." Mitchell described other newcomers as a "studious looking lot. Turned out later they thought they were coming out here for the purpose of laboratory work. Lots of talk about 'enlisting under false pretenses.' "[4]

Foulkes maintained that he was on hand to greet every arriving contingent and that he gave every man the option of returning to his original unit if he objected to gas warfare. Atkinson remembered both the interview and the offer to back out, but Ashley specifically denied ever hearing any such offer although he noted that "subsequent experience did not lead me to suppose that gas was more objectionable on moral or any other grounds than high explosives."[5] Another chemist who joined the unit at this time, John Thomas, recalled that several men did ask to be sent home upon hearing of the nature of the mission.[6]

Initial billets consisted of barns and tents in nearby fields. Gale in section 7 made room for new arrivals by spreading more straw over a barn flooring, an area eighteen feet square affording sleeping space for fifteen men.[7] Luther Mitchell's section 26 found billets in a girls' school. The earliest arrivals set to work digging experimental trenches on the Helfaut Common, filling sandbags, and route marching. Many of the sandbags had been procured from local French villages, and one of the soldiers noticed a note pinned to one: "Made by St. Mark's Girl's School at Le Gros. Dear Tommy, I hope that this will protect you from the German shells so that you will return safely."[8] Because of the variable winds, the Specials had to prepare practice trenches facing several directions, but the hard, flinty ground made digging unpleasant and difficult. "Our life seems to be one continual round of digging and we are all fed up with it," Gale complained after only four days of digging.[9]

An ex-captain of the Deccan Horse (an Indian cavalry regiment) named Percy-Smith, whose all-too-frequent use of a certain phrase quickly earned him the nickname "By God Percy" (some had it "My God"), commanded the first-organized Company 186. Maj. P. R.

Sanders, headmaster of a private school, Maj. Charles Garden, age forty-three and a mining engineer, and Maj. Edwin Berrisford, age twenty-five and a famed oarsman from Sheffield and later a clergyman, took command of the other three companies, 187, 188, and 189, respectively. Each company was made up of ten sections, numbered 1–10, 11–20, 21–30 and 31–40.

A Meteorological Service, initially set up to provide weather information primarily for flying, was already in operation at St. Omer, but Foulkes demanded an independent meteorological service for gas, and sometime in mid-1915 one of the meteorological superintendents, Ernest Gold, came over to Foulkes's operation. Colonel Gold, "Chief Flatulence Officer" to some of the bolder wags, and his assistants found billets in the hotel in the marketplace in St. Omer and established their office in a nearby house. At the suggestion of Foulkes, Gold obtained from London a supply of air meters which, when placed at suitable open spots behind the lines, yielded accurate readings of air speeds and wind direction at about four feet above ground level. Gold provided rudimentary meteorological training for gas officers who then tried their hand at the chancy business of front-line weather prediction.[10]

The initial gas offensive was to take the form of a surprise gas attack, lasting no less than thirty minutes on a front of 5,000 yards, as part of the upcoming British attack at Loos. Originally planned for early July, logistic delays were to force repeated postponements, and though at one point scheduled for 15 September 1915, the Loos offensive was not to take place until 25 September. In the short time believed available, Foulkes confronted seemingly insurmountable logistical and operational challenges. How soon and in what quantities could the War Office supply the gas and the cylinders? Far too optimistically, the Ministry of Munitions promised in late June to provide 1,600 cylinders (forty tons of gas) by 17 July, sufficient for a half-hour attack on a 5,000 yard front, and thereafter 150 tons per week, sufficient for two half-hour attacks per week over a five-mile front.[11] This was to prove a rash and empty promise.

The successful deployment and discharge of cloud gas necessitated solutions to a series of complicated logistic and tactical problems. The cylinders, transported from ships to an advance supply depot by train and lorry, had to be carried by hand the last distance to the front line. Deep emplacement pits then had to be dug into the front line to safely store them until needed. Under battle conditions the gas troops were to attach connecting pipes, throw one end over the trench parapet into no man's land, and synchronize the gas discharge by simultaneously turning on the valves. Upon contact with air, the liquid chlorine would instantly vaporize; the rest depended entirely on a favorable wind.

The arrival of the first gas-filled cylinders in mid-July permitted more realistic practice. Problems surfaced early on. A scarcity of the requisitioned flexible (spiral) copper pipes forced the substitution of a rigid iron pipe, which proved far less easy to work with and which was to perform quite unsatisfactorily under battle conditions. Interminable practice at the job of connecting and disconnecting the unwieldy pipes to the required number of cylinders aimed at a target time of thirty-five seconds per cylinder.[12] In late August a young engineer, William Howard Livens, brought to Foulkes a rubber-tube connector to replace the rigid and more cumbersome iron-pipe connectors. Foulkes, informed by Trench Warfare (a department of the Ministry of Munitions) that the chlorine gas would erode rubber, at first rejected the substitution. But Livens calculated that it would "do its job" long before any significant deterioration took place. Livens also devised a system of four-way connectors that avoided the awkward and dangerous exchange of pipes from one cylinder to the next during the discharge period. Without authorization he determined to experiment with both of these innovations during the coming gas engagement. An inventive sort, Livens would later rise to an independent company command within the expanded Special Brigade.

Most of the chemists were increasingly dismayed to discover that their work consisted of so little chemistry and so much plumbing and portering. New arrivals were greeted with the remark, "You don't have to be a chemist, all they want are navvies."[13] Ashley questioned the necessity of employing chemists for what was quite plainly plumber's work and was "gratified to hear that chemists were needed to give confidence to the infantry."[14] Gale reflected that "when the war is over we shall all be highly qualified navvies, scavengers, general removal and housebreaking experts."[15]

The exhortations to secrecy reached comical proportions. No one was to use the word "gas." Foulkes chose "accessory" as the code word for cylinder, but "Roger," "Oojah," "jacket," and "rat" soon won trench popularity. Capt. Walter Campbell-Smith, a late transfer from the Artists' Rifles, later recalled that at that time "we were not supposed to know what gas it was; it was called Red Star [but] it was chlorine."[16] Although Luther Mitchell continued his detailed diary throughout these days, he was scrupulously careful not to write anything about the nature of the mission of the Special Companies until after the Battle of Loos. "It had to be kept absolutely quiet before the attack." Frank Cousins, a schoolteacher from Durham in Company 187, perhaps too conscientious, refrained from writing in his diary at all during the month of August.

Daily routine at Helfaut began with reveille at 6 A.M., breakfast at
7:30, parade at 9, followed by company drill on the Helfaut common,
route marches, revolver drill, and a combination of orientation lectures
and hands-on training during the remainder of the day. Lectures fo-
cused on the whole range of chemical warfare: wind direction, chemical properties, distance judging, need for secrecy, protective practices,
and care of equipment. Practice trench digging continued daily. Nocturnal dummy gas exercises prepared the men for the real thing. Billet
cleaning occupied any slack daytime moments, "a great institution
out here," wrote Gale. "France will be infinitely cleaner when the
B.E.F. leave than ever before."[17] John A. Oriel in section 7 found the cylinder handling the most onerous part of the work: "We had to carry
them hanging from an apparatus which only the Army could possibly
have thought up and devised. It resembled very closely the "neck
yokes" I had seen in those horrid pictures of slaves being driven from
the interior of Africa to the coast."[18]

To accompany marching drills, the men quickly improvised appropriate verse to the stanzas of familiar songs and hymns. One of the fa-
vorites was an extemporized "Holy, Holy, Holy":

> Marching, marching, marching,
> Always bloomin' marching
> Marching in the morning,
> And marching late at night
> Marching, marching, marching,
> Always bloomin' marching.

Improvised stanzas of "Fred Karno's Army" provided a delicious parody of the experiences of a Special:

> 1. We are Fred Karno's Army,
>   The Roger Corps R.E.
>   We cannot march, we cannot fight,
>   What ruddy good are we?
>   But when we get to Berlin
>   The Kaiser he will say,
>   "Hoch! Hoch! mein Gott, They're a ruddy fine lot,"
>   And then he'll fade away.

> 2. Now when we joined the army,
>   In the good old days of yore,
>   They gave us each two ruddy stripes,

Hell only knows what for.
We carried jolly Rogers,
Until our backs were sore,
And when we'd let the blighters off,
We carried up some more.

3. Although we wear two chevrons,
   We daily do fatigues,
   Transporting pipes and cylinders,
   And marching leagues and leagues.
   And when we are not marching,
   We're polishing our straps;
   Hoch, Hoch, we all are corporals,
   Corporals,—yes, perhaps!

4. We go route marches daily,
   And step it out so grand,
   The Tommies shout as we march out,
   "All Corporals! well, I'm damned."
   Although we are all corporals,
   We do fatigues galore,
   Latrines and guards, and cleaning yards,
   Oh, what a ruddy war!

5. We go up to the trenches,
   And let off ruddy gas;
   We make such awful stenches,
   And wither all the grass.
   The infantry all hail us,
   As we take up our pipes,
   "Oh, damn and blast them, here they come,
   Those b____ with two stripes.[19]

In spite of minor complaints, life at Helfaut was not unpleasant; the soldiers inevitably invented less arduous duty for hot afternoons.

All that is necessary [are] a supply of maps and a flat grassy part of the plateau. The maps are spread out on the ground and the section then distributes itself on the grass with elbows on the maps and the thing is done! Another very pleasant exercise is estimating the speed of the wind and comparing the estimate with the speed as measured with the anemometer: this takes at least two hours for a section of 30 men, and is an easy way of filling up time.[20]

For G. O. Mitchell the weeks at Helfaut were "placid and easy."[21] As the units settled into quarters, personal pictures and clippings from home newspapers soon filled the walls of the barn billets, "but not War pictures, as literature relating to the War is not greatly appreciated out here."[22] An artist in section II of Company 187 covered the white-washed walls of his accommodation with caricatures of the section and portraits of selected individuals.[23] Shared packages from family provided special treats: "Gorgeous parcel from home, sweets, sardines, condensed milk, pickles, cake, it was a treat to taste English grub again."[24] Paydays afforded opportunities for celebration and time to spend in the villages nearby, although Gale thought the sudden rise in prices a form of daylight robbery. An "incurable ragtime maniac" livened up marches in Gale's section. Geoffrey Higson played bridge almost every evening. Sports occupied many afternoons, cricket and football in particular, played on the common, and in the evenings, concerts in a large barn at Helfaut: "Those who could (or would) sing, sang; those who declined had to contribute to the dixie of beer which supplied the innocuous if diuretic beverage. On other evenings a few of us would scamper headlong down the scrubby slopes to Gondardenne to consume the by-now-accustomed 'frites' and drink beer and grenadine."[25]

The first impression of F. A. R. Hopkins upon arrival at Helfaut was of a soldier "sitting beneath an apple tree reading (of all things) Hobbes's *Leviathan*. In retrospect it was summer all the time, and eternal blue skies, . . . lolling against a grassy slope engaged in what we called military sketching."[26] The chemists found time for bathing excursions, both at the quarry and in the river. Luther Mitchell thoroughly enjoyed his "soft time" at Helfaut.[27] Meiron Thomas, a late arrival, found himself billetted with a French family. They have ten rabbits, "which they rear and fatten *not* as pets, but for eating!!"[28] Many French women took in the soldiers' washing in return for a bar of canteen soap, a commodity in short supply in the villages. Frank Cousins described life during this brief Helfaut period as "pleasant days full of pleasurable anticipations of the future for the air was electric with rumors of big things to come."[29]

Some of the clearly overqualified recruits presented odd spectacles as gas corporals. D. A. Clibbens, who joined Company 186 in July, possessed a B.Sc. from London, a M.Sc. from Bristol, and a Ph.D. from Jena and Freiburg. Sewell, his section officer, considered Clibbens and three other graduates inappropriate for combat and assigned them duties as sanitary corporals. The four paraded every morning with their brooms. "In my own mind I dignified my own position with the title Non-commissioned Officer in Charge of Company Hygiene," wrote Clibbens.

The villagers of Hallines addressed him as "Monsieur, the officer of the sweeping brooms," and the children called him "Monsieur Clib." In their spare time, Clibbens and the other sweepers organized a local school for the youngsters of the village.[30] Atkinson estimated that fully half the men in his company had university degrees.[31] In retrospect, it seems clear that many such individuals would have better contributed to the war effort in laboratories than in the trenches.

In mid-August 1915 Foulkes staged a rehearsal gas attack. Following a night march with full pipe kit, the soldiers entered the practice trenches and connected the pipes. In Gale's words, "all our parapet pipes were raised together and the imaginary gas attack commenced." On 22 August, barely a month after the first recruits arrived at Helfaut and less than two months since his appointment, Foulkes arranged a demonstration at Helfaut for Haig and most of the generals of the First Army. Foulkes records that all went well and that Haig was pleased and satisfied, a tribute to the hard work of Monier-Williams. Liddell Hart has suggested that the demonstration might have been "too success-ful" and that it played an unfortunate role in converting Haig to an overly optimistic view of the gas potential.[32]

Meanwhile Foulkes had been shuttling back and forth across the Channel, visiting Millbank Experimental Laboratories, consulting with Robertson almost daily, lunching with corps and army com-manders, and investigating French gas apparatus. On 6 August he met for the first time with the Scientific Advisory Committee in London. The day following the demonstration for Haig, Foulkes crossed to En-gland, put himself up at the Grosvenor, and saw part of a show at the Hippodrome. The following day he visited Chatham, crossed the Channel back to France, reviewed plans with each of his company com-manders, then motored to the front to consult with corps commanders. On 31 August he consulted with Generals Herbert Plumer, Edmund Al-lenby, and Haig and in the evening reviewed final plans with Sanders and Percy-Smith, who were to supervise the widest gas fronts. It is dif-ficult to imagine how any commanding officer under similar circum-stances could have done more than Foulkes did to ensure the success of his unit's unprecedented mission.

Interminable delays in delivery of gas supplies and equipment, espe-cially the required number of cylinders, plagued the unit, already har-ried by lack of adequate training time. In late August, a two-week post-ponement of the Loos offensive had afforded some small relief to the rushed gas personnel whose preparations were already well behind schedule. As late as 1 September, only slightly more than half the re-quested 6,500 gas cylinders had arrived, and with only two weeks to the new Z day, Foulkes still had only three trained companies available. This was hardly his fault, however, since official sanction for the establishment of a fourth came through only on 1 September.[33]

Toward the end of August Helfaut was "alive with rumors" as to the date of departure for the front lines.[34] Training intensified—marches with full pipe kit, practice with time synchronization, more lectures on weather, and stagings of mock gas releases in the darkness. But as raw and untrained recruits continued to augment the force throughout August, there came to be less and less time to provide proper indoctrination and training for the latecomers. Foulkes admitted that the longest period of training anyone had was six weeks, and most had considerably less. Since many of the most recent recruits came directly from civilian life, such a limited period of training was hardly sufficient, especially in view of the specialized functions they were expected to perform.

On the morning of 4 September, only eleven days before the scheduled Z day, Percy-Smith and Sanders led thirty-four of the more experienced sections out of Helfaut.[35] "By God Percy" delivered a rousing morale-boosting speech: "Boys, you are going to take part in the greatest battle the Army has yet prepared for; advance is now at a standstill and the artillery and infantry are waiting for you to clear the way."[36] That a shortage of artillery shells existed was no secret to anyone—it was widely expected and hoped that the use of gas would in large measure make up for this deficiency and clear the path for safe passage of the infantry.

5
Up the Line to Loos

After two months at Helfaut, we went up the line,
The change and the bustle, bedad they were fine,
We had some fine strafes, which we'll ne'er forget
And we hear that the Huns have some nasty coughs yet,
We never had thought there could be so much mud,
Shure we sank to our waists if a minute we stood,
And I thought of the life, ooh, so careless and free,
Where the Mountains of Mourne sweep down to the sea.

British resistance to the urging of Foch and Joffre for a combined French and British offensive in Artois in the early autumn of 1915 is well known. At a conference on 27 July with Foch, Sir John French had argued unsuccessfully that an autumn offensive would be premature and that a smaller attack north of La Bassée in the area of Aubers Ridge would better set the stage for a larger, more promising offensive in the spring of 1916. French Generals Foch and Joffre were adamant on the necessity for an autumn offensive in which the British forces would attack side by side with the French south of La Bassée. Both Sir John and Haig, skeptical of chances to achieve a breakthrough at that stage of their preparedness, were initially reluctant to commit the full strength of their forces to Joffre's schedule. Upon learning of the proposed action, Sir Henry Rawlinson, IV Corps commander, wrote, "It will cost us dearly and we shall not get far."[1] Joffre was ultimately successful, however, in persuading Kitchener of the absolute necessity of mounting a strong Allied autumn offensive on the Western Front as a means of relieving German pressure on the Russians. In the official history, *Military Operations: France, and Belgium*, Edmonds concluded that under pressure from Kitchener at home and Foch and Joffre in France "the British Commander-in-Chief was therefore compelled to undertake operations before he was ready, over ground that was most unfavourable, and against the better judgment of himself and General Haig."[2]

Because of inadequate artillery, Haig's original game plan called for a limited attack with only two divisions, but the possibility of playing the gas card added another trump to his hand. Sir Henry Wilson, chief liaison officer to French GHQ, remained doubtful of the potential of the gas component, but Haig had been so impressed with the demonstration of 22 August that he subsequently dared to hope for a breakthrough after all, perhaps even a "decisive" one if the wind were to prove favorable.[3] He promptly laid down alternative plans for a more ambitious attack with six divisions, the path to be cleared by gas.[4] Rawlinson's correspondence at this time suggests that the British assumed the luxury of some flexibility as to day and hour of the attack. "No date has yet been set, indeed the actual date must depend on the weather."[5] Especially after successive postponements which afforded the Special Companies extra time for preparations, Haig became more convinced that "with gas, decisive results were to be expected."[6] Rawlinson, who was somewhat more cautiously realistic, wrote to A. Fitzgerald at the War Office in late August that "we are inclined I think to place too much reliance on the gas and not enough on the Artillery."[7]

Nor were the British granted the choice of terrain on which to fight what they considered a premature battle. Their preference for Flanders foundered on French insistence that their combined attacks go in side by side in Artois. Thus the main thrust of what was later to become known as the Battle of Loos confronted a seven-mile front from the town of Festubert on the north southward to the village of Grenay, opposite Lens, where the line was taken up by the French attacking simultaneously. The Vermelles-Hulluch Road just about bisected the British front. For the most part, this British sector of the line ran roughly along a north-south axis—the northern part of the line constituting the left wing, and the south the right (from the Allied point of view). Initial objectives were the small mining villages of La Bassée, Haisnes, Hulluch, Loos, and, on the southern flank, Hill 70 and Cité St. Laurent in the environs of Lens. This portion of Artois was for the most part fairly level, without ridges or hedges but dotted with rock quarries, brick works, and slag heaps. Except for the rock and brick outcroppings, the terrain was amenable to gas attack. But the flatness that made it suitable for the gas discharge was most unsuitable for the infantry advance because it offered little or no cover, unless, of course, gas cleared the way and neutralized the opposition. "As open as the palm of my hand," complained Rawlinson.[8] The abandoned slag heaps unfortunately provided excellent vantage points for German machine-gun emplacements.

Haig's First Army consisted of four army corps: I and IV Corps were to mount the main assault with their six divisions, while battalion-sized attacks from III Corps and the Indian Corps were to contribute the diversionary feints to the north, opposite Aubers Ridge and in the neighborhood of Festubert. Gen. Hubert Gough deployed his three divisions of I Corps along the northern wing of the main front, north to south, 2d, 9th, and 7th. The 2d Division stood astride the canal, the 9th Division faced the Hohenzollern Redoubt, and the 7th Division lined up on the 9th's right as far as the Vermelles-Hulluch Road. General Rawlinson's three divisions of IV Corps continued the line southward, 1st, 15th, and 47th. The 1st Division, its left aligned with the south side of the Vermelles-Hulluch Road, faced directly opposite a lone surviving cherry tree in no man's land called simply Lone Tree.[9] The 15th Division, next in line, faced the village of Loos itself, with Hill 70 beyond. The 47th faced a mineworks called the Double Crassier, with Lens to the southeast and abutting the French line on the right.

Initial plans called for the release of 2,850 gas cylinders in support of the I Corps, 2,250 for the IV Corps, and lesser amounts on the diversionary front, all finishing with a grand discharge of smoke candles. The total gas frontage stretched roughly 14,500 yards.[10] Such a distribution did not correspond conveniently to the company structure of the gas organization. Even with the promise of a fourth company (189), there were not sufficient companies to cover the six divisions of the main assault line. For all practical purposes, therefore, the company structure had to be entirely scratched at the last moment. Instead of four companies of ten sections each, Foulkes deployed his men in groups of sections independent of company organization. Percy-Smith took eighteen sections (including all sections of Company 186) to I Corps, while Sanders led sixteen sections (including all sections of Company 187) to IV Corps. As additional sections reached adequate strength, they joined the various units already deployed. Foulkes, putting the best light on things, called the regroupings "composite companies," but the last-minute changes could not have increased the confidence of either officers or men.

The shortage of cylinders forced a further reduction in the number of cylinders per emplacement—from fifteen to thirteen or less and north of La Bassée Canal only three cylinders per bay. A continuous gas discharge from the reduced number of cylinders would not be sufficient to outlast the half hour which British intelligence had estimated that German gas helmets afforded protection, and in any event it was thought that the enemy would be "well prepared for any [gas] attack so short as half an hour."[11] Foulkes compensated by increasing the number of smoke candles and alternating the gas and smoke discharges. Instead of a continuous thirty-eight minutes of gas followed by two min-

La Bassée Canal. (Courtesy of Liddell Hart Centre for Military Archives)

utes of smoke, Foulkes settled for twelve minutes of gas and eight minutes of smoke, followed by another twelve minutes of gas and eight
minutes of smoke.

On the morning of 4 September, sixty-eight London motorbuses,
"complete with their adverts of Johnny Walker, Pear's Soap, etc.," and
eight lorries pulled out of Helfaut, for Bethune, carrying the first contingent of gas men on their mission of retaliation.[12] Bethune lay about
twenty-five miles to the southeast of Helfaut on La Bassée Canal and
about six miles west of the front line. The villages and farms in its environs provided convenient forward billets for the British during most
of the war, and virtually every member of the Special Companies billeted here at one time or another during the next four years. Several sections found quarters in the village of Busnes, near Lillers and almost
due west of Bethune, where they remained for two weeks before moving up closer to the front lines. G. O. Mitchell found the village "quite
a pretty one, with the usual big church, fairly good shops, and decent
country round, although very flat."[13] A colliery village, Vermelles, a
few miles east of Bethune and very close to the front line, provided billets for a few sections of Company 187.

Some lucky corporals settled into private homes, and according to one of them, "There were two ways of getting into the bedroom which I shared with Lefebure; one either went through Madame's bedroom or one stepped through a shell hole in the wall. When turning in late at night, we naturally entered . . . by stepping through the shell hole, but Madame did not think that was quite proper."[14] The largest billet, assigned to most of the sections from Company 186, turned out to be a former chicory factory situated on the east side of Bethune along La Bassée Canal. It was a large, unattractive brick building constructed expressly for the drying and processing of the nuts and beans. The floors on the upper levels consisted of perforated iron grates and the openings that passed for windows contained no glass. Some of the men fabricated coffin-like beds from cylinder cases.[15] The nearby canal afforded a convenient opportunity to swim, though one infantryman reported that the water was "putrid and grew a vivid green scum when undisturbed by shell bursts, which, while they dissipated the greenery, stirred up the black and stinking mud from the bottom."[16] Gale's graphic description of his portion of the chicory factory is likewise bleak:

> Our new billet is a cheerless hole, especially built to catch all the draughts in creation. Our share of the billet is a brick work tunnel at the base of the main building, open at both ends and very draughty. The main structure is a large brick drying house with three perforated steel floors about 6 feet apart and these are only accessible by crazy ladders and stairways in a doubtful state of repair. Life here is decidedly crowded in more ways than one, not to mention the mud that filters downward through the floors from the occupants overhead, and the language that filters upwards from the recipients of said mud! The lucky sections are those who, preferring curses to mud, annexed the top floors of the billet. We, in our tunnel, are free from mud, but the draught is enough to blow the coats off our backs. The floor is brick and very wobbly. To keep warm we all slept close together with our spare clothes on top of us and our feet wrapped up in our puttees or tucked into our cardigans.[17]

The more ingenious of the men "promptly organized shower baths from perforated tobacco tins at the ends of bent pipes from the factory boiler."[18]

One of the most unusual billets, at Verguin, was that of H. P. Islip, Company 189, who described it as "one of the best billets I ever had in France—a stone-built pig-sty which was scrupulously clean. Its rightful owner was fortunately not at home."[19] Quarters near Grenay, base for some sections of Company 188, included a chicken house.[20] The officers settled somewhat more comfortably into a local chateau.

Frequent marching along La Bassée Road gave rise to the following stanzas sung in irreverent parody to the tune of "Onward Christian Soldiers":

> Onward Christian Soldiers
> Up La Bassée Road,
> With your pipes and spanners,
> What a ruddy load.
> We are not down-hearted
> We have had some rum.
> We don't care for old Von Kluck
> Let his legions come.
> CHORUS: Onward Christian Soldiers,
> Up the ruddy road—
> Where old Fritz is waiting
> To give us hell, I'm told.[21]

Until the cylinders reached the Bethune area, life there at first differed little from life at Helfaut. Hopkins located a piano and reported that "scarcely a night passed without Alderson or I being called upon to officiate at the piano."[22] Popular musical comedies of the day, "Tonight's the Night," "The Passing Show," and others, supplied most of the favorite songs. Grantham considered the sole job of the commanders as "nothing more than to keep us out of mischief" and mentions serious fishing and frequent water polo.[23] Ashley spent "lots of time in town and swimming in the canal."[24] The men occasionally watched the Bethune observation balloon, dubbed "the Sausage," drifting overhead, its occupants monitoring the enemy activity below from their vantage point in the sky. Bethune was close enough to the front lines, however, for the soldiers to hear the deafening roar of intermittent shellfire: "Some of the large shells make a fearful roaring noise when travelling through the air, rather like a tube train."[25]

On the same day these first gas sections decamped for the front, 4 September, Robertson summoned Foulkes to St. Omer and dispatched him with an important message for Haig. The offensive had been postponed another ten days, from 15 September to 25 September. An enigmatic comment in Foulkes's personal diary refers to a "slight contra temps" with Haig, but it does not indicate whether it concerned the postponement, which of course was not Foulkes's decision, or something else. Whatever it was, Foulkes "put things right before leaving him."[26] In any event he welcomed the ten extra days in which to refine gas preparations. Meanwhile the Germans were hoisting signs above their trenches asking the date and time of the expected offensive.[27]

Soon after arrival in the area, the gas officers set out to reconnoiter the front lines, familiarize themselves with the lay of the land of the particular bays to which their sections had been assigned, and locate appropriate sites for the cylinder emplacements which they then marked with a number or a peg in the trench. Map skills proved more useful than chemistry in the process. Grantham compared the difficulty of surveying a map of the front to the challenge of constructing a map of Hampton Court maze—from inside.[28]

At the front, the war had already fashioned its own geographic parameters and dimensions out of the once verdant Artois countryside. Each side had long since constructed a line of barbed-wire entanglement fronting no man's land, a morass of holes, churned-up earth, desolation, and occasionally, rotting corpses. The width of no man's land varied from as little as about thirty feet to several hundred yards. In 1916 a stretch along the Somme at one point was so narrow that the Germans were able to use British electricity.[29] A jagged series of bays and traverses along the front-line trenches created a zig-zag pattern that prevented enfilade (lateral) firing along the length of the trench should the enemy storm one part of the line. Facing no man's land, a protective wall of sandbags formed the trench parapet. At the bottom of the trench below the parapet was a raised portion of the trench floor called a firestep. Short trenches called saps led in one direction into no man's land for reconnaissance and in the other to the latrines. Communication trenches, also intentionally crooked and winding, ran perpendicular to the front line, many several miles or more in twisting length. These led back to the support line about 100 to 200 yards behind and roughly parallel to the front line. The support trench incorporated dugouts which usually housed section or company headquarters. Behind the support trench was the reserve trench, typically about half a mile further to the rear and also roughly parallel to the front, which housed battalion headquarters, advanced dressing stations, and railheads. Still further to the rear were, respectively, the divisional and corps headquarters.

Once inside the reserve line, most local place-names lost all usefulness. Though some Ninth Avenues and First Communication Trenches existed, soldiers quickly sign-posted most every trench and intersection with English, Scottish, or Welch road names. The vast majority of trenches echoed the names of fashionable London streets: Saville Row, Curzon Street, Regent Street, Cromwell Road, Oxford Street, the Strand, and Rotten Row. A network of trenches at Givenchy replicated the thoroughfares of Whitehall. Trenches such as Lee Way, Stansfield

Avenue, and Binegh Redoubt offered dubious tribute to the senior officers of the particular area. The Hertford Territorials aptly dubbed their trench Hertford Street. Important trench intersections became Piccadilly Circus, Charing Cross, Oxford Circus, Kensington Station, Waterloo, Cambridge Circus, Trafalgar Square. Shrapnel Corner, Suicide Way, and Dead Man's Alley denoted the obvious. Trenches accommodating dressing stations (first aid) were invariably Harley Street, London's well-known West End street that houses physicians' offices. During periods of great troop movement, such as brigade relief or large-scale offensives, signs designated communication trenches "up" and "down." Postings "TO BERLIN" or "TO ENGLAND" not only added a touch of humor but designated the way to safety or danger in the clearest terms. One soldier noticed a "TO BERLIN" sign with the pencil addition "1,000,000.1 miles."[30] This was the new subsurface world the gas troops entered in the autumn of 1915.

Leisurely days came to an abrupt end as small groups of Specials began to thread their way up the various communication trenches to deposit equipment at the front lines. Gale in section 7, in support of the 26th Brigade of Gen. G. H. Thesiger's 9th (Scottish) Division, found this part of the line

> very well made and comparatively safe, the northern end of our line provided with dugouts. . . . A fair amount of firing was going on, the occasional swish of shell flying over followed by a dull boom in the distant German positions, the singing of shell fragments and nose caps, and the 'ping' of snipers' bullets were quite sufficient to remind me that the Bosches are only about 100–150 yards distant.[31]

Directly opposite the "Ladies from Hell," as the Germans were said to call the Scottish kilted troops, loomed the German strongpoint named Hohenzollern Redoubt, a 20-foot-high flat-topped fosse, or slag heap, nearly 300 yards in length, bristling with nests of machine-gun emplacements, and reinforced by well-defended communication trench-tunnels, Little Willie and Big Willie. This formidable salient was to be a major objective of the gas attack and one of the most desperately contested positions along the whole front for much of the war. Visual examination was safe, of course, only by periscope.

Cousins recorded his company's first look at the 15th Division's trenches along the south side of the Lens Road:

> The trenches are in chalk and the lines of them can easily be traced. The depth of the trench is well over nine feet. We heard the

ping of the bullets and the shriek of our shells followed by the dull thud of bursting. We saw the German trenches protected by wire entanglements (about 1 1/2 feet above ground) on the hill ridge through periscopes and spy holes. The nearest trenches were 150 yards away and more or less ran North and South. One incident is of interest. Lt. Smeaton lifted his periscope an inch or two too high and two bullets arrived one just over the trench and the other into a sandbag.[32]

Divisional war diaries disclose elaborate instructions regarding infantry support for the Special Companies once the cylinders began arriving. Foulkes apprised the 15th Division in late August of the weight and dimensions of the cylinders, the required allocations of picks and shovels per partition, and so on, together with detailed requisitions for wagons to transport cylinders from the railheads to the divisional dump and for loading parties at the dumps. The division also agreed to place two infantrymen per partition bay under the command of the gas personnel from 8 P.M. on the evening before the discharge, primarily to operate the smoke candles. These infantry received instruction on cylinder-handling in the event of casualties among the gas personnel. In addition, Foulkes also arranged for priority access to divisional telephones for his gas commanders.[33]

Upon arrival in the front trenches, the gas personnel prepared the cylinder emplacements by first digging away part of the firestep and then excavating a pit about two feet deeper than the level of the trench bottom, using timber to shore up the sides to the level of the trench floor. They then covered the excavated emplacements with several layers of sandbags to await the arrival of the cylinders. Foulkes assigned up to fifteen batteries to each gas section, each battery accommodating up to thirteen cylinders. Two men worked a single battery.

Throughout these proceedings Foulkes urged the utmost secrecy even among British infantry. The word "gas" was never to be whispered. Elaborate codes disguised the real meaning of telephone messages. Orders prohibited lights or fires in the front lines, and Gale, while on duty there, remembers turning in generally at dusk for this reason. The presence of the Specials in the front lines elicited understandable curiosity on the part of the various infantry units manning the trenches. The Special Companies concocted a variety of imaginative explanations. Among the more implausible was that the new arrivals were installing heating stoves to keep the trenches warm during the coming winter.[34] All equipment, pipes, cylinders, connectors, and tools were packed in unmarked boxes. Circulars threatened draconian punishments for anyone caught using any other word except "accessory" when referring to the gas apparatus. Rawlinson, skeptical that the secret was not already out, referred to the cylinders as the Jolly Rogers,[35] and one infantryman remembers them dubbed ''Loos Wallahs.''[36] On at least one occasion gas officers appear to have taken the admonitions a bit too seriously. Arrested for suspicious behavior at the front lines, they compounded their plight by refusing to disclose anything about themselves or their mission. Guardsmen escorted them at point of bayonet to brigade headquarters where they were eventually identified and released.[37] Robert Graves, then a member of an infantry unit at Loos and later well known as a prolific author and one of the most articulate war critics, considered the security precautions a huge joke, claiming that French civilians as well as the German troops knew all about it.[38]

Another problem, the shortage of trained officers, persisted right up to the final days. Some of the promised officer contingents did not arrive from England until mid-September; to make up the deficit, Foulkes borrowed twelve volunteer infantry subalterns from Territorial battalions. Four of these, Capt. R. E. Otter, Lt. F. D. Charles, Lt. F. H. Wallis, and Lt. A. B. White, all from the London Rifle Brigade, later wrote detailed reports of their activities with the gasmen at Loos.[39] They arrived at Helfaut on 3 September, and after only one day of orientation lectures, each took command of one of the gas sections later to comprise Company 189. Walter Campbell-Smith, borrowed from the Artists' Rifles, remained permanently in the Special Companies and rose from second lieutenant to lieutenant colonel. Campbell-Smith, who had an M.A. from Cambridge and was a Fellow of Corpus Christi College, applied himself immediately to the new work at hand and adapted quickly. In view of the short training time available, however, he anticipated serious problems when it came to the real thing, especially with regard to the awkward system of pipe connections:

> We had these gas cylinders weighing about 1 cwt; then we had pipes which consisted in general of two pipes, one bent at right angles 4–5' long with a bend about 1' from one end and a shorted pipe also bent at right angles, one end attached to the cylinder and the other to the pipe so that the length of the pipe was sufficient to reach from the top of the cylinder to the top of the parapet. It was obvious to us that we should lose time in transferring the pipe from one cylinder to another and that it would be difficult.[40]

On 13 September, after barely a week's preparation, Captain Otter and Lieutenant Wallis led their sections to Verquin, and then, together with four other sections, to the front-line trenches in support of the 47th Division. On the same day, Lt. A. B. White took command of an additional section of Company 186 and two days later proceeded to his allotted front astride La Bassée Canal in support of the 6th Brigade, 2d Division. Also on 13 September, another six officers and 106 men under a Lieutenant Higgins (13th London Regiment) bolstered Company 186.[41]

Meanwhile Foulkes continued to shuttle back and forth between London and France. While in London he found time for the occasional matinee, but spent the greatest part of his time in meetings with Jackson and the other experimental chemists. In France he consulted with Robertson, Haig, Rawlinson, and Allenby, as well as his own gas officers, Monier-Williams, Percy-Smith, and Sanders, and also found time later to inspect virtually every emplacement along the line. Ironically, on the morning of 15 September, the original Z day, a tantalizingly perfect westerly breeze wafted over the area. "Another ideal day for the use of gas," wrote Rawlinson, "and it is a thousand pities that the attack could not have come off as at first arranged."[42]

Back in Helfaut, Monier-Williams did his best to provide a modicum of training for the continuing stream of recruits before sending them on to join the others in the barns and factories around Bethune.

> A boiling hot day. All our section packed into a 3 ton lorry, and after the usual uneventful journey, arrived at village of Philosophe. This had evidently been a mining village and a more dingy looking hole I have seldom seen. After a short march we reached the small town of Vermelles. Here our section were billeted in an end cottage of a row facing the enemy lines. I have seen a good number of ruined towns in my time, but nothing to beat Vermelles. . . . There was scarcely a house standing in the place.[43]

With zero hour less than ten days off, Foulkes still lacked both men and officers, but the most critical shortage was 1,000 gas cylinders. On 16 September Haig wrote urgently to Robertson, demanding that employees at the gas factories work night and day rather than the usual eight-hour day: "The situation was a *special* one and *special* measures must be taken."[44] At a final Allied conference on 18 September, Haig brought up the shortage of cylinders and Foulkes received a good deal of criticism. But French defended Foulkes and later told him privately "not to mind what anyone thought—I was under him personally" and that he was satisfied.[45] On 19 September another six sections arrived from Helfaut: two (3 and 22) to beef up I Corps, two (21 and 25) to IV Corps, and two (32 and 33) to support the diversionary actions of the Indian Corps and III Corps.

As for the flexible timetable, Haig and Rawlinson were to be rather abruptly disillusioned. As late as 16 September Haig felt that if the winds were not favorable the gas attack ought to be postponed and that "no attack should take place without gas."[46] But at a consultation at Hinges that same day Sir John informed Haig, Gough, and Rawlinson that the attack was set for 25 September, "gas or no gas." Rawlinson, who as late as 29 August had been under the impression that the attack could wait for a favorable wind "as long as a week," was not pleased.[47] "How can we attack without gas? . . . We must wait for the wind, I say."[48] Yet in spite of this seemingly explicit declaration on the part of French, two days later Haig still seemed to be speculating about the possibility of postponement if the winds should not be favorable on 25 September.[49] Somewhat enigmatically, on the same day he assured a worried Kitchener of every expectation of success "if the wind were only favourable on the 25th."[50]

Under the circumstances, Haig asked Rawlinson and Gough to formulate yet another alternative plan in the event weather were to prevent any use of gas. "I cannot attack on so wide a front without gas," replied Rawly (as he was known to close friends), and he went on to half-heartedly suggest various weaker commitments: "If we cannot use gas it is a very serious handicap," and he suggested that Haig press for an attack on 24, 25, or 26 September, as the weather dictated. "A day will not make much difference to the French who can go in on the 25th as arranged but 24 hours will have no effect on the cooperation between the two armies." On 19 September, however, the reaffirmation came over the telephone: "We must attack on the 25th gas or no gas."[51]

Haig had set up First Army headquarters at Hinges, not far from Bethune, and from a nearby house in the same village Foulkes proposed to oversee the gas operation. The gas commander laid out on a trestle table a detailed trench map of the entire battlefront, marking the location of each section officer with a small flag which could be positioned to indicate wind direction. During the night preceding zero hour, as his officers sent in hourly wind reports in secret code, Foulkes proposed to adjust the flag pins, pencil in the velocity, and so provide a visual up-to-the-minute display of the wind conditions over the entire gas front. Meanwhile, civilian workers at the Castner-Kellner factory at Runcorn in north England filled the gas cylinders with chlorine and shipped them off to the port of Boulogne; then the cylinders traveled by train the twenty-five miles to Audruick, where Foulkes had established a storage shed and rail siding. The first shipment arrived on 18 September, and Foulkes had arranged for the transport of the gas cylinders from Audruick to the trenches in three stages. Trains carried them to the terminus of the railhead near Bethune, where gas personnel opened each box, removed the cylinders, loosened the dome caps, replaced the cylinders in the box, and refastened the box lids with only one screw. Infantry officers occasionally countermanded these orders, not wishing this work to be done in their areas.[52] John Thomas reported that "the infantry were scared stiff of our gas and would not wish to be in our mob for anything."[53] Gas secrecy was apparently not entirely tight.

Horse-drawn General Service wagons supplied in groups of five by the various divisions took the cylinders on the next stage of the journey from the railhead to local dumps where Foulkes had assigned separate unloading and loading sites. To reduce noise, layers of sacking muffled the wagon wheels, and soldiers tied several layers of partially filled sandbags onto the hoofs of each team of two horses.[54] Parties of soldiers hauled the cylinders the last stage of the journey by night, from dump to front-line trench. Each gas cylinder weighed about 125 to 160 pounds; two iron handles facilitated carrying by rope slings or poles. As each wagon pulled up, gas personnel unloaded the boxes, unscrewed the box lids, removed the cylinders, and slung them by the two handles onto the carrying ropes or poles. The dome cap protected the gas valves during transport. The carriers, one at each end of the pole, wore large white patches on their backs with a number in black corresponding to the number of the intended cylinder gas emplacement.[55] Guides then led the way in the darkness along the duckboards through the communication trenches whose endless twists and turns added additional barriers that impeded the progress of the carrying parties. This carrying-and-portering was among the most arduous of the Specials' many tasks and was especially burdensome for shorter individuals such as Charlie Chance, an older schoolteacher, who due to lack of height always bore "the heavy end of the stick" whether in front or rear.[56] After stowing the cylinders in their trench emplacements, the Specials covered them with a protective layer of sandbags.

Where possible, gas officers commandeered divisional infantrymen for the portering, a recruitment understandably much resented. Requisitioned infantry carrying parties of the 47th Division regarded the unwieldy cylinders "with a certain holy dread."[57] The 2d Division complained bitterly that the cylinder carry-in interrupted all other traffic in the communication trenches for six hours.[58] Robert Graves and his company of Welch Fusiliers were later to perform this duty and found it extremely onerous: "This was worse than carrying the dead; the cylinders were cast iron, heavy and hateful. The men cursed and sulked. . . . I felt like screaming." This painful experience may account somewhat for the contempt for the whole concept of gas warfare which Graves expressed through his quasi-fictitious company commander in his autobiography, *Good-bye to All That*:

> It's damnable. It's not soldiering to use stuff like that, even though the Germans did start it. It's dirty, and it'll bring us bad luck.

We're sure to bungle it. Take those new gas-companies—sorry, excuse me, I mean accessory companies—their very look makes me tremble. Chemistry dons from London University, a few lads straight from school, one or two N.C.O.s of the old-soldier type, trained together for three weeks, then given a job as responsible as this, of course they'll bungle it. How could they do otherwise?[59]

Sewell noticed about this time a variation of a well-known verse scribbled on a sandbag by a South Wales Borderer: "God made bees, bees make honey. / The S.W.B. do the work, the R.E.s draw the money." Dalton recalled from 1916 a slight variation: "Some men work, some men shirk. Bees make honey, / We do all the _____ work! R.E.s get the money."[60] Most often, however, the Specials had to perform the carry-in themselves.

Strangely enough, the least flawed and best-organized carry-in seems to have been accomplished by the section led by newcomer A. B. White and performed by borrowed infantry from the 6th Brigade, with two men to a cylinder, an extra man as support, plus a noncommissioned officer in charge of each group of four cylinders. Sentries patrolled marked routes in and out of the communication trenches and the operation worked efficiently and smoothly. Following the carry-in, White detailed six men to guard the cylinders, withdrawing the rest of the section to support billets where they spent the last three days before the attack. Later, when the pipes arrived, White ordered these hung on pegs along the parapet, ready at hand when the time came for connection. The inexperienced White seems to have arranged things more ingeniously and professionally than many of the specially trained gas officers.

On 20 September Foulkes made a tour of inspection along the whole gas front. Each bay along the main gas frontage contained eleven to thirteen cylinders, double that number of pipe connections, assorted nuts and bolts, and two spanners (wrenches), one of which was adjustable.

> The top of each cylinder was surrounded by a dome cap which protected both the turning-on tap and the outlet valve. The spindle might have either a small rectangular projecting rod, or it might possess a convex wheel handle; each requires the use of a different type of spanner. The outlet valve was closed by a blind nut which had to be removed before connecting the jet-pipe.[61]

Each gas section had available two Vermorel sprayers to neutralize the inevitable gas leaks in the trenches. The Specials had been issued new, carefully synchronized watches, although Ashley's malfunctioned the first night and never worked again. All Specials wore identifying brassards of red, green, and white to prevent their being mistaken for deserters if found in the trenches after an attacking wave had gone over the top.

On 21 September both the British and the French preliminary bombardments commenced. That same day General Foch met with French, Robertson, and Wilson and warned that "not too much reliance" should be placed on the gas and that the tactical plans should be fully capable of execution independent of gas if necessary.[62] The French attack was not to include a gas component. Since Kitchener had committed Haig unconditionally to the attack on 25 September in support of the French and, most importantly, irrespective of the weather conditions, Haig could not wait indefinitely for ideal weather conditions as the Germans had done at Second Ypres. If the British and French assaults were to be synchronized, any waiting on the wind was out of the question. As he had furthermore been ordered to shelve alternative plans for a smaller attack, Haig had to hope for that favorable wind at dawn on 25 September.

On 23 September two seemingly unrelated events took place. In Britain the income tax went up to three and sixpence in the pound, and in France it began to rain heavily. The former underscored the heavy expense of the war effort, while the latter magnified enormously the physical difficulties of the gas handlers. The thunderstorms, which continued intermittently right through to the day of the offensive, transformed the once dry trenches into deep streams of fast-running water.

The last several nights prior to the attack saw feverish activity on the part of the gas troops as they hurriedly wrestled the last-arriving complements of cylinders into place. Sewell[63] remembers the congestion in the communication trenches during the night of 22/23 September as a battalion relief operation ran into his infantry carrying party:

There were in theory "up" and "down" trenches for this critical and dangerous night's work, but what with a battalion attempting to relieve "up" a "down" trench and confusion over transport it was not until dawn that the first of the P.B.I. began to filter into the front line, wearing grey flannel gas helmets most conspicuously rolled on top of their heads, and staggering under the 140 pounds weight of the cylinders.

The actual installation, of course, was wholly the responsibility of the Specials. "My 'Comicals' worked like beavers, and we got our quota nicely to bed before the strafe started again." Late the next afternoon Sewell supervised the transport of the cylinder pipes to the front line.[64]

One of Grantham's "circular" letters, distributed among as many as forty friends and relatives back home, describes his journey up the communication trench Thursday night, 23 September:

> It continued to rain and we continued to plod on and on now hidden from sight of everything and slipping about often into holes knee deep with water, always ankle deep in mud . . . on, on, on we struggled—it seemed almost an interminable age—the BEF men keeping up a steady flow of grousing and bad language, the rest in silence except for an occasional expletive as they tripped over a telephone wire or slid into some hole. At last . . . we arrived soaked through and plastered with slime up to and including our caps.[65]

The pipes, bundled in kits, and usually brought in following the cylinders, presented their own difficulties. Maneuvering the cumbersome and unwieldy bundles, some reaching ten feet in length, through the twists and turns of communication trenches and traverses proved both extremely fatiguing and frustrating:

> I shall never forget that journey down the communication trench. In order to localize the effect of shell explosions, the CT is zig-zag from beginning to end. The result was that we had to carry the pipes right above our heads in order to get them along the trench, otherwise at every corner they would get stuck. The CT is 3 1/2 miles long and the journey took us between seven and eight hours. Rain was falling during the whole of the journey. In many places the trench was over a foot deep in water.[66]

Right up to the last hours, Monier-Williams shuttled raw recruits from Helfaut to the front, ninety-seven noncommissioned officers as late as 24 September.[67] Among them were two sections of Company 189 led by Lt. A. E. Kent and Lt. Campbell-Smith, who reached the lines of the Indian Corps near Neuve Chapelle, opposite Aubers Ridge, at literally the last hour. Expecting 800 cylinders, they received only 160.[68] Their bays were scattered along appropriate salients in the line, not clustered side by side, as were those along the main line of attack. L. W. White, one of the last Specials to arrive in trime for the battle, joined section 33, already in the line at Neuve Chapelle, after only a few days practice in the trenches on Helfaut common. The gas cylinders here had already been dug in under the firing step. All along the line Royal Engineers had constructed duckboard bridges over the fire-trenches to facilitate advance of the infantry. Machine gunners had oiled their weapons to prevent gas corrosion.[69] Everything finally seemed to be falling into place for the British gas retaliation. Sir John French met with Foulkes on 23 September, after which the commander in chief confided to his diary, "All is in order and all we want is a favourable wind."[70]

Now it became simply a matter of waiting. Ashley passed much of the time walking the trenches or sitting on sandbags playing chess.[71] Of course, none of the soldiers were to know the precise moment of attack until hours beforehand, but an unmistakable air of subdued expectation pervaded the trenches. "It is rumored that the 'Big Push' with a curtain-raiser by the Special Companies R.E., is coming off in a few days' time."[72]

Z day minus one dawned, Friday, 24 September 1915. Apart from a few infantry sentries, gas personnel took over the greater part of the front line during the twenty-four hours before zero hour. The rains persisted.

> Still raining! Everywhere in the trench there is water, varying in depth. In some places it is a foot or two deep. . . . We brought our food in sandbags with us, and although everything is sodden, and cheese, bread, bacon and sultana are mixed up together, we have had quite decent meals. We scrape a little crevice in the side of the trench, make a fire there, and boil our tea and cook bacon—those who have any.[73]

The cook serving Campbell-Smith's section provided no hot meals the last several days, "being scared lest smoke from the cookhouse would draw enemy shell fire."[74] John Oriel in section 7 complained that by Friday he had no food left, having been up the line five days with no replenishment of rations.[75] Those Specials who had completed installation of their cylinders remained in the trenches throughout the day. Geoffrey Higson brought up the last of the pipes to the 7th Division front: "Still wet and muddy—over the ankles. We are in a fearful mess, but not excessively cold." John Thomas and his section 5 spent the day "moving from trench to trench and from dugout to dugout until evening."[76] They made cocoa by heating water with candles. G. O. Mitchell and his partner were up early checking out their emplacements:

> After we had got everything fixed up to our mutual satisfaction we went back to our dugout. During the course of the day, I watched the bombardment of the German line from a favourable position. Our heavy and field artillery were blasting their barbed wire and

front line off the face of the earth. It was a fine but terrible sight, the accuracy of our fire being remarkable. This had been going on for three days![77]

The last shipment of cylinders, dispatched from Runcorn on 22 September, arrived by ship at Boulogne on Friday morning, the twenty-fourth, and Foulkes arranged for special lorry transport directly from the port to the advance dumps at the heads of the various communication trenches. The cylinders reached the advance dump the same afternoon and the men of section 2, Company 186, completed their installation in the front lines. The continuing British bombardment was unremittingly fierce, with the occasional shell falling short, and several of Luther Mitchell's trenchmates received shrapnel wounds during the afternoon. Sniping fire continued throughout the evening. Mitchell was to "stand to" all night. Because the German guns and gunners had been withdrawn deep into the dugouts and recesses of the German front line, virtually all of the shelling was British. Men of the London Civil Service, with the 47th Division, thought no one in the German front lines could have lived through that day's bombardment.[78] Meiron Thomas, having joined the Special Companies too late to actively participate in the battle, nevertheless went up to see the front lines and wrote to his mother that Friday evening:

There is nothing left of the German front line trenches or wire. They have been exploded to the winds of the air so that everything should be plain sailing, although one never knows. In a way I am annoyed at being left out. . . . I should have tried hard to get into the trenches to witness the operation[s]. They will be talked of in history for the remainder of existence. That's all I can say.[79]

Gasman Ronald Purves, an agricultural student from Scotland and a transfer from a cavalry regiment, found refuge deep in a mine sap along the Bassée Canal, where he spent the night of 24 September. Writing by candlelight, he committed to his diary the harrowing ordeal of the forty-eight hours preceding zero hour:

There is an awful roaring, whizzing, screaming and banging of shells. A real hell must be going on in the German trenches. We left Chicory Factory at 5 o'clock on Thursday afternoon [23 September] & marched along to Annequin via Beuvry. Artillery ammunition columns galloping along past us to the guns. Great flashes of lightning going across the sky & a drizzly rain commenced, getting heavier & heavier until about 8 o'c when we had got our pipes on our shoulders. Mc_____ & I had our own set and a double set of spare pipes for the 1/4 mile or so up to the communication trench, Wilson's Way. Our shoulders felt as if cut to the bone with weight of pack and pipes, and we felt absolutely done up when we dropped them and passed them on. . . . It was awful work with the 12' pipes, getting them round the traverses. The mud was liquid and it was plastered up to our knees. We were soaked to the waist. Waterproof sheets saved our shoulders. It was too much for most of them, so we left all the pipes & took our packs up to the dug-outs, Mac and I going to this mine, a few yards from our cylinders.

When Purves tried to return for the pipes, he and Mac got lost twice and after walking several miles out of the way ultimately retrieved the pipes and slept in the trench sap. After breakfast of tea, bread, jam, and maconochie ration (beef and vegetables), they cleaned their own pipes, as well as some of the others, which had become thoroughly fouled during the carry-up.

German whizzbangs came over a bit in the forenoon, one landing outside the back parapet [parados] & the wind put our candle out, 20 yards down the mine. Spoke to a lot of the Argyle and Sutherland Highlanders who are in the trenches just now. They are going in the charge tomorrow for La Bassée & are fairly cheerful about it. They have seen a lot of fighting before, the 2 Battalion. I got a French bayonet along the trench from one of them, probably thrown over by a shell. Frenchmen are lying dead outside the trench; probably some are over me just now. British aeroplanes are up & saw none being shelled. The bombardment is hellish! Dirt is often dropping on us with the vibration of the bursting shells. One blow-back of a British shell made a piece land in the trench, ripping off a corner of a traverse 5 yds away from me. One of the A & S [Argyle and Sutherland] picked it up. It was very hot. I've got it in my pack now. I really can't describe this time here just now. It's not bothering me at all, but makes one feel a little queer. I do hope the wind changes. It's wrong for us just now.[80]

Late Friday afternoon, 24 September, the last gas section, loaded with pipes and spanners and commanded by borrowed officer F. D. Charles, arrived at the Loos front, where each man put on his identifying brassard and manned his battery. This last contingent brought the total number of men to 1,404 and the number of gas officers to 59, in charge of 5,500 chlorine gas cylinders.[81]

This last day, Foulkes, having completed final gas arrangements, also motored to Hinges. There, together with Haig, Monier-Williams, and Gold, he awaited zero hour. Throughout the day Gold labored over his meteorological charts. The wind remained southeasterly at about fifteen miles per hour, clearly unpropitious. But low barometer readings in the Bay of Biscay promised a westerly change, and upon this everything depended. As the hours passed, Gold became more and more perplexed. For some unknown reason the usual weather reports from the French coast and from inside France, which had hitherto arrived daily, did not arrive.[82] Without this information there was no way to confirm the expected turn of the wind from southeasterly to westerly. At 2 P.M. Rawlinson, Gough, and Gold met with Haig at Hinges to discuss the weather and zero hour. Gold could offer no conclusive weather prediction.[83] As to zero hour, "Goughie" suggested dawn and "Rawly" 10 A.M., and it was left open for the moment. The French were to go over at 10 A.M.. As late as 6 P.M. on Friday, the wind remained southeasterly, and heavy rain had again begun with no signs of stopping.

At 10:30 that night Lt. A. B. White, canal-side, left his section 5 in the front line and walked the 900 yards back to 6th Brigade headquarters to await final confirmation of zero hour. John Thomas, in this section, remembers first being ordered "to stand by our emplacements all night." Later orders allowed taking turns, four hours off and four on.[84] Percy Higson, with the 7th Division, slept that night on the firing platform of his front-line trench, covered by a waterproof ground sheet.[85] Frank Cousins, with the 15th Division opposite Loos, had supper at 12:30 A.M. and also slept on sandbags on his firing platform.[86]

On this, the last night before the battle, Foulkes sat up all night with Gold. By midnight he received the last of the "all ready" messages from each of his officers. To this point, he later alleged, the gas operation had been a "model of efficient staff organization."[87] He and Gold spent the night receiving localized wind reports and plotting directions on his desk map—positioning the flags in the appropriate directions and penciling in the velocities as he received them. By midnight the southeast wind had veered to the west, but it softened as the night wore on. Gold was acutely aware that light winds of less than three to four mph are extremely fitful, and locally subject to unpredictable and sudden changes of direction. Richard Butler, Haig's chief of staff, came in at frequent intervals to view the latest display. Only sporadically did the flags conform even to minimal conditions. Gold, frustrated at not being able to guarantee a favorable report, later wrote: "I shall never forget the night before the battle of Loos. . . . I still sigh and shudder, however, at the ghastliness of the whole business."[88] Also with Gold most of that night, Brig. Gen. John Charteris, head of British intelligence, remembered Gold's attitude as "very doubtful, but on the whole inclined to think the wind would increase and hold for the extra hour or so required."[89]

When Rawlinson wrote the last passage in his diary at II P.M., Friday, 24 September, prospects still did not look good: "It is a bit of a gamble but in war we must gamble if we are to do any good. If the wind is right we may do a big thing after all."[90] As the minutes ticked away past midnight a distinctly unpropitious calm settled along the whole of the front, especially noticeable on either side of La Bassée Canal. In Henry Williamson's novel, *A Fox under My Cloak*, a sergeant with the 1st Division near the very center of the gas frontage remarks to Lt. Philip Maddison, "I don't like the look of this quiet air, Sir. The men are saying that the gas will hang about, and they'd rather go over the bags [the parapet, which was made of sandbags] without it."[91]

Richard Gale remembers his section 7 commander, whom he called Mr. Dunn, about 3 A.M. handing him a copy of the program of gas and smoke discharges, with specific times noted only in reference to a still unannounced zero hour. It was the last time Gale was ever to see Mr. Dunn alive.[92] Notification of zero hour reached the last of the Special Company officers by telegraph just after 4:30 A.M., on 25 September. Section commanders then distributed final written specifics of the gas attack to their various bays. John Thomas recalls his section leader coming along "carrying little boards on which were printed instructions for the attack."[93] Lieutenant Charles, with the 15th Division, received his message at 4:40 A.M. In his case, it was he who passed on the time of zero hour to the infantry now moving up into the front-line trenches. L. W. White recalls a humorous moment as each infantryman received the customary offer of a measure of rum prior to going over the top: "The Ghurkas in our bay (there were two of us "chemists" in each fire bay) were having their rum rationed and insisted on sharing it with us. I had never tasted rum but not wishing to offend the dark little men with their kukris in hand, took much too big a swig and nearly choked."[94]

The imperturbable Haig went to bed at his usual hour and slept soundly until 2 A.M., when he was awakened with news of the latest weather reports. Were it not for Kitchener's commitment to the French, the unfavorable weather prospects might have prompted a decision to cancel the gas discharge. But Haig was committed to the attack nonetheless, and he had come to place such hopes in the use of gas that he could not contemplate a satisfactory outcome without it. To cancel the gas attack would in Haig's mind foreclose all hope of success, and to postpone the infantry attack had been disallowed in advance. In deference to French urging, the British were to fight at best a chancy battle on a front they would never have chosen, with severely inadequate artillery, tied to an inflexible timetable which might well undermine chances for gas to clear the path that artillery could not.[95] Since Haig did not have to make a decision until 3 A.M. he went back to sleep for another hour. When at 3 A.M. his aides woke him again from a sound sleep to make the final decision, Gold's prognostication was slightly more sanguine.[96] Haig set zero hour for 6:30 A.M., wind or no wind, gas or no gas, and promptly went back to sleep.

At 5 o'clock, an hour before dawn and only fifty minutes before gas zero hour, Foulkes and Haig consulted a last time. Foulkes remembers the wind as "almost calm, SSW, very unfavourable."[97] It was clear that the minimum conditions were not to be met after all. Haig wavered. He telephoned Gough at I Corps headquarters and asked whether it was still possible to cancel the gas. General Gough replied that it was too late.[98]

Haig then asked Foulkes for reassurance that, regardless of orders, in the face of locally unfavorable wind conditions, the gas officers fully understood that they had the authority to cancel the gas discharge in their respective sectors. Foulkes replied with clear assurance that they did.[99] Haig's private memoirs attest to his grave doubts during those last moments:

> I went out at 5 A.M. Almost a calm. Alan Fletcher lit a cigarette, and the smoke drifted in puffs toward the N.E. Staff officers were ordered to stand by in case it were necessary to counter the order to attack. At one time owing to the calm, I feared the gas might simply hang about *our* trenches. However, at 5:15 A.M. I said "Carry on." I went to the top of our wooden look-out tower. The wind came gently from S.W. and by 5:40 had increased slightly. The leaves of the poplar trees gently rustled. This seemed satisfactory. But what a risk I must run of gas blowing back upon our own dense masses of troops![100]

With Gold, the president of the Royal Meteorological Society, standing by, one may wonder whether Haig sensed any irony in his taking notice of the direction of Fletcher's puff of smoke and the rustling of poplar leaves. About 5 A.M., along the southern gas front, Captain Otter, in front of the 47th Division, and Maj. E. S. B. Hamilton, with the Royal Army Medical Corps, observed a slight improvement in wind direction. "How providential," everyone said, but the improvement was only temporary.[101]Fox, in the firing-line trenches astride the canal, remembered the moments just before dawn:

At intervals we joined the sentry on the firestep and gazed across the German lines; once or twice an enemy machine gun opened up, the bullets skimming our parapet with deadly precision, making bits of sandbag fly; a Verey light soared over and dropping close to our trench, illuminated the scene for a few moments, . . . some rats came out of a hole at one end of the bay, scrambled up the side of the trench, gazed at us warily while sniffing the air, and disappeared over the top; orders were given quietly as the sentries were relieved; there was a tenseness of excitement, mingled with a foreboding of the morrow. The sky slowly lightened away to the East, and as the order "stand to" was passed along, the infantry manned the front line trench in the chill of the early hours; it was September 25, 1915.[102]

6
Loos—The First British Gas Attack

As Haig and Foulkes agonized over the weather at headquarters, the infantry and the Specials huddled nervously in the crowded trenches awaiting dawn in a drizzling rain. The long weeks of preparation were over. It was finally time to connect the pipes and open the valves, time to gamble, time to retaliate. The role of the Special Companies in the complex drama that began to unfold with the Saturday dawn of 25 September is best related in several stages: first, the comparatively small gas discharges on the northern diversionary fronts; next, the indecision as to whether or not to release the gas on 2d Division front; then the main gas discharge itself from 5:50 A.M. to 6:30 A.M.; and finally, the subsequent infantry assaults.

The diversionary attacks consisted of three separate feints to the north, commencing up to two hours before the major assault. Significant gaps separated each of these three attacking forces. The earliest began before dawn when a small gas contingent with the 8th Division of III Corps opened a limited number of cylinders and smoke candles on the farthest subsidiary front, near Armentières. No gas diaries survive to provide details. In the environs of Neuve Chapelle, opposite Aubers Ridge, two brigades of the Meerut Division (Garhwal and Bareilly, both mixing Indian and British battalions), supported by a short gas discharge, composed the second feint. The Indian Corps's wholly British 19th Division, in front of Festubert, comprised the third diversionary effort.

Led by Campbell-Smith, gas personnel on the Meerut Division's front had installed their cylinders opposite Aubers Ridge and distributed candles over a wider frontage.[1] Every hour throughout the night, Campbell-Smith had conscientiously reported weather conditions—always unfavorably—but at 4 A.M. word came reaffirming the gas discharge. "I remember being very upset that the gas was going to be used."[2] About an hour before zero hour a chance German trench mortar bomb scored a direct hit at one of these gas emplacements, bursting the cylinder heads and drenching the trench with chlorine, the first of many such accidents.³ Campbell-Smith nevertheless moved up and down the line, visiting every emplacement "warning our corporals to turn the gas off if the wind at their emplacement was not clearing it. . . . As I went along the line the message giving Zero hour was being passed along by word of mouth. To my horror I came to a bay where the message being passed was Zero hour at 5:15 not 5:50." Having corrected the zero hour by working back to where the mistake originated, Campbell-Smith and his men opened the valves at 5:50 in an uncertain wind.

A vivid memory is just at or after Zero hour of a cylinder or pipe leaking fast into the bay and no one in the bay. We had the cylinder turned off in no time but gas was thick in the trench.⁴

It was difficult having emptied one cylinder from one set of pipes; it was not only difficult to undo the nuts which formed the unions, but when you had undone them a considerable amount of liquid dropped from the pipes into the trench and fumed there and certainly a minute or more than a minute was lost in changing from one cylinder to another, so that there was an appreciable time when each emplacement was actually letting off no gas; there was a break in the continuity of the cloud. The other thing I remember is there was a leak of both joints and that under the conditions of battle [that] was almost unpreventable; from the high strain I do not think it could have avoided having some leaks because it was not until the pipe got at all dirty that they were likely to get the threads crossed and in actually swinging out the parapet pipe which must be done at the last moment so that the Germans did not see them coming over the parapet top they had to swing out the parapet pipe to a right angle and then tighten up the union, and many men tightened up the unions as quickly as they could to turn on the gas and did not tighten them up sufficiently so that there were many leaks at that junction of the parapet pipe and the connexion pipe.⁵

At 6 A.M. the first wave of the units from the Bareilly Brigade, including battalions of the Black Watch, went over the top and "through the first line like butter." Moments later, the second wave met gasping soldiers of the Black Watch stumbling back, having run into their own gas and apparently not having kept their gas masks on.⁶ Campbell-Smith had the misfortune of meeting one of these at this most inopportune time: "I was rather disconcerted by one of these warriors who came back into the trench saying 'Damn your bloody gas' several times and with great vehemence. He was coughing badly and I offered him an ammonia ampoule and pressed him to inhale it but he would have none of that and departed again over the parapet to rejoin his comrades.''

Nearby, L. W. White, one of the gas corporals, was also standing by for zero hour with a battalion of the 3d Ghurka Rifles (Garhwal Brigade). Promptly at 5:48 a big mine which had been tunneled under the German lines detonated, and two minutes later twenty colored rockets fired from brigade headquarters lit up the dawn sky, the signal for the onset of the ten-minute gas discharge.

> As the time of the attack drew near my comrade and I connected up the iron piping to the cylinders (there were about six) ready to carry the gas over the parapet and a few feet into no man's land. . . . But at zero hour neither of us could turn on the gas because either the spanner provided was too short or the valves were too tightly closed. Then the Ghurkas went ''over the top.''[7]

Many of the Specials were to encounter troubles such as White described, and few managed to discharge all their allotted gas. With the same brigade infantryman 2d Lt. George Grossmith[8] watched nervously as discharged gas drifted in an uncertain wind.

> At 5:59 our first line got over the parapet and formed up going forward immediately. At 6 the guns ceased and artillery lifted 100 yards. From this point the tragedy began. . . . At the time the gas cloud was being released the wind was blowing at the rate of two miles per hour (very slow indeed). As our front, at this point of the line, faced southeast this meant that the gas travelled ''half-right'' from our front. The gas rolled out of the cylinders in dense, sickly looking yellow clouds, and seemed to pile up after a time instead of going forward. This was no doubt due to the gas being generated faster that the wind could carry it away. Now on each side of the gas, for a hundred yards, there were ''smoke candles'' which generated a harmless dark brown smoke to go over with the gas, screen everything from the eyes of the enemy and especially from the artillery. We got up over the parapet and started on our way. . . . The gas hung in a thick pall over everything, and it was impossible to see more than ten yards.[9]

The gas and smoke so obscured the view that Grossmith's unit became disoriented and the survivors inadvertently circled back to their own lines. Undamaged enemy firepower wiped out most of Grossmith's battalion and most of the other leading battalions of the Meerut Division. Twenty-one-year-old Grossmith was wounded in the thigh at about 7

Table 6.1 Order of battle at Loos (north to south), showing location of gas and other personnel

Diversionary Forces		
Indian Corps	Meerut Division	Walter Campbell-Smith
		L.W. White
		George Grossmith
	19th Division	
Main Attacking Forces		
I Corps (Gough)		
	2d Division	
	5th Brigade (north	Percy-Smith
	of canal)	Jack Sewell
		Martin Sidney Fox
		D. M. Wilson
		John A. Oriel
		Donald Grantham[a]
	6th Brigade (south	A. B. White
	of canal)	John Thomas
		Ronald Purves
		Robert Graves
	9th Division	R. C. Gale
		Luther Mitchell
		George Pollitt
	7th Division	Higson brothers
		G. O. Mitchell
		Charles Ashley[a]
IV Corps (Rawlinson)		
	1st Division	Henry Williamson
	15th Division	F. D. Charles
		Frank Cousins
		R. Dawson
	47th Division	R. E. Otter
		F. H. Wallis

[a]Precise location uncertain. Donald Grantham was with 2d Division, brigade undetermined. Charles Ashley was with I Corps, possibly 7th Division.

o'clock, remained on the ground hardly daring to move throughout the day, and managed to crawl to safety only when darkness fell, writing the preceding account from the hospital two days later.

Foulkes admits that only a few of the cylinders were opened on the Aubers front, but attributes this to an intentional shutoff due to a change in the direction of the wind rather than to any defect in the apparatus.[10] It is not clear why Foulkes deployed gas on any of these subsidiary fronts—particularly the Armentières front, where its earlier appearance compromised the chance of surprise later on the main

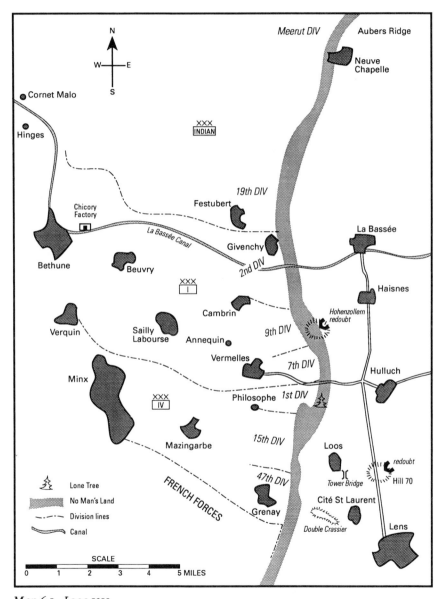

N
W —|— E
S

Cornet Malo

Hinges

Meerut DIV   Aubers Ridge

Neuve
Chapelle

XXX
INDIAN

19th DIV

Chicory
Factory   Festubert

La Bassée Canal   La Bassée

Givenchy
2nd DIV

Bethune   Beuvry   Haisnes

XXX
I

Cambrin   Hohenzollern
redoubt

Verquin   9th DIV

Sailly   Annequin
Labourse   Hulluch

Vermelles   7th DIV

Minx   Philosophe   1st DIV

XXX
IV

Mazingarbe   redoubt
15th DIV   Loos   Hill 70

🌲 Lone Tree   47th DIV   Tower Bridge
No Man's Land   Grenay   Cité St Laurent
Division lines   Double Crassier   Lens
Canal

FRENCH FORCES

SCALE
0   1   2   3   4   5 MILES

Map 6.1. Loos 1915

front—since the amounts of gas were too small to be decisive. Nor does Foulkes allude in his book to the earlier infantry zero hour on these northern fronts.

The attack of the third part of the diversionary effort, that of the 19th Division (58th Brigade, Indian Corps), coincided with that of the main force just to its south. Here, and along the main gas frontage from La Bassée southward, the artillery bombardment intensified for the last hour beginning at 5:30 A.M. Plans called for the forty-minute alternating gas and smoke discharge to commence at 5:50, zero hour for the infantry being 6:30. The historian of the 19th Division was later to write:

Dawn on the 25th, a thoroughly miserable morning; a thin rain was falling and what wind there was was obviously unfavourable, for it was, at the best, only a breeze which changed direction continually.

The gas was discharged and hung in a thin cloud, first over our trenches in an exasperating manner, and then began to drift slowly—very slowly—towards the enemy's trenches. The smoke candles had been lighted and created a pall of dense smoke in front of our trenches, thereby doing more harm than good.

The lead battalions of the 58th Brigade advanced into a stream of machine-gun and rifle fire, and within the first fifteen minutes twelve officers and about three hundred of the 9th Welch lay either dead or wounded. No one advanced more than eighty yards. The 9th Royal Welch Fusiliers fared no better and their commander was killed. Shortly after the lead companies of the second waves of the 9th Cheshires and the 6th Wiltshires scrambled over the top, orders went out to suspend the attack. Officers were later to conclude that the gas and smoke had been of no assistance whatever.[11]

Meanwhile a paralyzing indecision seized gas officers up and down the main frontage as the wind velocity and direction was nowhere very favorable. Along the 2d Division sector especially, the approach of dawn brought a clear deterioration of wind conditions from marginal to decidedly unfavorable, and the gas officers of Percy-Smith's "composite company" stationed there faced the approaching zero hour with great apprehension.[12] Several gas officers on the left (north) side of the canal did in fact try to cancel the gas discharge, among them Jack Sewell.

The wind was now practically nil and it was drizzling, so on receipt of zero hour only one hour before it was due I rang up 5th Brigade HQ and asked them if this meant I was to carry on. They said "Yes, why?" I explained that I had reported unfavorably on the wind all night and would not hold myself responsible for the effect of gas on our own men. An agitated voice said he would report to Corps, and I received the order "Carry on."[13]

Captain Percy-Smith also tried to countermand the orders for gas release, cautioning the trench commander that the wind was unfavorable. When the latter reported this by phone to the 2d Division, its commander, Gen. Henry Horne, reconfirmed the original order: "The answer was 'The order is to turn on the gas.' Later on: 'The gas officer refuses to open the cylinders,' and the reply 'Then shoot the b____.'"[14]

Robert Graves, on the right (south) side of the canal with the Royal Welch Fusiliers (19th Brigade), corroborates the peremptory nature of the order: "It seems that at half-past four an R.E. captain commanding the gas-company in the front line phoned through to divisional headquarters: 'Dead calm. Impossible to discharge accessory.' The answer he got was: 'Accessory to be discharged at all costs.'"[15] Section commander A. B. White, sensing impending calamity, also remonstrated:

By 5:30 A.M. I had everything ready to start at zero, and I went back a short distance to ascertain whether the wind was favourable. Finding it blowing very lightly from the SSW and varying considerably in direction, I decided not to carry on and warned the men to do nothing without further orders. At 5:40 A.M. a mine was blown up in front of my line. The charge appeared to have been too weak as no debris was thrown up, only an immense cloud of smoke. From the direction in which the smoke drifted I was confirmed in my impression that it would not be safe to carry on. At 5:48 I got the Brigade on the telephone and informed the General [A. C. Daly] that I was unable to carry on. He replied that he had already spoken to the 2nd Division about the wind being unsuitable and that he had received a direct order to carry on. In these circumstances he ordered me to let the gas off. I returned to the front line and ordered the gas to be turned on about 5:58 A.M.[16]

John Thomas's recollection parallels A. B. White's account.[17] Just before zero hour Thomas suggested to White that they uncover a few cylinders, remove the dome caps and oil the nozzles so as to be better prepared for the discharge, but White preferred to leave them protected until the last possible moment lest they be hit by stray shell fragments.

We had our smoke helmets on our heads in readiness to pull down when the discharge began. However, to our consternation, a runner came rushing round shouting that the discharge was cancelled.

Martin Sidney Fox with gas cylinders in front-line trench. (Courtesy of Royal Engineers Museum)

Scarcely believing this, Davies asked me to see what was happening to the Section on our left. I ran round the few traverses that separated us, to find them in the act of turning on the gas. Pulling my smoke helmet down as I ran back, I found Davies in a cloud of yellow gas. He had turned one cylinder on but there were leaks at every joint of the parapet pipes.[18]

The less than acceptable wind conditions led to some indecision and hesitation elsewhere along the line as well, but nowhere else did the gas officers try as strenuously to countermand orders as astride the Bassée Canal with the 2d Division.

At 5:50 A.M. the waiting was over, and up and down the seven-mile main front, wind or no wind, the gas Specials threw their pipes over the parapet and turned on the valves with their spanners. No member of the Special Companies would ever forget the suspense and strain of the next forty minutes during which the deadly chlorine and thick smoke hissed from the opened cylinders and candles. It now became painfully evident that a synchronized gas release under battle conditions was far different from the dummy practices on the languid Helfaut common. No matter where the position, the rain and trench mud had coated pipes, spanners, and cylinders with a slick slime.

> To attach a pipe to twelve cylinders in succession and turn the tap on and off in a period of 38 minutes does not sound a difficult task, for the gas took less than 2 minutes to flow out of each cylinder and we had two pipes. However, working as hard as we could, and without intermission while smoke was being sent over, we managed to empty only ten cylinders, which we later discovered was more than the average. The difficulty was caused by the release of pressure making the nuts so cold that they would not fit easily onto the new cylinder. . . . One man, we were told, was so frustrated that he carried his cylinders forward and then tried to burst them by firing at them; another followed his example but turned the taps on without attaching any pipe.[19]

The frustrated gas soldier in this story was Sergeant Major Morrison of Company 186, who was killed by a jet-stream of liquid chlorine which struck him as he fired at close range.[20] John Thomas's diaries disclose similar problems in section 5.

> Streams of gas [were] escaping from every joint in the pipes, and Skinner [was] busily spraying both Davies and myself with "Hypo" solution from his Vermorel Sprayer in an effort to neutralize the chlorine with the "hypo" solution. I fastened onto the leaks and tightened the joints with my spanner, and when the first cylinder became empty proceeded to deal with the second. The escaping gas had so chilled the pipes by now, that it was almost impossible to unfasten the joints. There was a slight drizzle of rain also, and this turned to snow on the pipes and the outside of the pipes became covered with a slippery surface of ice. We had got the second cylinder on when the word came along to "Turn off." Whilst we were on our knees turning on, there was a terrific din going on in the trench. "Runners" were rushing past with urgent orders and stumbling over us as they ran, whilst others were placing short ladders against the side of the trench to assist those who were to follow "over the top."

Lt. D. M. Wilson, a chemical engineer from Ipswich, also astride the canal, blamed gas contamination in the trenches not on uncooperative winds, but on faulty apparatus: "The wind was favourable and all went well until we had to change the parapet pipes in each emplacement

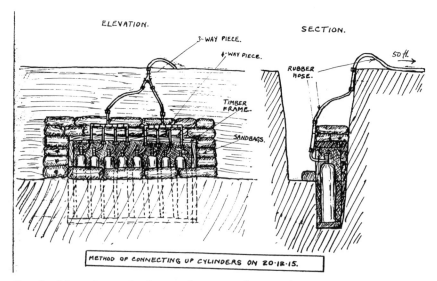

Sketch of front-line cylinder emplacement showing four-way connections. (Courtesy of Imperial War Museum, Richard Gale Diary)

from the first cylinder to the next. When the pipe was disconnected the residual gas flowed back into the trench and caused a number of gas casualties."[21] Nearby, gas corporal Ronald Purves crouched and waited.

> The bombardment was pretty hellish, absolutely indescribable. At 5:40 A.M. Sergt. Reilly came along and gave the order to let off the gas at 5:50 A.M., and we did. Leaks of Cl_2 came out at the joints, but after some struggling, got things going. Mac turned on the first one as I threw out the pipe, & then did nothing. So went at it as best as I could, choking, coughing, half-blinded, and feeling as if the last moments had come. It's impossible to put any of the sensations on paper; but I shall not forget it after I get home. At my 6th or 7th cylinder, Rayner came along and told me to shut off because our own men were being gassed. My own bit was thick with gas, and I couldn't see except in a blink or two. A hail of shells, both British and German, were landing all round, and a rattle of machine guns was everywhere.[22]

Where the Specials Companies released the gas in contrary winds or dead calm the results were predictably disastrous. Jack Sewell, who also protested the discharge in vain, watched helplessly from the fire-step.

I saw the first brown and white smoke from the candles along the parapet begin to mingle with the greeny-yellow cloud of chlorine, but rising straight up into the air and drifting along our own front line. . . . The cloud quickly hid everything from sight, which was probably a mercy. . . . Once committed to an attack such as this, the wretched Section Officer could do nothing but watch and pray, but the strain on our nerves was considerable as we had received no orders from higher authority as to our individual responsibility.[23]

Consequences for the infantry were nonetheless disastrous, as illustrated by the report of an infantryman in the 5th Brigade:

The gas, when set free, travelled away from our trenches—though its direction was NE rather than E. No trouble occurred until almost 6:25 A.M. when our trenches were suddenly enveloped in dense volumes of gas which rolled up from the canal on our right, where it had apparently collected, and possibly blown back. Within 5 minutes our two leading platoons had only 7 and 9 men left respectively who were fit to carry on.[24]

A. B. White, on the south side of the canal, was another of the officers who had tried unsuccessfully to protest the discharge.

At first the gas drifted slowly toward the German lines (it was plainly visible in the rain), but at one or two bends of the trench the gas drifted into it. In these cases it was turned off at once. At about 6:20 the wind changed and quantities of the gas came back over our parapet, so I ordered all gas to be turned off and only smoke candles used.[25]

The necessity of wearing the awkward and uncomfortable gas mask during the entire operation compounded difficulties. A small insert of mica allowed a certain degree of cloudy vision,[26] but, unfortunately, the proper use of these primitive gas hoods made the wearer uncomfortably hot. To allow greater freedom of movement and comfort, Charles Ashley removed his gas hood before zero hour, laying it and his revolver on the parapet behind him.

In addition to these gas-related difficulties, the onset of the gas attack elicited an intense retaliatory artillery bombardment. "They are shelling us for all they are worth," Luther Mitchell wrote. Grantham compared no man's land that morning to a "gorse bush on a hot summer day—it just crackled and split all over."[27] Shells bursting along the line shattered some of the fragile pipes, connectors, and sometimes the

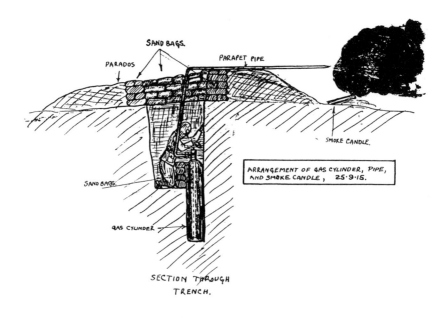

SAND BAGS.

PARADOS

PARAPET PIPE

SMOKE CANDLE.

ARRANGEMENT OF GAS CYLINDER, PIPE, AND SMOKE CANDLE, 25·9·15.

SAND BAGS.

GAS CYLINDER

SECTION THROUGH TRENCH.

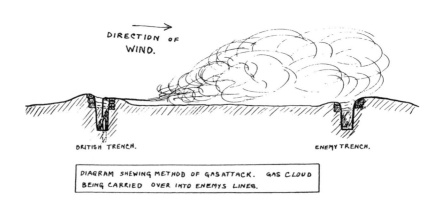

DIRECTION OF WIND.

BRITISH TRENCH.

ENEMY TRENCH.

DIAGRAM SHEWING METHOD OF GAS ATTACK. GAS CLOUD BEING CARRIED OVER INTO ENEMYS LINES.

Sketches of trench cross section at the Battle of Loos, 25 September 1915. (Courtesy of Imperial War Museum, Richard Gale Diary)

chlorine gas cylinders themselves. Parapets collapsed, bay emplacements caved in, tons of earth poured into the trenches, and lingering
everywhere was the frightening smell of deadly chlorine gas. "Some
bays were blown in almost completely burying the cylinders and their
crews, connecting pipes were blown about and severed, while some cylinders were burst, pouring gas into our trenches."[28] Graves's account of
this part of the action is gratuitously uncharitable:

> Thomas [Graves's fictitious infantry officer] had not over-esti-
> mated the gas-company's efficiency. The spanner for unscrewing
> the cocks of the cylinders proved, with two or three exceptions, to
> be misfits. The gas-men rushed about shouting for the loan of an
> adjustable spanner. They managed to discharge one or two cylin-
> ders, the gas went whistling out, formed a thick cloud a few yards
> off in No Man's Land, and then gradually spread back into our
> trenches. The Germans, who had been expecting gas, immediately
> put on their gas-helmets: semi-rigid ones, better than ours. Bun-
> dles of oily cotton-waste were strewn along the German parapet
> and set alight as a barrier to the gas. Then their batteries opened on
> our lines. The confusion in the front trench must have been horri-
> ble, direct hits broke several of the gas cylinders, the trench filled
> with gas, the gas-company stampeded.[29]

The large amounts of gas which had by this time leaked into the British trenches were having a deadly effect. Some men, such as Wilson,
fortunately suffered only mild gassing. In section 26, exploding shells
filled the trench with dense smoke, and Luther Mitchell, returning
from another traverse where he had rushed to apply an emergency field
dressing, found his mate Stuart "half suffocating with our own gas. We
all had gas helmets on, but they got so stuffy that the temptation is to
remove them for a breath of air, which proves to be a breath of chlorine."[30]

Opposite the Hohenzollern Redoubt, the 9th Division faced only
marginally more favorable winds than the 2d Division. Stationed here,
in support of the 26th Infantry Brigade, was Richard C. Gale.

> At 5:30 we again stood by for 5:50, by now it was lighter and the
> breeze a little more marked. One minute more, the intensity of our
> artillery rising in a roaring crescendo every moment, what an im-
> mensity of time that last minute seemed, at last zero hour arrived,
> the gas was turned on, and to the accompaniment of an inferno of
> fire of all calibers, the greenish wall of gas slowly grew from our
> parapets, rolling across no-man's-land to the Redoubt. In addition,

A

SECRET.—(Not to be carried forward in the Assault).

TIME TABLE OF GAS.

Attacks South of the LA BASSEE CANAL.

(Minutes).	
0	Start the gas and run 6 cylinders one after the other at full blast until all are exhausted.
0-12‡—0-40	Start the smoke. The smoke is to run concurrently with the gas if the gas is not exhausted by 0 12
0-20	Start the gas again and run 6 cylinders one after the other at full blast until all are exhausted.
0-32—0-40	Start the smoke again. The smoke is to run concurrently with the gas, if the gas is not exhausted by 0-32.
0-38	Turn all gas off punctually. Thicken up smoke with triple candles. Prepare for assault.
0-40	**ASSAULT.**

‡ On the 3-cylinder and no-cylinder fronts the smoke will be started at 0-6.

Note :—From 0 to 0-40, front system of hostile trenches will be kept under continuous shrapnel fire. Defences further in rear under bombardment of H.E. shell of all calibres.

At 0-40 artillery fire will lift as required.

1st Army Printing Section, R.E. 465

Gas timetable for the Battle of Loos, Hohenzollern front. (Courtesy of Imperial War Museum, Richard Gale Diary)

smoke candles were used to render the gas cloud more opaque and form a screen of invisibility for our infantry. It was not long before the enemy guessed what was happening, and rocket signals, calling for help were sent up to warn their gunners. An aeroplane passing overhead dropped a smoke signal, giving the range to the gunners, and soon the air was thick with shrapnel and the earth trembling from the impact of high explosive shells. While the gas attack was in progress, the Camerons (5th Queen's Own) prepared for their share of the proceedings with the greatest unconcern, and gave us their caps and scraps of tartan for souvenirs. Tea has just been handed round, with a stiff dose of rum added to it. Meanwhile the time passes and the gas will soon be turned off—6:28 A.M. The gas and smoke cloud rolls on, now a great wall of greenish yellow fog.

Then silence. A shouted order and "the Jacks are up" and "Over the top" and the long awaited 'Big Push' has begun.[31]

Experiences of gas Specials all along the line were similarly horrifying. On the 7th Division front, G. O. Mitchell and his section crouched amid the 1st South Staffordshires.[32]

The day broke dull and a slight drizzle was blowing about 1/4 [degree] left from us about 5 mph. The S.S.R. [South Staffordshire Regiment of the 7th Division] was occupying our part of the line. We received our orders and zero time fairly early on. Zero was 5:50 A.M. We started our performance on the minute. I got a big mouthful with the first cylinder and then, *of course*, pulled my helmet down. We had only two pipes for twelve cylinders and had to change over when the one was empty. God, what a game! The rotten apparatus they had given us was leaking all over the place and we were working in a cloud of gas. We sweated ourselves to death and only got eight off. All gas had to be turned off at 6:28 A.M. At 6:30 the infantry had to go over the parapet. We finished on time.

A sergeant infantryman with the 6th Gordons (20th Brigade) complained that he had never been taught anything about gas, that the helmets were not much good, and that the trenches were full of gas.

Half of us was gassed, you see, those helmets wouldn't take the gas, and we were choking there and spitting and choking and I got terribly sick and I was sick and vomiting and I couldn't cut it there any longer and there were others a lot like me just the same.

As a result of this gassing the sergeant was out of action for several months, but, like the vast majority of gas cases, recovered sufficiently to return to France following sick leave.[33]

Rawlinson's three divisions of IV Corps, 1st, 15th, and 47th, occupied the remaining frontage from the Vermelles Road south to where the line joined the French units near Grenay. The 15th and 47th Divisions represented the first of Kitchener's New Armies and were experiencing their first combat of the war. The 1st Division faced Lone Tree, the 15th stood opposite Loos, and the 47th faced the Double Crassier in front of Lens. The German bombardment had seriously damaged the gas pipes here. Lieutenant Charles reported a southwest wind at "very little over 1 mph," close to an acceptable direction, but with far too little velocity.[34] The troops in 15th Division were wondering if the wind conditions justified the gas discharge.[35] Here, waiting anxiously as zero hour approached, was Frank Cousins:

Gas cylinders in the front line at Loos. (Courtesy of Imperial War Museum)

> Rain was very heavy and the trenches a swamp. . . . At 15 to 6
> o'clock we finished final preparations, though the wind was very
> doubtful. We had quite given [up] all idea of using gas when word
> came to start in 5 minutes. The guns talked all night. At 5 o'clock
> the guns were at it hammer and tongs. At 10 to 6 we threw over a
> smoke candle and the wind carried over the gas at an angle of 30 de-
> grees. At once the Germans sent up a red and green light.[36]

It is curious that Cousins displayed such grave doubts about the wind
since he was posted in one of the more favorable sectors. Lieutenant
Charles, nearby, gave the order to turn on the gas at 5:50 A.M.:

> The Germans, who had not fired a shot all night, immediately
> plastered our parapet with shrapnel, machine-gun and rifle fire.
> The shrapnel did a large amount of damage to our pipes, and,
> through this fact and the eagerness of the men to turn on the gas
> before tightening up the connections, our trench was very soon
> filled with gas. . . . The infantry in the trenches, finding the heat
> inside their smoke helmets trying and experiencing some diffi-
> culty in breathing, were inclined to draw them up to get a couple of
> breaths of fresh air, with the result that quite a number of them
> were more or less seriously gassed. Directly these men found
> themselves coughing they wrenched their helmets off and stag-
> gered down the trench, making it very difficult for us to work or

even move at all. Also at this period the wind changed slightly and some of the smoke . . . poured down the trench.[37]

Cousins's account continues: "Walker very soon got gassed but I carried on. I was very busy and barely noticed the shrapnel and whizz bangs which came over in chunks. I fired off six cylinders having to stop because of the veering of the wind. A triple candle finished it."[38]

Promptly at 6:30 all gas and smoke discharges ceased, whistles sounded, and all along the line the infantry clambered up the assault ladders and over the parapet into the din of no man's land. Most soldiers had about a hundred yards to cross, following the gas cloud. John Thomas, on the south side of the canal, watched the first infantry disappear into the morning mist:

The wind was so light that it scarcely carried the gas away, and it hung about in depressions and shell-holes between the lines. Into this the infantry advanced only to find themselves choking and gasping for breath. In no time the men sent over were stumbling back into the trench, some wounded, most coughing and struggling for breath from the effects of the gas into which they had stumbled. The enemy reacted, after a short pause, with violent machine-gun fire that swept the parapets like hail and covered everyone in the trench with the earth dislodged by the bullets. The bullets raked the parapets like spitting tongues of serpents and spelt death to any head that showed above the trench. In no time I was busy bandaging some of the wounded, but any that could walk, made for the dressing station as fast as they could.

Though most all gas personnel with the 2d Division discontinued the discharge as soon as it became evident that its effect was counterproductive, the advancing infantry in this sector suffered heavy gas losses. Foulkes blamed casualties here, however, on uncut German wire. On the 9th Division front, "light and variable" winds blew the gas back upon the advancing infantry, but the Royal Scots Fusiliers advanced so quickly that they bypassed the gas and advanced ahead of it, overrunning the Hohenzollern Redoubt during the morning.[39]

Gasman G. O. Mitchell watched with fascination the first wave of 7th Division battalions scramble up the ladders and out of the fire-trench.

The Staffordshires went over where we were as if they were on parade, at the slope and dressing by the right. There was very little rifle fire but it was an inspiring sight. Pretty soon the German artillery opened. Their fire wasn't particularly heavy, but they were sending over some heavy stuff and I had a few near squeaks. Soon the wounded began to come back, and we saw some horrible wounds and bandaged up a good number. All at once a number of men (un-wounded) came back with a tale that they hadn't been able to get through the barbed wire. My opinion was that they had got "wind up." Soon an order came on "Every man stand to, German counter-attack!" My feelings can be imagined, but it was only a rumour! The only Germans coming over were prisoners under escort. There was a few young lads among them, but the majority looked no different in age and appearance to our lads. A goodly number looked as if they had suffered from our little efforts.[40]

Rawlinson observed the drama of IV Corps unfold from the top of a fosse about three miles from the front: "The view before me was one I shall never forget. Gradually a huge cloud of white and yellow gas rose from our trenches to a heighth between 200-300 feet, and floated quietly away towards the German trenches."[41] In his opinion, "It was a wonderful sight."[42] A slight southerly wind eddy pushed the drifting gas more in a northerly direction along no man's land rather than easterly across it, especially where a distinct bulge in the line placed the 1st Division directly in the path of any gas blown northward from the 15th Division. The advancing units of the 2d Brigade, on the south end of the 1st Division, suffered severely from these gas pockets drifting along from the south, their 2d King's Royal Rifles alone reporting some 200 men incapacitated due to gas.[43] At regular intervals Rawlinson relayed news from the front by telephone back to First Army headquaters. At 7:15 A.M.: "1st Division getting on slowly, being delayed by own gas." At 8 A.M.: "1st Division still hung up by our gas." At 8:30 A.M.: "1st Division lost 2000 of our men from our own gas."[44]

It was here along the 15th Division front opposite the town of Loos that the much-celebrated Scottish piper, Peter Laidlaw, of the 7th King's Own Scottish Borderers, won the Victoria Cross. Laidlaw "jumped up on to our parapet and piped away, though gas fumes surrounded him, and enemy rifle fire was sweeping our trenches."[45] The Scottish Division watched the gas cloud drift forward: "The effects of the white clouds of smoke rolling slowly towards the enemy trenches was extraordinary. It looked as if a curtain, stabbed here and there with red bursts of shrapnel, had been drawn across the Division's front."[46] Moments later the first companies of the King's Own Scottish Borderers went over the top, disappearing into the thick curtain of chlorine gas, and followed at short interval by the Camerons, the Sutherlands,

Infantry preparing to go over the top at Loos amid clouds of chlorine. (Courtesy of Liddell Hart Centre for Military Archives)

and another battalion of the Black Watch. Cousins's remarkable account continues:

> One poor lad fainted at the parapet and then went over. In came a lad with a pierced vein which we turnequed [applied a tourniquet]. He was still there at 2 o'clock. He too wanted to go over again. Then a fellow came in gassed. Then we got a man in who was shot thru' the stomach and gradually bled to death. Then came a man with a smashed leg. We helped all these. One Black Watch officer came in with a shattered leg. We got him across our trench and his remark was typical: "What a damned mess there is in this trench!" We were busy in the trenches till 11:30. Then I went over the top and I worked between the two trenches making men comfortable and giving water.[47]

A lieutenant with the 10th Scottish Rifles (46th Brigade) reported that when the gas was released not only was the wind variable, but "the wind was actually in our faces."[48]

In the most southern sector, manned by the 47th Division, a bizarre phenomenon allowed advancing soldiers to completely bypass the gas cloud: "Unfortunately there was very little wind and when the gas was eventually released . . . it hung about in a bank only a few yards in front of the trenches so that when we went over the top we soon passed through the gas into the clear air beyond."[49] It was here on the southernmost sectors of the British line that the 15th and 47th Divisions were able to make the greatest advances, overrunning both Loos and Hill 70 and entering the northern outskirts of Lens by midday.

The Specials were under orders not to withdraw from the trenches immediately after the gas discharge, but to wait an hour or two to allow support troops priority passage through the network of communication trenches. It was during this time that Ashley recalls one of the infantry officers mistaking the gas crews for infantry laggards and waving a revolver at them. They saved themselves by pointing quickly to their red, green, and white brassards. Just after the first wave had gone over the top, Ashley noticed that the revolver he had laid on the parapet was missing. Although it would seem to be a strange time for souvenir collecting, Ashley assumed that one of the advancing infantrymen must have taken it.[50]

Soldiers awaiting the order to go over crouched high on the firestep to avoid the gas below. Crashing German shells filled the air. The trenches stank with a "gas-blood-lyddite-latrine smell."[51] The rain intensified. Successive waves of infantry passing through the trenches and over the top caused massive congestion. Escort parties with captured Germans struggled backward against the advancing tide. Stretcher-bearers were forced to lift the wounded clear up over the tops of the trenches to get around the corners. It was difficult for the Specials to keep out of the way, but Graves's allegation that the gas soldiers "stampeded" is nowhere corroborated. Many of the Specials used the time by Vermorel spraying to neutralize the pockets of gas still lurking dangerously in the trenches. A captain with the Royal Scots Fusiliers, going over in the second wave several hours later, found the front-line trench "stocked with gas cylinders and there were a number of dead and wounded lying at the bottom. . . . We soon had all the wounded out of the trench and put on the top outside to be clear of any gas which might be lying in the foot of the trench."[52] Donald Grantham, a sprayer for section 4, also spent so much time attending to dead and wounded that his diary might well be mistaken for one written by the Royal Army Medical Corps:

Heard a man gassed and found Garside unconscious, brought him round and got him into a dugout nearby. . . . Then into firetrench

Smoke cloud from the trenches. (Courtesy of Royal Engineers Museum)

where I found Harris dead with a bullet hole clean through his head. Helped drag him into a dugout. This was about 8 [A.M.] and I did not get his blood washed off my hands for over ten hours. Did a few bandages and helped wounded down. Carried a man with wounded foot right out, then carried another part way. Helped others. Returned to our dugout then went and fetched Aldridge (badly gassed) from firetrench and carried him right out to Dressing Station.[53]

Throughout the rest of the day, section by section, or in small knots, the gas corporals began to thread their way back to their billets near Bethune. Ronald Purves, slightly gassed, was one of the first to seek medical attention.

By 6:30 A.M. got out down by Bay 19, feeling my way down. When I got down to Back Street I took my respirator off. It was in an awful mess with coughing and spitting. I passed down the communication trenches which were full of infantry men ready to go over. A few wounded men were going down too, some in an awful mess. I think I gassed all the way down to the first dressing station where I got a little ammonia, and that helped a little. While sitting in the dressing station a shrapnel bullet struck one of the RAMC men on the face and rolled off him on to the back of my neck. Fortunately it was spent and did no damage. I have it in my pocket. Tims and I

wandered down together and stopped first at the 2nd dressing station, No. 1, Harley Street. There got ammonia and hot salt water.
Still we were pretty bad, spitting up green matter. Got to a Territorial R.A.M.C. post and got bovril, biscuits, and plenty tea and then
felt better; but they said we were to go to hospital. . . . [Instead
they walked back to the Chicory Factory.] By the way our smoke
helmets were practically useless. Section 22 came in by degrees,
but 5 or 6 are missing. Pollard is finished off for the rest of his life, I
am afraid. On Saturday night, Tims and I went to sleep about 7
P.M., and woke about 7 A.M., so felt a lot better, though still pretty
choky. . . . Had a wash in the canal and a good swim.[54]

Gas Lieutenant Charles thought things had gone nicely. He heard reports of "practically no opposition" and that the infantry had advanced
through the fourth enemy line within the first twenty minutes. At
about 7:30 in the morning Charles led his section out of the front lines,
hindered considerably by still advancing files of infantry and cavalry
proceeding in one direction and streams of wounded and German prisoners going the other.[55]

Shortly before noon, G. O. Mitchell and his mate Griffiths abandoned the trenches.

I was in a very exhausted condition, couldn't breathe properly and
had a deuce of a headache. Going down the communication trench
and across the fields near Vermelles were streams of wounded of all
descriptions, a sight I don't want to see again but will have to I'm
afraid. We were a terrible time getting down the trench owing to
the wounded, especially a badly wounded sergeant on a stretcher; a
chaplain was acting as stretcher-bearer. The Huns were sending
over occasional shrapnel and just after we got out of the trench,
over came some 5.9" shells. . . . I was absolutely done when we
reached the village and fell out. We joined up just before the c'oy
moved off and then we had a deuce of a march back to the chicory
factory. After having something to eat and drink, got down to it and
slept till Sunday, September 26th.[56]

Sewell and his section quit the line about the same time: "Casualties
began to pour down, some obviously affected by gas. At about 11:00
A.M., I got out, and met the remainder of my men at a rendezvous behind our gun lines, as there was no question of forming up in all that
confusion. Fifteen bedraggled and coughing men were all that were left
out of thirty-two."[57]
John Thomas recalls an incident similar to that of G. O. Mitchell, a

frantic moment when orders came to man the firestep to repel an enemy counterattack. He quickly loaded his Colt revolver, but the alarm proved false. It was late afternoon when he left the trenches, leaving there a number of Royal Fusiliers "in a pitiful state," groaning and struggling for breath. "It is doubtful if any of those managed to survive. It rained heavily all the way back and I remember thinking that we couldn't be wetter if we were walking in the canal itself." Luther Mitchell, like most Specials, found the trek back to base camp a nightmare:

> Our trench has many wounded and dying men in it and it was friteful [sic] to see them. They were patient though. The whole of the communication trench was sprinkled with blood and many poor fellows were trying to make their way to Vermelles to the dressing station there.[58]

By mid-afternoon streams of casualties had swamped most first aid posts. A doctor working at the 15th Division dressing station remembered the day as "a sort of long nightmare with the only thing clear being the necessity for dressing more and more people every minute."[59] To Gale the journey back was "a horrible nightmare of mud, blood, and destruction." L. W. White walked over dead bodies.[60] R. Dawson, a gasman also with the 15th Division, after making his way back to Mazingarbe, responded to a call for volunteers and returned to the front to escort German prisoners. Ashley and his section seem to have been among the last out of the front line that day, reaching the chicory factory wet and exhausted late in the afternoon, their comrades assuming them to have been casualties.

Before returning to base, Cousins and several other Company 187 chemists led a reconnaissance party across no man's land to assess the effect of the gas attack. Coming upon a curtained dugout, Walker pulled down the curtain and Cousins alone descended backwards down a flight of about fifteen steps into the darkened dugout. There, about twenty-one feet below ground, barely visible in the dim light of a pit lamp, he could make out chairs and table and hear German voices from deeper within the gloom. "Kamerad, Kamerad," came the voice. Using a little German, French, and English, Cousins concluded that the dugout held a colonel—the speaker—a captain, and five other German soldiers, who had all survived the day's attack and had taken refuge from the danger aboveground:

> The officer explained their presence in the dugout by the gassing of their own men and particularly enquired if we were English. See-

ing my lack of equipment, he wanted to know if I was an officer. I assured him that I was and ordered him out but let him get his cigars. He presented me with a tin of fruit and a cigarette. He and his party filed out and on arrival at the top I found Walker with rifle and fixed bayonet.

Six months later, Cousins retold his story for the *Sapper,* and in this version a less polite tone is suggested:

After some moments I began to get impatient, and ordered him out of the dugout. At that he switched on an electric lamp he wore on his breast, whereat I lost my temper, and said things. He apologized, and then gave a command in German, whereat the other officer, he and his five privates filed out with their hands up. I brought up the rear, and on arrival at the mouth of the dug-out found a comrade with rifle and bayonet. . . . At the time we were struck with the youthfulness of the officers. The colonel looked to be about 30 years old. As to the privates, they were trembling with fright, and were not at all the fearsome Huns of the papers.[61]

Cousins handed over his seven prisoners to an officer of the Camerons. Unarmed and virtually single-handed, the Durham schoolmaster had captured two fully armed German officers and five soldiers. "I have often laughed at the incident," he wrote several years later. "A little cheek and bad German will carry through an awkward situation." He collected a few souvenirs as well. His prize find was a German helmet with prominent brass spike, taken from a Bavarian officer, bearing the date "1914" and "J.R. 157" and inscribed "Mit Gott für Koenig und Vaterland," which he later posted to his mother. Following Cousins's unexpected adventure, he returned to his original front-line gas trench and tied up the gas pipes and stowed them away in the bay, by which time everyone else had long since left the front lines. Alone, he worked his way back along Quality Street. "Two snipers were very busy and I got the chalk in the neck." Cousins's Company 187 had suffered seven killed, eight wounded, nine missing, and fourteen gassed.

For his action Cousins earned the Distinguished Conduct Medal, an award for noncommissioned officers comparable to the Distinguished Service Order for officers, and more prestigious than the Military Medal. On the obverse was a picture of the king and on the reverse the words "For Distinguished Conduct in the Field." News of the schoolmaster's feat duly appeared in the Durham press, and he became something of a local celebrity and war hero. It was cause for an especially proud celebration by the principal, masters, and pupils at his Johnston Technical School.

Exhausted and ailing, most of the men of the gas companies spent the entire next day, Sunday, sleeping. An ever-circumspect Meiron Thomas wrote again to his mother, "I don't suppose I dare mention even yet what happened to our little affair or how it succeeded or failed."[62] When Lieutenant Charles and his section returned to the front line to retrieve any unused cylinders, pipes, spanners, and other bits of equipment, they encountered a scene of appalling destruction and congestion.

> There were batteries of guns practically wheel to wheel with their ammunition limbers some hundred yards in rear; the latter kept galloping up with supplies. A little behind were massed regimental transports, bridging trains, machine-gun limbers and even cookers with hot food or tea going. The main Lens road a chock-a-block with G.S. wagons, limbers and fresh infantry going one way, whilst wounded men and relieved troops, mostly smothered in mud and with only their smoke helmets on their heads and nearly all with their swords still fixed, were going in the opposite direction. It was impossible for my men to work as two batteries of field guns were in action some 30 yards in rear of our old front line and the enemy was making excellent practice with heavy H.E.[63]

The imbroglio between Haig and French over belated reinforcements at Loos is well known. When the 21st and 24th Divisions finally advanced to the attack at 11 A.M. on 26 September, neither artillery nor gas umbrella shielded them, nor was opposing machine-gun fire seriously neutralized, and their futile attack failed abysmally.[64]

Foulkes ordered some sections back into the front lines for a second gas release on Monday afternoon, 27 September, in support of the Guards Division attack on Hill 70. In heavy rain and with a "perfect" wind blowing at five mph, the Specials discharged 450 cylinders. In the words of one gas officer, "the gas went away a treat."[65] Within minutes of the discharge, however, Lieutenant Charles noticed a great number of fires burning in front of the German trenches, apparently to lift the gas over their positions. Nothing could be seen through the haze of gas and smoke but the flickering fires all along the line.[66] When the infantry advanced, both here and along the canal at Givenchy, enemy machine-gun fire drove them back.[67] A corporal with the Guards on that occasion noticed "plenty of evidence of the gas attack carried out by the Special Companies, whose cylinders were still in position and surrounded, it seemed, by bodies, stench and havoc of all kinds for miles."[68] Purves heard from one of the 10th Scottish Rifles that "Huns in the big crater had been well gassed and were lying dead, black in the face." In macabre fashion Purves concluded, "So we did some good."[69]

But, in truth, the British attack at Loos had been an unmitigated failure. After localized gains on the first day, subsequent but belated assaults on the second German line proved futile, and German gunners mowed down advancing soldiers in droves—on what the Germans referred to as the *Lechenfeld von Loos* ("the corpse field of Loos"). The British suffered just over 50,000 casualties, including the only son of Rudyard Kipling (60,000, counting some equally futile subsequent subsidiary assaults). Three divisional commanders were killed, T. Capper of the 7th, G. H. Thesiger of the 9th, and F. D. V. Wing of the 12th. Subsequent analysis of the battle was to cost Sir John French his job. The simultaneous French assaults to the south, both in Artois and Champagne, fared even worse.

British gas casualties, too, were high—2,639 casualties, including seven dead, during the first three days of the Loos offensive according to Dr. Claude Douglas, Royal Army Medical Corps. These figures yield a gas casualty ratio of 4.4 percent of total casualties, a high percentage compared to later experience.[70] Although none of them went over the top with the infantry, the Special Companies lost 14 percent of their forces, including twenty-two killed, though not all by gas.[71] Under these grim circumstances the first British experiment in gas warfare came to a temporary halt, and a feeling of keen disappointment pervaded the Special Companies. Thomas and his section felt "quite crestfallen" at the result. Leonard Eastham, Company 187, considered the gas component "a near complete disaster."[72] Gas had not proved decisive. It had not cleared the way for the infantry. It had certainly not been the war-winner Foulkes had hoped it might be.

7
Boomerang Ally

Just before the Loos attack General Gough had conjectured that "gas might be a boomerang ally—a tremendous but treacherous friend."[1] Gough's premonition proved to be more accurate than he could have imagined. What went wrong? In short, everything possible. Though many of the problems derived from intractable wind force and direction, human factors accounted for an ample share of the blame. Faulty apparatus, loss of surprise, inadequate manpower, hasty training, insufficient numbers of cylinders, ambiguous authority, flawed fail-safe measures—each contributed a share to the disappointing results.

The decision to go ahead with the gas offensive under less than minimally required wind conditions ultimately rested with Haig, although it is difficult to imagine his insisting on gas in the face of vigorous personal objections from the gas commander. Foulkes admitted in his diary that at a final interview with Haig early on the morning of 25 September 1915 the wind was "almost calm SSW very unfavourable for a gas attack, but the battle could not be postponed."[2] These words clearly suggest that while Haig felt constrained by a schedule not of his own choosing, he had long since determined to play the gas card given even marginal weather conditions, a position to which Foulkes seems to have acquiesced.

Both Haig and Foulkes may have allowed the overall gas attack to proceed despite uncertain wind conditions because of misplaced confidence in local discretionary authority which should have averted or aborted the gas discharge on those fronts where particularly unfavorable conditions prevailed. This fail-safe system, however, seems to have been flawed, for gas officers who tried to exercise discretionary authority in the end allowed 2d Division higher command to overrule their own judgment. Evidently mere section commanders Sewell and White did not think they had the authority to directly refuse such peremptory orders, and even company commander Percy-Smith eventually acquiesced as well. Foulkes claimed to have discussed this issue thoroughly with all the generals on several occasions. Horne, the divisional commander in question, had attended Foulkes's lecture on the subject on 22 August and was present three days later when the gas commander briefed I Corps personnel. General Gough, Brigadier Gen. A. S. Cobbe from the general staff, and General Capper were all present as well. Foulkes had lunched with 2d Division on 20 September, only five days before the offensive.[3] He had likewise had many consultations with Percy-Smith and the other gas officers. There seemed no lack of prior consultation and communication. Either Foulkes had not convinced the infantry commanders to allow the gas officers to make the final decision or he had not sufficiently impressed his gas officers that the final decision was theirs to make, both of which he later alleged had been made clear to all. An infantry soldier with the Indian Corps did recall that the gas release was to proceed "only if the wind was favourable."[4] Given the vagaries of localized wind, clearly the officer on the spot ought to have exercised his own judgment. This problem was to surface repeatedly because infantry commanders, for the most part unversed in the dynamics of cloud gas warfare, tended to adhere more rigidly to carefully laid tactical plans than gas warfare allowed.

Lack of adequate communication between officers and commanders during battle might be blamed on the absence of "voice control," which so frequently crippled commanders in the First World War and which walkie-talkies solved in the Second. During the critical moments at Loos, however, the 2d Division maintained uninterrupted communication with the front lines via telephone and General Horne insisted on the order to proceed *despite* communication with the frontline gas officers.

Gas blowing back on British lines, a most exasperating problem, ought also to have been remedied by discretionary countermanding authority on the part of the gas officers. "Not only is our gas no bloody good," an infantryman groused, "but it even blows back and kills our own men!"[5] The worst blow-back occurred along the 2d Division front, and Foulkes admits in his diary that here the wind was blowing "right along our line from right to left and in many places didn't even reach the German lines."[6] Many gas officers did, at least, abort the discharge when the gas blew back into their own trenches.

Foulkes had placed great store in the element of surprise, but in spite of the Special Companies' extraordinary efforts, their attack did not catch the enemy entirely unprepared. It is difficult to imagine what more Foulkes or the gasmen could have done to complete such a complex installation in the front lines in a more clandestine manner. German observation posts afforded excellent views of many of the British trenches, and it was commonly thought that from these vantage points the Germans had spotted the gas installations.[7] Among captured enemy documents in the archives of the Imperial War Museum is an anonymous German account of the 25 September gas attack. The author alleges that German patrols had heard "unusual hammering on metal" which gave away the gas secret and that not only was his section not taken by surprise, but it had ample time to take quite extensive countermeasures.

> We had to prepare 20 inches square wooden boxes filled with straw and tar and in the rear they ordered several thousand emergency masks to protect mouth and nose. At that time just a piece of cloth with some mull with two ribbons to fasten in the neck also some medical liquid to wet the masks. We waited for weeks—nothing happened, of course the British had to wait for favourable weather and wind, and we were already blamed for creating false alarm. Then on the 25th September we suddenly saw a white thick cloud close to the ground slowly creeping towards our trenches. Immediately we gave alarm, lighted our tarboxes, put on our masks and waited. The heat of our tarboxes lifted the gas over our trench and fell down again behind the trench. The cloud was about 500 yards deep and you could see up to 5 yards only. Right behind the gas the British infantry carelessly advancing with trailing arms. It must have been a strange vision for the British when they suddenly saw the German trench in flames and being surprised by a murderous rifle and m.g. fire at close range.[8]

H. E. Braine, an officer with the 19th Brigade, 2d Division, corroborates this statement: "I myself saw the Bosch light fires on their parapet and put their machine guns on the top of it and do whatever they liked."[9] There were other similar reports of German machine-gun crews building bonfires around the gun emplacements.[10] These were not isolated incidents—the following year along the Somme, soldiers of the 20th Division reported German troops similarly fighting gas by lighting parapet fires "to make the cloud rise."[11]

Nor had the gas operation proceeded entirely successfully in a technical sense. Gas leakage was widespread, caused in large part by wrong-size spanners, unwieldy pipes, and unexpectedly difficult connections. G. O. Mitchell was not alone in complaining bitterly about "rotten apparatus." Gale called the rigid iron-pipe connectors a "ghastly failure."[12] Even Foulkes admitted that "nearly all the pipes were defective."[13] Much of the leakage resulted from residual gas that escaped when gasmen changed parapet pipes from one cylinder to the next. Wilson later contended that for security reasons this pipe changing had not been practiced at Helfaut, but in any event, practice with empty cylinders would not have revealed a leakage problem.[14] Lt. A. B. White complained of faulty connections and broken copper pipes. Nearly his entire section suffered some degree of gassing. Four went to the hospital and two others were gassed so severely that they could not walk.[15] Campbell-Smith later testified that few of the gas casualties would have survived 25 September had the gas used been phosgene rather than the less-toxic chlorine, so great was the gas concentration in the trenches during and just after the discharge.[16] Only Livens's experimental rubber pipes and his four-way connection system, which he had used without authorization in his section, had worked well. Foulkes later maintained that he had suggested the infantry vacate the front-line trenches during the gas release, but that their commanders had "refused categorically" to do so—such an evacuation was "unthinkable."[17]

The chlorine caused a greening of the buttons, cap-badges, and other metal parts of the Specials' uniforms, a harmless but clear evidence of gas leakage. Fox and many in his section regarded this tarnishing a singular mark of distinction, proof positive that they had really been in the gas war, but Lt. H. L. P. Acland of section 6 ordered his men to polish the tarnish off. Fox called them the "shiny sixth."[18]

An ancillary complaint concerned the necessity of wearing the gas mask, which most soldiers thought a terrible hindrance. The PH mask in general use at this time was a gray flannel helmet soaked in hypo (neutralizing chlorine), phenol, and hexamine (neutralizing phosgene). A celluloid window allowed vision and a mouth tube allowed breathing. When worn properly during exertion, the hood admitted an inadequate supply of air, causing a suffocating sensation. A motorcyclist with the 28th Division blamed the crash of his vehicle on poor visibility caused by his steamed-up helmet.[19] Troops who wore their helmets rolled up on their heads complained that the heavy rain falling later in the morning soaked the chemicals which then ran down their foreheads and caused a good deal of eye irritation. A battalion commander of the South Staffords threw his away in disgust early on the morning of 25 September.[20] Likewise, Grossmith felt so stifled wearing the mask that he discarded it during the battle.[21] A Camerons infantryman in the 15th Division going over on the next day found lots of gas hanging about "but we took off our gas masks otherwise we would have exploded."[22]

Infantry commanders placed far too much reliance on the incapacitating effects of the gas on the enemy, "relying on the gas to work wonders!"[23] A battalion commander with the 2d Division reported that "no wire cutting had been done on the battalion front as reliance was placed entirely on the expected effect of our gas."[24] Officers with the 10th Scottish Rifles (15th Division) believed the gas would neutralize both enemy infantry and artillery to a depth of three miles![25] Henry Williamson had been led to believe that the gas would "lay out the Germans for a couple of hours after one whiff," promising a "walk-over."[26] This overconfidence in the potential of gas was to reappear throughout the war.

Reports from the advancing infantry battalions were uniformly critical of the gas—it was not strong enough, it was released in insufficient wind, it had negligible effects on the enemy, it was not worth the carry, it hindered the attackers more than the enemy. On 25 September Rawlinson had received reports in mid-afternoon that the Germans were suffering more from shellfire than from the gas.[27] General Gough, commander of I Corps, concluded that cloud gas exhibited three inherent flaws which severely restricted its usefulness: the immense manpower required for the carry-in and installation, the waste of gas traveling across no man's land, and the absolute dependence of gas on the vagaries of the wind.[28] Brig. Gen. H. T. Thuillier, later Director of Gas Services, commanded the 2d Infantry Brigade (1st Division) in support at Loos: "The impression I derived from the officers who were under me was that they were not at all happy with them [the gas cylinders] there and thought they were dangerous altogether."[29] Maj. Gen. F. W. M. McCracken, commander of the 15th Division and victim of a good deal of British gas, suggested that in the future the gas cylinders be discharged in batteries from remote control, that the parapet pipes be buried in the parapet to avoid being thrown back into the trench, and that the smoke candles be provided with an upright holder to enable the candlemen to maintain adequate cover.[30] Foulkes seems to have totally ignored each of these very sensible suggestions.

Assessments at headquarters were likewise dubious. Few there had shared Haig's enthusiasm for gas in any event. After the Loos debacle, Wilson's skepticism seemed fully corroborated. Lt. Gen. R. D. Whigham insisted that "whatever success was gained was not due to gas."[31] The unanimous view was that prevailing wind conditions had not justified the gas attack.

Even in those sectors where wind conditions had been most favorable, the effect of the gas appeared to have been indecisive at best. Opposite the Hohenzollern Redoubt and the town of Hulluch, the infantry had been able to penetrate several lines of enemy trenches, but George Pollitt, commander of several gas sections in that very sector, severely discounted the gas contribution:

On that occasion [Loos offensive in general] the wind was all wrong, but immediately along the German position [the Hohenzollern Redoubt] a cloud of gas did float onto the German lines on a small front. It caused few if no casualties because the Germans saw it coming and could and did run in front of it and it never caught them up.

Pollitt claimed to have followed the cloud for about 1,000 yards without seeing a single German.[32]

Yet contrary to all indications, Foulkes contended that in spite of unfortunate accidents the gas had been a near-total success and had made a positive contribution to the British offensive. Foulkes also convinced himself, again contrary to all evidence, that the gas attack on 25 September had been a complete surprise. By 1938 he claimed that had it not been for the unexpected gas, the advance would have been repulsed all along the line and "perhaps tens of thousands of additional lives would have been sacrificed."[33] As late as 1962 Foulkes was still insisting that the gas at Loos was "much more successful than generally supposed."[34] Haber characterizes Foulkes's appraisal as "a travesty of the facts."[35] Less harshly, Trevor Wilson reflects the view of most recent scholarship when he states that the British suffered more than the Germans from their own gas.[36]

Foulkes was not oblivious, however, to the widespread impression both in the army and at home that the use of gas had proved more a hindrance than a help. Years later he would admit to his own gas veterans that the Loos period had been one of "extemporization" and "peculiar difficulty."[37] At the time, however, he was astute enough to recognize that the Special Companies had a public relations problem and that he would have to become a skillful propagandist. Toward this end Foulkes ordered each section and company officer to compile a written report on the effects of gas in his sector, but his circular of 8 October complains that very few officers complied.[38] He also sought to add questions about gas effectiveness to the questionnaires administered to all German prisoners, but GHQ refused.[39] On his own, Foulkes personally gathered twenty-five pages of selective favorable battlefield anecdotal evidence, mostly from captured German documents and alleged statements of German prisoners. But he ignored the well-known tendency of prisoners to ingratiate themselves to their captors, which renders all such statements highly suspect.

Armed with his selective evidence that the gas attack had been a success, he urged continued and even increased use of gas. Following a visit to GHQ, he alleged that French and Robertson "both were very well pleased with the results of the gas attack on the 25th" and later claimed that GHQ "was never in doubt, during the whole war, about the value of our gas attacks."[40] Undaunted, Foulkes congratulated his companies for their "very gallant and devoted" performance and expressed enthusiastic optimism for greater success in future gas operations.[41]

8
The Specials' First Winter

Not easily dissuaded by disappointment or deterred by criticism and convinced that improvements in equipment and slight operational modifications would solve whatever gas problems existed, Foulkes set about remedying the more flagrant deficiencies and determined to try again. Equipment improvement took obvious priority. The ten-foot length of pipe sections had proved too unwieldy, both in transport and in the firing trench. Foulkes ordered them sawed in half and the ends threaded for easier coupling under hurried conditions. Awkward pipe joints, both the rigid iron and the "flexible" spiral ones, had been the cause of much of the gas leakage. All reports indicated that Livens's rubber pipes, which he had employed without authorization, had proven superior to the others, and after the battle Foulkes ordered them as standard equipment. Meiron Thomas of Company 188, by then a master at masking forbidden topics in innocuous language, wrote to his mother not too informatively about the "idiotic looking" scientist-officer:

> Previous to our last "straffe," in direct contravention to all orders he used certain "stuff," and when the O. C. inspected the line previous to the show, this man was pulled over the coals as an idiot, etc. *Now* the boot is on the other leg, and this "stuff" proved so much more efficacious than that the others used, that it has to a great extent been substituted, and to my mind will do away with a lot of the trouble which marred our last performance. That is all I can say.[1]

One can only imagine what the uninformed original reader of these lines made of the information. Livens's "stuff" were pieces of rubber hose used for connecting one end of the pipes to the gas cylinder and the other end to the parapet pipes. Armed only with Foulkes's oral authority to procure the required supply, the brash Livens rushed across the Channel, demanded and got the required lengths of rubber hose, and personally commandeered taxis, ships, and trains to get them to Helfaut in record time. As early as 28 September 1915, each section set to work assembling its quota of fresh pipe kits. This they did by cutting rubber tubing into suitable lengths and binding the hose to metal sockets with copper wire; one end included a spigot for connection to the cylinder and the other was connected to the parapet pipes. One soldier recalls sitting in Cambrin churchyard "making up the rubber four-ways" under Livens's direction.[2] Tested successfully under high pressure, the new hose connectors proved superior. When the kits were finished, the Specials inserted cork plugs into the pipe ends and wrapped them with canvas to prevent debris from clogging the openings.[3] Another significant benefit of this four-way system was that it allowed completion of all connections in advance of the moment of discharge. Each cylinder now discharged into its own set of piping, both delivery and jet, whereas before only two delivery pipes served each emplacement.

Another change deployed four men instead of two in each battery emplacement containing about twenty-four cylinders. To avoid a repetition of the confusion caused by fuzzy responsibility, Foulkes publicized more clearly the principle that sectional gas officers must assume ultimate on-the-spot responsibility for the order to discharge. Although Foulkes contends that he made this clear before Loos, Fox mentions it as if it were new policy.[4]

On 10 October the Prince of Wales and Lord Wolseley, old soldier extraordinaire and ex–commander in chief, visited the Special Companies on push-bikes, and after dinner Foulkes arranged a gas demonstration in a field behind the billet:[5] "H.R.H. expressed a wish to let off a cylinder of gas. This was quickly provided, there being volunteers to the number of the whole Company for this special fatigue. H.R.H. turned the gas on but retired at once coughing violently with suitable remarks. A corporal turned it off." The royal spanner became a prized souvenir.[6]

With improvements under way, Foulkes ventured a second, but much smaller, gas discharge in support of Haig's renewed attack on 13 October on the Hohenzollern Redoubt, the nearby quarries, and the town of Hulluch, all of which had been in British hands only briefly after the three days of heaviest fighting at Loos. For this attack, Foulkes arranged the cylinders in a denser concentration and ordered their discharge two at a time. Gas officers Sanders and Garden were this time fully cognizant of their discretionary authority. Thus contrary winds in the morning did not give rise to the angst experienced on 25 September. Moreover, the smaller scale of this operation allowed infantry units to accept a flexible zero hour as well. The infantry would either wait for a more favorable wind or advance without gas. Opposite Cambrin to the north the wind died away just before zero hour, and this time section commanders of Company 186 countermanded the discharge order, preventing the release of gas which would have blown back on their own lines.[7] Conditions improved by midday, and at 1 P.M., opposite the Redoubt, the primary target area, the wind turned very favorable. There the Specials opened the valves, and in textbook fashion the gas glided over the enemy lines powered by a five mph wind. The infantry followed. Sid Kemp, a signaller with the West Kents, watched the attack from battalion headquarters:

> The gas attack was on and I saw it rise from those cylinders, form into a white cloud, and this cloud rose to about 6 to 8 feet from the ground. The whole lot joined up together, and with a west breeze behind it, just went towards the German lines. Behind the gas, walking in orderly fashion, was the infantry, but they were keeping behind the gas and not belting into it.[8]

Kemp's account illustrates an almost perfect military use of gas, but success on this occasion was possible only because of the flexible timetable, for near-perfect wind conditions rarely exist over a large front at a predictable moment.

Although the modified equipment resulted in far less gas leakage, the trenches still filled with fumes. Under battle conditions there was no foolproof way to totally prevent blow-back or gas leakages caused by accident. Geoffrey Higson was badly gassed when several of his "Alices," as he had christened his cylinders, leaked at their pistons.[9] Overcrowding of assault infantry huddled in the trenches exacerbated the effects of even small amounts of leakage and blow-back. Infantryman Frederick Hunt remembers being crowded together in the Hulluch trenches "like herrings in a box, shoulder to shoulder, . . . so congested that it was almost impossible to put your hand in your pocket." The men realized they were being poisoned by the gas, but they were too tightly packed together to take protective measures. Hunt lost consciousness and woke up in a hospital boat. After several anxious days in a base hospital near Boulogne, he survived and recuperated in England.[10]

Given the difficulty of the task and their relative inexperience in this new mode of fighting, the men of the Special Companies displayed surprising ingenuity and courage. Quick thinking and somewhat rash action during this engagement earned for James Lennox Dawson the coveted Victoria Cross, the highest decoration given in the British Army.[11] The twenty-three-year-old Dawson, a Presbyterian from Tillycoultry, Clackmannanshire, had joined the 5th Battalion of the Cameronians (Scottish Rifles) in November 1914, but as he was a chemist, he had transferred to the Special Companies in late July 1915 and had won a promotion to sergeant in Company 187 in August. Foulkes later remembered him as "a bespectacled chemist's assistant."[12] During the attack on the Hohenzollern Redoubt on 13 October, Dawson's trench filled with gas. Spotting three leaking gas cylinders, he climbed up onto the parados in full view of enemy fire, hauled up the leaking cylinders, rolled them some sixteen yards away from the trench into no man's land, then fired rifle bullets into them to let the gas escape. Dawson, the only Special to win the Victoria Cross, received his decoration personally from King George V on 15 December in a ceremony at Buckingham Palace. Wilson, who had replaced Dunn (killed at Loos) as commander of section 7 of Company 186, later received the Military Cross for throwing a lighted phosphorous bomb out of the trench.[13] Fox earned no decorations for his routine but no less dangerous work as a section runner between the gas emplacements and section headquarters in the support line.

Owing to the cancellation of the original orders and the necessity of "standing by" for several hours after zero, there was certainly a good deal of "running" to be done. It was a matter of considerable concern, to note how a trench mortar, visible as it soared over toward our Line, seemed to have the fiendish characteristic of following me along.[14]

Although the 13 October gas operation was a far greater technical success than those of September, the infantry assault, as before, failed abysmally. Foulkes blamed German hand-grenade superiority. In Pollitt's opinion, the advancing infantry of the 46th Division went over too slowly, and this delay vitiated the advantage afforded by the gas because the Germans had time to recover.[15] Rawlinson, too, admitted that a delay of ten minutes in the 1st Division enabled the enemy to recover and re-man the trenches after the British bombardment ceased.[16] The losses of the gas companies in this second engagement were three men killed, eighteen wounded, and seventeen gassed.[17] The official history concluded that very little of the British gas ever reached the enemy lines, and although Foulkes later wrote that "this could not have happened," there was no doubt that the gas on this occasion had not contributed any more substantially to the infantry attack, except in localized sectors, than during the September operations.[18]

Returning from the 13 October front-line engagement, many of the gas sections moved to new billets also in the Bethune area. The men in Company 188 found new quarters south of Bethune in the town of

"A hot tub at MMe Danchys, followed by dry togs, omellotte and coffee, soon altered our outlook on life, and we felt none the worse." (Courtesy of Imperial War Museum, Richard Gale Diary, 13 November 1915)

Sailly Labourse, which they invariably called "Sally's the boys," where a colliery bathroom provided opportunity for their first bath in over two months, a luxury Luther Mitchell found indescribable. Sections 26 and 27 bedded down in an unused portion of the colliery, a long low tunnel previously used as an oven. Since there were no doors at the ends of the tunnel and no other openings, occupants had to choose between darkness or a terrific draft. Mitchell and his companions mostly chose the darkness. The Germans had previously occupied Sailly, and Mitchell heard that they had commandeered people's houses, burned churches, and forced men to dig trenches and then had shot them—typical but unsubstantiated atrocity tales.[19] Grantham noticed village children singing "Tipperarie."[20] Company 187 settled in north of Bethune at the village of Cornet Malo.

Livens continued to work on improvements in the discharge operation, one of which facilitated the opening of the cylinders. His new device was a "pinch cock," which clamped on the rubber hose and was strong enough to withstand the pressure of the cylinder gas. The cylinders could thus be connected to the pipe system ahead of time with the cylinder taps opened. At zero hour, all that had to be done to effect discharge was to unclamp each of the pinch cocks one by one.[21]

During October a continuing stream of reinforcements reached the Special Companies from Helfaut and were distributed among depleted sections of the four companies. One draft of thirty chemists included a prolific diarist, R. F. Dalton, who joined section 3 of Company 186 at the chicory factory. More than forty years later, when time had softened harsh memories, he would write almost fondly of the good times in this dreary place—of awkward attempts to kill the abundant rats with entrenching tools and of the ingenious improvisation of a stove by Tom Joyce, another recent transfer from the Royal Fusiliers:

> The stove, a perforated oil-drum resting on bricks, was connected by an ingenious system of old rainwater pipe lengths through a broken window pane to the open air. Sleeve joints at the ends were cut from milk tins. . . . Wood from cylinder boxes . . . and Army ''dog biscuits'' were used as fuel.[22]

During most of this time the Specials were hard at work making up pipe kits and practicing the wearing of the new phenate tube smoke helmet. They also received goggles and flexible eyepieces to protect the eyes from tear gas shells. It was a time of reflection on battles past and battles to come. In the evenings many gathered at neighborhood *estaminets*. One gas corporal recalls one such wine shop in Bethune where he and his mates enjoyed an 1869 claret ''in perfect condition.''[23] Others remained in billets, writing letters or playing cards by candlelight.

In early November Captain Garden and twelve gas corporals, including Grantham, embarked for Alexandria with 6,000 gas-filled cylinders for use at Gallipoli; but the British command there refused to initiate chemical warfare—fortunately, for it is difficult to imagine a position less advantageous for the release of gas than that of the Allies at the foot of the Gallipoli cliffs. The Turks everywhere occupied the higher ground, and the problems of gas blowing back down upon the crowded British positions would have been insuperable. Evacuation in any case took place shortly after. Extensive leakage during the voyage caused understandable concern to the ship's crew, and stories circulated of a near mutiny. The party returned to France, mission not accomplished.

Company 186, billeted still at the miserable chicory factory, rotated daily to the front lines to maintain and guard the gas cylinders, in groups of three men per section and relieved every twenty-four hours. Fatigue parties retrieved empty cylinders and carried them back to railheads, repaired damaged emplacement pits, and prepared more new pipe kits. Occasionally they traveled in lorries, although riding did not always make the trip easier. Luther Mitchell recalled a suffocating ride when all thirty-two in the section shared one lorry already half-filled with slightly leaking gas cylinders.[24] Offensive gas activity continued sporadically well into the new year, mostly small harassing attacks at dawn, as weather permitted.

In November, heavy rains again transformed the trenches and dugouts into rivers of mud and muck. Fitted with thigh-length gum boots, leather jerkins, and thick leather gloves, the men learned to wade instead of walk. Duckboards became even more essential, but frequently sank from view into mud the consistency of thick soup.[25] A missing or misaligned section of duckboard plunged the wader into the soft sticky slime. Gale remembers a trench aptly renamed Pudding Lane.[26] As they waded through stretches of opaque knee-deep water the gas soldiers used ash poles to measure mud depth. John Thomas, taking time out from his reading of a translation of Homer's *Iliad*, wrote in his diary in mid-November that the water at his emplacement reached his navel: "No knee action was necessary to go through it. One slouched along in a semi-swimming stroke, keeping one's hands high to keep them dry."[27] Along Harley Street communication trench ran an overhead trestle supporting a rail for the transport of slung stretchers, and the men frequently had to grasp the rail hand-over-hand to keep from being sucked downward into the mud. One trench ran under a roadway, with water up to one's chin. The flooded trenches swarmed with frogs, toads, gnat larvae, and rats, "huge fat loathsome creatures as big as cats" and engorged from feeding on unburied human bodies.[28] The higher water table in the low-lying areas of Flanders precluded deep trenches, and Specials had to construct breastwork parapets of sandbags aboveground. Following an all-day rain on 13 November, Gale reconnoitered the front-line trenches: "We found everything in an awful state; floods of mud and water everywhere, trenches collapsing, and cylinders disappearing into the mud. . . . In the front line the slush was knee deep . . . and the reserve trenches about waist deep."[29] The heavy rains flooded the tunnel billets of Sailly Labourse, soaking blankets and generally creating wet, cold, and miserable conditions. By mid-December the deeper dugouts presented an even sorrier spectacle: "The steps leading down to the dugouts by this time had been worn away and the only way to enter was by sitting on one's backside and sliding down to the bottom. Getting out was effected by creeping and clawing the sides with hands and fingers."[30]

Rain made life generally miserable for everyone but greatly exacerbated the trench work of the gas Specials. Tending the cold and slippery cylinders and pipes became doubly onerous. The thick mud sucked the gas cylinders downward in a viselike grip: "I had to lie on my stomach in the mud in order to connect the pipes to the nozzles of the cylinders. We lit candles to see what we were doing."[31] Gale's section tried unsuccessfully to drain a trench almost submerged in mud and water by running a pipe along a mine gallery under the embankment and out into a shell crater on the canal bank. Some emplacements were accessible only by "crawling out across a sea of mud."[32]

The coming of winter added darkness and cold to the dampness, with nights "black as Hades."[33] Repeated cancellations, called "wash-outs," added to the sense of frustration. Night after night sections of Company 186 waded "up the line," heaved away the sandbags, connected up the pipes, and, more often than not, just before zero hour, got word that contrary winds had washed out the stunt and had to repeat the whole operation in reverse. Luther Mitchell remembered a particularly cold December night spent waiting for a favorable wind in an abandoned dugout near the front line: "I slept for an hour or two and woke up shivering. During the rest of the night I stood outside the dugout stamping my feet in the endeavour to keep them warm."[34] The next day concentrated German shelling devastated most of his trench ramparts, killed two Specials, and wounded many others. The wind remained stubbornly unfavorable, and after posting guards, the company returned to base on 23 December. Back at the colliery, to an exhausted Mitchell "our brick-kiln tunnel seemed like a palace." But on rare occasions everything worked well, as on one of the last gas operations before Christmas: "Left Factory at 2:15 P.M. The wind was perfect [westerly], and blowing at the rate of about 3 mph. At 10 o'clock we turned on the gas, it was a fine sight to see the gas cloud slowly creeping across no-man's-land to the German lines. . . . The new pipe kit worked well, and we had no bad leaks."[35]

Except for a few sections guarding cylinders in the front lines, most of the men returned to home billets near Helfaut by Christmas: Companies 186 and 188 at Bilques, 187 at Heuringham, and 189 at Helfaut itself. Food stores were plentiful, and Tom Joyce in Company 186 was able to scrounge sufficient surplus tins of bully beef and maconochie for unauthorized distribution to grateful infantry billeted at the bleak Brickstacks trenches, for which Joyce came to be known as Corporal Santa Claus.[36] Christmas Day brought food parcels from home supplemented with gifts from London newspapers. The *Daily Chronicle* treat consisted of a half pound of B.D.V. tobacco, 100 cigarettes, and one pound of Mackintosh's coffee and chocolate, one such package distributed to every two men. *Daily News* Christmas puddings completed the feast.[37]

Foulkes spent Christmas Day in France, his diary showing routine conferences with Livens, Pollitt, and Sanders.

On New Year's Eve some of the gasmen built an enormous bonfire out of spare cylinder boxes. A local *estaminet* put on a big dinner. At midnight they all sang the obligatory "Auld Lang Syne," after which "By God" Percy-Smith, quite inebriated, announced that the Germans were already defeated, and "if not, then by God they soon would be."[38] The disapproving Luther Mitchell remained in the kiln tunnel awaiting the return of drunken comrades: "The merriment was carried on until the old year was out and the new year in. The boys are some of the best, but on such occasions are liable to lose control of themselves, and although I do not encourage such conduct, I can quite understand it."[39] The same evening, a German shell made a direct hit on the front-line trench emplacements which Mitchell had prepared, penetrated the breastworks, went right through one of the gas cylinders, and lodged in the ground—all without exploding. Had it detonated, all twenty adjacent gas cylinders in the emplacement would also have exploded, killing or severely gassing anyone nearby. As it was, the three men on guard escaped with only slight gassing.[40]

In early January, Sewell and Pollitt examined the gas cylinders left in the front-line emplacements through the first months of winter. As feared, the heavy cylinders had sunk deep into the mud, so orders went out to retrieve all cylinders from the trenches.

> We toiled up night after night to our old piece of line to dig them out. It had fallen in in many places and was held only by sentry groups standing on duckboards or huddled round braziers. Reliefs were carried out over the open. Enormous rats ran freely up and down. I took up only my tallest and strongest men for this job. We found one communication trench, Piccadilly Circus, full of water, and managed to float out the empty cylinders, but the full ones had to be forced out, the hollow base acting as a vacuum, and then carried down the line. It was most exhausting. Cross used to wait for me with a scraper to clean off my trench coat and waders before he could remove them and always had a large tot of rum ready—bless him![41]

Fox, too, warmly recalled the welcome tot of rum, one sixty-fourth of a gallon, "working wonders" upon return from long hours in cold and wet conditions.[42]

John Thomas and his section 5, having spent Christmas in the trenches of La Bassée, were in base camp at Bilques during the first week of January when a call came for volunteers to return to the trenches for yet another gas operation. Strangely enough, far too many stepped forward, including John Thomas, and lots had to be drawn to select six from each section for this secret operation. Thomas was among those chosen.[43]

My pal, Skinner, was not amongst the "lucky" ones, and Barneston, Walker's pal, also missed the draw. Since pals always wished to work together when possible, I was asked to swap places with Barneston, but I did not wish to miss the "show" and so kept my place.

And so it was that on Thursday the 13th of January, 1916, we climbed into a fleet of old London buses and journeyed towards the front. As usual we had no idea where we would land up.

Having guessed incorrectly that they were headed for Ypres, the unit ended up in the village of Pont-de-Nieppe, just west of Armentières, in support of the 25th Division. "Our billet was in the bedroom in a house still occupied by a woman and her three children. The six of us in this billet were the six from section 5, West, Walker, Duffy, Duff, McGregor and myself. We soon settled in and began 'drumming-up' quantities of tea, and frying bacon on my little Primus stove."

The composite unit spent some days testing gas cylinders and lubricating the nozzles, spindles, and dome caps in a nearby barn. They had arranged for madame at the billet to cook for them, but found that she was siphoning off most of their provisions for herself and children.

Luckily for us there was an artillery battery close by and the cook there took us under his care, and from then on we fared like fighting cocks. The fact that we were all corporals caused some comment wherever we went, and the N.C.O.s at the battery were puzzled about this and quizzed us about our job. Since any mention of "gas" was forbidden, we said we were concerned with a drainpipe scheme for the trenches which were very waterlogged in this area.

On several evenings we paid a visit to Armentières, a mile or so away. The centre of Armentières was a shambles; houses in all states of collapse, and troops moving in single file. On the western side, however, there were still some little cafes open, generally in the cellar, where eggs and chips and coffee could be bought. Ofttimes the coffee was laced with army rum, when it became "cafe-avec" and cost half a franc more. Twice or three times we managed to visit these cafes in the evenings to enjoy "pomme-de-terre frits," "des oeufs," and "cafe-avec" until we were merry enough to sing to our heart's content, and to forget the war for an hour or two.

On January 17, (my birthday) we left for the trenches at 6:30 P.M., and reached our emplacements at eight o'clock. The trenches here were very different from those in the La Bassée area. Here the ground water level was so high that the trenches were only some two to three feet deep, so that breast-works had to be thrown up to protect the men from frontal fire, leaving little or no protection from shells falling close behind the line.

Presently the carrying parties arrived bringing the gas cylinders, after which we were busy putting them into the emplacements already prepared for them, and protecting them with a double row of sandbags.

The following morning, after spending a considerable time in cleaning the mud from our clothing and equipment, some four of us ambled along on the road that leads to the village of Ploegsteert [Plugstreet to most Tommies]. . . . We proceeded some 50 yards along the Ploegsteert Road after being warned that parts of the road were under observation by a German Sausage balloon. We must have been seen, for a salvo of shells came screaming along and straddled the road where we were, sending us scurrying for shelter. We jumped the roadside ditch and dived for some shell-holes in the field. Two more salvos came along and fell near us, but fortunately no one was hit. Our clothes, however, were more muddied than ever after lying in the shell-holes which were partially filled with water. We had been under severe shell-fire many times before, but always in the shelter of the trench. This new experience of being caught in the open shook us quite a bit, and increased our respect for the German artillery.

Later that same day, West and I were warned for trench-guard duty that evening. Two or three men were always kept in the trenches after gas had been installed in case gas cylinders were hit. The men were relieved every twenty-four hours. At the same time we were told the gas attack would probably take place on the morrow, the 19th.

This last news was disappointing, since we had lost a night's sleep already, and West and I could not expect many hours of rest in the trenches. We would consequently be tired and washed out just when every faculty needed to be in their most alert condition. In pouring rain West and I left for the line around four o'clock in the afternoon. After relieving the guard and seeing that all was well at the emplacements, we searched around for some shelter for the night.

Eventually we found a low shelter in the support line. It was too low to allow of sitting up in, so we had to creep in and rest on our elbows to do anything. There was, however, a sheet of corrugated iron overhead, together with two rows of sandbags over that, so we felt safe from anything but a direct hit. We tried to warm some cocoa, using several pieces of candle. The mutual heating of the bits of candle resulted in melting each other far more successfully than heating the cocoa, so we were obliged to drink it lukewarm and eat some bread and cheese with it. Sleep was out of the question, we were wet and cold and thoroughly uncomfortable.

Thomas and West were soon joined by two men from the Royal North Lancashires who regaled them with discomforting tales of German mines under the front lines in this area. According to these infantrymen, sixteen men of the Lancashire Fusiliers had recently been killed when one of these exploded under their position.

The news concerning the enemy mine under our emplacements was not so amusing, and led me to ponder whether I had been wise to volunteer for this "do." What if the enemy should blow up the mine in reprisal for the gas attack! . . . These thoughts and similar morbid ones flitted to and fro in my head during the remainder of the night, and it was a relief to see the morning light appear.

With the daylight came the smell of frying bacon, as the men in the front line trooped back in small batches to the cookhouse in the support line. They carried the tea in their canteens and the bacon in the canteen lids to eat at leisure in the line.

About eleven in the morning the sun came out and made things much more cheerful. With the clearing sky came a German plane flying low to see what was afoot. Soon one of our planes came up and they began to circle and stalk each other. . . . Very soon there was a fierce fire from both sides as they tried to wing their respective enemy planes. When the planes had gone, our fellows filed in from the communication trench, about 150 all told. They brought the news that everything was to be ready by 12 mid-day, so we repaired to our emplacements and connected the parapet pipes and made everything ready.

From mid-day on there was to be a slow bombardment which was to increase in intensity until 4:30 P.M. when the gas was to be released. We were "standing-to" at our emplacements from about 3:30, and as zero approached we got our P.H. helmets on our heads, in readiness to pull down and insert the skirts inside the neck of our tunics immediately before turning on. From a little vantage point we could watch our 60-pounder shells, during the last 50 yards or so of their descent, smash into the German barbed wire to send it flying in fragments into the air. Some moments before "zero," when every gun behind us was belching fire and steel over the enemy line, I happened to look towards the west where the last rays of the setting sun was brightening the evening sky. In a flash my thoughts travelled westwards to St David's Pembrokeshire, and to the Cathedral where I was once a choirboy, and to the haunting chant of the "Nunc dimittis," "Lord, now lettest thy servant depart in peace, according to Thy word!"

The next moment the four of us at the emplacement were busy turning on the gas until all the cylinders were empty. As soon as the pipes appeared over the parapet, a fierce rifle and machine gun fire was opened on them, and soon every enemy gun in the neighborhood fired until the air was full of bursting projectiles. In fifteen minutes all the cylinders were emptied and by then the machine guns had been silenced. But some heavy trench mortars were still active, and their shells fell near the front line with a tremendous crash. These, together with the artillery barrage kept throwing showers of earth over us as they exploded in our near vicinity. Once the cylinders were empty we searched for some cover and found a low shelter behind the emplacement. We crept into it and listened to the din of the bombardment, wondering whether it would be blown up by a mine in revenge for the present attack.

When the fire had died down a bit, to our surprise, West produced from his valise, a bottle of whisky, still more than half full. Where he got the whisky from I don't know, for retailers were forbidden to supply spirits to the troops. They were allowed to sell beer and wine only. The bottle passed from mouth to mouth and was warm and comforting. Some of us not much used to strong spirits soon felt the effects, and McGregor began to swear at the Germans, and leaping out, and jumping on to the parapet, he emptied his revolver in their direction.

Later we sandbagged the emplacements, for like soda-water syphons, there always remained a small quantity of chlorine in the bottom of the cylinders which could lead to casualties if they were hit. On our way out of the trenches we saw how many a shell had hit the communication trenches during the enemy retaliation. We reached billets about 8:30 P.M., and set about brewing some tea before curling up to sleep.

This was a "combined stunt." Gas was used on a sector of the front, whilst on the extreme right of our sector gas was replaced by smoke. Under cover of the smoke a raiding party of the infantry went over to the German lines causing much damage and many casualties, and returning with prisoners and much valued information.

Later that day we returned to the trenches to collect our pipes, etc., which could be used again when necessary. . . . The battery sergeants now knew what we had been up to. They asked, jokingly, how the draining work was getting on. We replied "We shall soon have all the water from the trenches running through to the river Lys."

On Sunday, 23 January, the familiar London buses returned to pick up the gas volunteers for the drive back to Bilques. Yet another gas operation had ended. Riding on the open upper deck, tree branches brushing his face, a philosophic Thomas ruminated about the fresh westerly breeze which purged the atmosphere of the scent of chlorine, on early signs of the return of spring, and on what had to happen before the spring wheat of Europe might be "redeemed from its mauling bath of mud and blood."

During the January releases, the British had experimentally added 20 percent sulfur chloride to the chlorine, a mixture called Blue Star. The heavier sodium chloride kept the cloud closer to ground level. But it deposited a small liquid pool at the end of the parapet pipe which emitted fumes for some time afterward, and for this reason the chemists shortly discontinued use of Blue Star.[44]

Foulkes had maintained his usual feverish pace throughout these months. Altogether he made twenty-two Channel crossings between the time of his appointment and the end of 1915. In addition to conferences with French, Lord Frederic Cavan, Arthur Crossley, L. J. Barley, Jackson, the Scientific Advisory Committee, and many gas officers and infantry commanders, he attended experiments at Wembley, and Birmingham, visited various factories both in England and France, and found time to attend eight London shows, lunch fairly frequently at the Savoy, Christmas-shop at Harrods, and, during two visits to Paris, tour the Invalides and dine at Maxims.

As of 12 January 1916, the strength of the Special Companies stood at thirty-four officers and 1,519 men, and still, not a single pioneer.[45] The period of improvisation was drawing to a close. In spite of disappointing results, Foulkes's powers of persuasion succeeded in securing not only a continuance of the gas mandate but a large-scale unit expansion as well.

9
Expansion into the Special Brigade

The General was so pleased with the Strafes that we made,
That himself said he'd make us into a Brigade,
So, dear Mary, we're down at a spot called Hallines,
Where we miss our shower-baths and our splendid latrines.
Though the life here is not quite so gay as Bethune,
Shure the weather is fine, we'll be all bathing soon,
We've a river that rushes by, Mary, to me,
It recalls the dark Mourne rushing down to the sea.

Although the results of nearly four months' experience with the chlorine gas cloud were almost without exception disappointing, Foulkes continued to persevere as though everything had gone well. In the face of apparently insuperable problems inherent in cloud gas warfare, he determined to make it work through manpower reorganization, further improvements, and an expansion of the gas companies to brigade strength. That he was successful in coaxing both Haig and the War Office to authorize such an expansion is another testimony to his uncommon powers of persuasion.

Each of the existing four Special Companies became the nucleus of each of four new battalions (see organizational chart in Appendix A). In this manner, too, the unit was an anomaly, for the Engineers normally were not organized in battalions. Likewise the old sections formed an experienced nucleus for each of sixteen new companies. The new companies consisted of six rather than ten sections. Foulkes assigned the letters A to Q (omitting I) to the sixteen new companies and numbered the new sections 1 to 96.

Foulkes recruited his new battalion commanders from within the ranks of the existing gas units. Percy-Smith, who would have gotten the first battalion, instead transferred back to his former Indian Cavalry Regiment, and Foulkes reassigned Monier-Williams from the Helfaut post to the command. Sanders, Berrisford, and Sidney Bunker, a twenty-seven-year-old research chemist, took charge of the other three battalions. The ranks of the new gas companies resembled somewhat the "Pals" of Kitchener's New Army battalions in that when the commanders broke up the four existing companies to become the cores of the sixteen new ones, they redistributed the men in such a way as to keep together those who were friends or who had worked together in the existing companies. For example, when Monier-Williams distributed the men from Company 186 to the new A, B, C, and D Companies, he divided the personnel of former sections 5 and 8 into six groups, each of which became the nucleus of the six new sections of A Company. The three other battalion commanders formed each of their four new companies in similar fashion from the ranks of former Companies 187, 188, and 189. Berrisford arranged to have 78 chemists and 26 nonchemists in each of his four new companies. Most of the additional officers required were promoted from the ranks of the original chemist corporals.

The working unit remained the company, grouped loosely in battalions but capable of independent deployment in the field, its size commensurate to the needs of one British infantry division. At this point sixteen British divisions were operating in France. Since the usual trench frontage of a division was approximately 1,500 yards, Foulkes calculated that a company of about 200 men grouped in six sections of 36 men each and spread out 250 yards to a section could appropriately cover the area. The War Office formalized these changes on 1 February, effective retroactive to 17 January 1916. To find the necessary 2,000-odd new men, Foulkes reinstituted a recruiting program both in England as well as throughout the army, and beginning in March, from 100 to 400 new men began arriving almost daily, along with motorcycles, lorries, boxcars, and other equipment.

The earlier decision to enlist all chemist recruits as corporals had been partially based on the assumption that in the heat of battle it might become necessary for them to exercise authority over infantry; but this eventuality never materialized. The new recruits, whether chemists or ordinary infantry, joined as pioneers rather than as corporals. An unintentional consequence of this new policy was the near impossibility of these pioneers ever being promoted to corporal, since every company contained too many already. Foulkes hinted that the original chemist-corporals should voluntarily give up their two stripes, but no volunteers stepped forward.

In late February Foulkes constructed a fifth battalion consisting of a further four companies. Its mission was the delivery of gas by Stokes mortar, a gun invented by Wilfred Stokes in 1914.[1] The mortar battalion employed a four-inch model of the Stokes devised for firing gas shells, as distinct from the three-inch model used by the infantry to fire high-explosive bombs. Designed by Stokes especially for chemical use, the

J section of the No. 3 Company, 5th (Mortar) Battalion, with four-inch Stokes mortars. (Courtesy of Royal Engineers Museum)

four-inch model was mobile, relatively silent, and capable of delivering gas in a fast yet simple manner.[2] The Stokes mortar was "drop-fired," that is, loaded and fired simultaneously by simply dropping the shell down the barrel. Gunners could fire these shells in rapid succession, at a rate limited only by the time it took to pick up a bomb and drop it into the mortar barrel—observers sometimes counted up to fifteen mortars in the air before the first hit the ground.[3] Constant improvement of both propellant and fuse resulted in safe firing as well as impact bomb detonation. Each Stokes mortar shell delivered as much as two liters of liquid gas, but Foulkes was unsuccessful in obtaining sufficient supply of these gas shells until mid-1917; in the meantime the mortar companies employed the Stokes gun mostly for laying down smoke screens.

Foulkes chose George Pollitt, Percy-Smith's replacement as Company 186 commander, to take over this fifth battalion, designated somewhat awkwardly as "No. 5 (Mortar) Battalion, Special Brigade, Royal Engineers." In mid-February, Foulkes solicited the just-organized sixteen cylinder companies for volunteers to form the nucleus of the new mortar companies. Many of the corporals, tired of humping heavy cylinders, were more than happy to try a change.

Inexplicably, Foulkes assigned numbers 1 to 4 to the companies of this fifth battalion instead of continuing the letter designation of the

Four-inch Stokes mortar and accessories. (Courtesy of Royal Engineers Museum)

cylinder companies. To further confuse matters he identified its sections by letter and its subsections by number, just the reverse of the system used in the cylinder companies and the rest of the army. All five battalion commanders found headquarters in the villages surrounding Helfaut: Heuringham, Bilques, Wizernes, Grand Bois, Petit Bois, Pihem, and Biancque, all also within four miles of St. Omer. Four additional Special Sections came into being at this same time in England, charged with the development of flame-throwing capabilities and later designated Z Company.

The question of personal weapons also demanded reconsideration.

Initially, Foulkes had armed all the original chemists with revolvers, partly because he thought rifles might impede the movements of the gas workers in the cramped trenches and partly because rifles were associated primarily with assault troops of low rank.[4] There were, however, several exceptions. Transfers from infantry units had commonly brought their rifles along with them and retained them. In addition, a large number of corporals had acquired unauthorized rifles found scattered on the Loos battlefield.[5] Soldiers on front-line guard duty, whether infantry or chemist, required rifles as well. Since the gasmen in the mortar companies might be expected to advance with the infantry, Foulkes judged the rifle to be a more appropriate weapon in their case, and men in those companies traded in their revolvers for rifles.[6] With these exceptions, all men in the cylinder companies retained the revolver, a questionable decision which Foulkes was to reverse in 1918.

The Special Companies had employed chlorine (called Red Star) in 1915 because it was the only suitable gas available in the quantities required. Allied experiments with the far more toxic phosgene, carbonyl chloride ($COCl_2$), began in June 1915, but production delays and management problems at the Calais plant caused long delays in supply. Mention has already been made of the disappointing results with Blue Star. The Germans, meanwhile, had first used phosgene in December 1915 and were employing large amounts of it in gas shells against the French in that desperate battle of attrition at Verdun, which had begun in February 1916.[7] In order for phosgene, a light gas, to be discharged in cloud form, as Foulkes intended, it had to be mixed with a heavier gas to keep the cloud from rising harmlessly into the atmosphere too soon. The natural choice was chlorine, thereby solving the weight problem and combining the lethal effects of both gases. In late January 1916, following lengthy experiments with various proportions, Foulkes decided on a 50 percent mixture of the two gases, which came to be called White Star. Phosgene was not only ten times more lethal than chlorine but also gave no immediate warning of its presence by inducing severe coughing, as did chlorine. This insidiously delayed effect made it especially injurious because the lung damage went unnoticed at the time of ingestion. The Special Brigade adopted the White Star mixture as the staple cylinder filling for most of the remainder of the war.[8]

Continuing gross mismanagement at the Calais phosgene plant induced Foulkes in March 1916 to volunteer two hundred of his own men for temporary assignment there, a detachment which became permanent. This Special Factory Section was based at Les Attacques, a few miles up the St. Omer Canal from Calais. The men worked in three shifts of eight hours, twenty-four hours a day, seven days a week, until a few days before the Armistice.[9]

By the spring of 1916 the total number of Special Companies reached twenty-one, roughly brigade strength, including sixteen cylinder companies, four mortar companies, Z Special Company, and the Special Factory Section, a total at fullest strength of around 6,000 men. Commensurate with the increased responsibilities of his much-augmented force, Foulkes took the rank of colonel. With relatively minor sectional renumbering in 1917, this size and organization represented the final wartime structure of the Special Brigade.

Foulkes's brief experience with gas warfare had clearly demonstrated the inadequacy of synoptic weather charts of all Europe in predicting local wind conditions, and in 1916 he succeeded in expanding the Meteorological Section (commonly called Meteor) to allow the posting of professional weather observers up and down the line of prospective gas operations. Using cup anemometers and wet-bulb and dry-bulb thermometers these observers gathered complete weather information at the "fundamental hours," Greenwich mean time 7 A.M., 1 P.M., 6 P.M., and 1 A.M. Hydrogen-filled balloons, their course followed by specially modified telescopes and suspended Chinese candle lanterns at night, gave readings of vertical wind currents taken at height intervals of five hundred feet. Observer teams attached to each division took similar readings, but without benefit of balloons. Single observers distributed all along the line took localized readings of wind direction and velocity, alerted local units to the opportunity for gas attacks, or warned of conditions suggesting an enemy gas attack. A meteorological staff at each army headquarters funneled weather information by priority telegraph to Meteor's headquarters at Hesdin, not far from St. Omer, where Gold compiled a twenty-four hour forecast.

Foulkes shuttled back and forth between France and London as before. In early March he came down with a severe cold, developed a high temperature, and spent two weeks in the hospital. Leaving too soon, he suffered a relapse, was readmitted, and was not to return to work until 27 March following recuperation in Boulogne and England.[10]

Since the beginning of the gas retaliation, a turf battle had been simmering over the relationship between the defensive and the offensive sides of chemical warfare, the former organized under the Medical Service, under the jurisdiction of the adjutant general's office, and the latter operating under the general staff. All concerned agreed that unification of gas services would be preferable, but there was no agreement as to which side would take over the other. During discussions with the Chemical Warfare Department in February 1916, Foulkes urged unsuccessfully that the defensive branch be "amalgamated" into the Special Brigade. As Foulkes lay in the hospital with a fever of 103 degrees, Brigadier General Thuillier, Royal Engineers, became Director of Gas Services, with overall responsibility for both offensive and defensive gas warfare. Foulkes became Assistant Director of Gas Services on the offensive side, and S. L. Cummins, Royal Army Medical Corps, took over as Assistant Director of Gas Services on the defensive side.[11]

The new arrangements left Foulkes with full operational responsibility for the Special Brigade and with little interference from Thuillier, but he had to contend with a welter of civilian advisory groups, both political and scientific, the most important of which was the Scientific Advisory Committee, later renamed the Chemical Advisory Committee. Detractors from this group and in army commands displayed increasing resistance to gas. Kitchener remained extremely lukewarm. A memorandum in March 1916 reports his opinion that "by June the gas war might be dropped" because successful defense made gases "of little or no effect" and that "the day of surprise by gas was over."[12] This was certainly not Foulkes's view, and the men of the Special Brigade heard little about these tensions in the higher command. Whatever opinions others might have harbored, the brigade officers spoke publicly of their gas mission only in the most positive terms. When referring to the Battle of Loos, lecturers "were careful to say that the gas attack was entirely successful."[13]

Throughout the remaining winter and spring months of 1916 the indoctrination and drilling of the newly recruited pioneers proceeded in the training villages around Helfaut. "I thought I should have died," wrote one nineteen-year-old recruit after his first cylinder fatigue.[14] Each day began with a half hour of quick-time marching, followed by a full day of drills, lectures, and practice, varied throughout the week. There were lectures on infantry training and organization, care and use of the revolver, military engineering, cylinder mechanics, treatment of duds and leaky cylinders, the new four-way connectors, technology and use of Vermorel sprayers, reconnaissance and intelligence, map reading, and first aid. The pioneers endured the obligatory exposure to gas-filled chambers, long practice sessions with gas masks, physical drill, helmet drill, revolver drill, meteorological practice, frequent kit and arms inspections, trench digging, emplacement construction, elementary surveying, signaling practice sessions, route marches, and practice on passing messages in trenches. One soldier recalled a practice session in which the message "two spanners are missing" came out the other end of the squad as having something to do with two spaniels.[15] The officers, too, attended required lectures on subjects ranging from field sanitation to gas lessons learned at Loos.[16]

Thomas Parkes, a twenty-one-year-old chemistry student from the Midlands, having specifically requested assignment to the chemists' sections, expressed annoyance at the typically pedestrian duties of a pi-

Q Company at revolver practice in the chalk pit at Helfaut. (Courtesy of Royal Engineers Museum)

oneer. "Helped C.O.'s chauffeur to clean car. How glad I learned Chemistry." And after digging trenches, "Simply navvy's work."[17] Frequently companies spent the night in the trenches on the common to become accustomed to sleeping out, and occasionally they fought nocturnal mock battles, as Luther Mitchell recalls:

> Last night we had some sport in the nature of night operations. It was a very moonlit night and consequently absolutely unsuitable for the work. J Company had to endeavour to break through from Wizernes to Helfaut across the Common and L Company had to attempt to stop us. We were the attacking party and had, at the commencement of operations to scale some heights—as our noble ancestors did the Heights of Abraham,—what? At the top the sport began. An enemy outpost claimed to have captured us and we told them they were all dead—hence lengthy arguments. Eventually we were all dismissed, after several more or less unsuccessful attempts at a rally and retired to our billets.[18]

Parkes recalled the practice night operations with the same cynical eye: "Night operation. To deploy through a wood in open order to locate a damaged aeroplane. Quite a farce. Section officer knowing nothing of how it should be done. Had we been up the line we should have all been captured or killed long before we moved off."

In addition to cylinder training, the mortar battalion practiced the deployment and operation of the Stokes mortar under the guidance of the brigade's Artillery Advisor, Capt. A. J. de C. Rivers. The guns came in two-inch and four-inch models, but the mortarmen usually fired the latter. The two-inch mortars, called "toffee apples," had a tendency to leak and were not popular with those who had to handle them.[19] The base-plates, when dug securely into the soil, provided a foundation for the mortar. Among the men digging model emplacements on Helfaut common and practicing rapid base-plate laying was the conscientious diarist Jack Oakey, who happened also to be Foulkes's brother-in-law.

Each section had to prepare a position properly sandbagged, etc. When the mortars were delivered the subsection [12] gun-teams were practiced in rapid base-plate laying. If we had known then what we knew later our whole method of base-plate laying would have been different. I should have gone in for slow and sure construction of foundations. The trouble arose out of the fact that our mortars were 4″ Stokes. The barrels were much heavier than the 3″ Stokes as used by the infantry, and the shell, a crude affair, a good deal heavier. The base-plate and legs were exactly the same as those issued for the 3″ mortar. I was the only officer in the battalion who had any practical experience with the 3″ and not much at that, having fired only 20 rounds at the enemy and as many at the Trench Mortar School.

The mortars were a constant source of employment for subsections when nothing much was doing. Mortars were cleaned and washed. To clean the bore which was smooth but not polished, and keep the rust out of the pores of the metal, hot water and much soda was used. I had to buy the soda for this purpose as the issued quantity hardly sufficed for the cooks. Each section painted a different coloured ring around the barrels, stands, base-plates, pick and shovel handles; even the cartridge rammers were so decorated. . . . But one soon found that mortars tended to become interchangeable between sections in the line. When out of the line it was quite right that a section should have its own mortars and stick to them. When I took over C section one of the first things I did . . . was to paint a big pink six-pointed star on mortars and boxes. N.C.O.s i/c teams always strove to keep the same mortars, for there were undoubtedly great differences between the reliability of the different mortars. Some of them seemed to have far fewer misfires than others. . . .

Our shell for the 4″ was a tin canister containing 5 or 6 lbs of red phosphorus encased in a piece of sheet iron, having a big heavy phosphorus-bronze base into which the cartridge was placed and a wooden plug at the top end; through the plug ran a hole and in the hole passed the Bickford fuse, which burst the tin. When in action one lighted the fuse end and then dropped the shell into the gun. If it failed to discharge, which was frequently the case, the gun crew got behind the gun and waited for the shell to burst in the barrel; when smoke and sparks had cleared away one proceeded to clean the barrel.

At times Major Pollitt would have us out at 5 or 6 A.M. on the common to practice various forms of barrages, and officers had to take notes of the number of duds and the grouping of the shells fired by mortars at particular spots.

On one occasion [1 May] there was an inspection of firing by the artillery advisor of the Brigade, Captain de C. Rivers, on which occasion each section of the company had to fire so many rounds and all had to be done according to the drill which was Artillery Gun Drill applied to Mortars. The Grande Finale was a company shoot from the prepared positions. When firing began and the smoke was thick . . . a bright glow appeared in front. The glow arose from a burning house. A shell had fallen on a thatched roof and in time the cottage was burnt out.

The old woman living there had her pig burnt—it ran back into the flames, and she claimed the loss of several thousand francs in cash which she said were hidden in a mattress and burnt.

A court of inquiry failed to determine who had fired the wayward mortar nor did Oakey ever learn the amount of damages the woman recovered. Of greater concern to the gasmen, however, was a fire which started in a gorse patch near their position and at one point during the drill virtually surrounded the men of A section.

As elsewhere in the army, streaks of humor and individuality helped to brighten and ease the grimness of routine trench life. A subsection commander, N. Morrison, camouflaged his mortar position elaborately with bits of gorse, rag, or grass on wire netting, transforming thereby a dreary task into the creation of "Hanging Gardens."[20] Oakey writes quite seriously of a trivial incident in which Major Pollitt caught him attempting to substitute a ringer during a company inspection:

When it came to D-12's turn I borrowed 4 or 5 men from B section which had been inspected. . . . Unfortunately I borrowed a man with red hair, so that soon as the major saw him he recognized him and so learnt the truth. The skipper was horrified and the major was wroth but no more was heard of it. I was most unlucky as ev-

ery section had borrowed of the others for the same purpose and
had not been detected.[21]

Outbreaks of measles and mumps interrupted training and quaran-
tined whole villages from time to time. In mid-April an attack of measles hospitalized Capt. Claude Douglas, the Oxford physiologist now
attached permanently to the Special Brigade from the Royal Army Medical Corps. During the month there were twelve cases of mumps, forty-
seven of measles, and one of diphtheria in the brigade. In May, Foulkes
ordered the entire unit inoculated against typhoid. The next month an
epidemic of diphtheria among the children of Helfaut for a time placed
all *estaminets* out of bounds.[22]

Heavy snow had fallen during late February, and many of the gasmen
spent evenings tobogganing down the nearby steep slopes on sleds constructed out of empty cylinder boxes.[23] During frequent free afternoons,
life seemed reminiscent of the carefree routine in the early days at Helfaut. "We have plenty of occupation but are not over-worked," wrote
Grantham. And in another letter in June: "All I have to do today is to
censor letters, paint my name on kit bags and spend as much time as
possible fishing."[24] The men found ample time for sports, mostly football matches between sections or battalions. On 1 February, Haig
watched "for some minutes" as 1st Battalion defeated 3d Battalion.
Cousins, then in H Company, wrote of company football finals, "obstacle wheelbarrow" races, cross-country racing, and a 100-yard dash. He
summed up the daily routine as "helmet and cylinder drill in morn-
ings, Rogers [cylinders] in afternoons, *estaminets* at night." Cousins
also played chess in the evenings.[25]

During frequent visits to England, Foulkes attended popular London
shows ("Peaches," "Half Past Eight," "Tonight's the Night"), an Albert Hall concert, and a dance with his wife, Dorothy. He took young
sons Tom and Howard for camel and elephant rides at the Regent's Park
Zoo. On one particularly full day in May, he witnessed in the morning
a demonstration of Vincent's flame-thrower at Wembley, lunched at
the Piccadilly, saw a matinee performance of "A Kiss for Cinderella,"
dined at Prince's, and in the evening took in a second play, "My Lady
Frayle."[26]

Gradually the injection of new blood, improved equipment, and a
good stint of hard training began to yield a salutary effect. Improving
morale and a growing esprit de corps replaced the disheartened mood of
the last months of 1915. In late May even the cynical Parkes noticed an
improvement. John Thomas's diary for 20 May epitomized the new air
of confidence: "The coming year should prove a successful one for us.
We hope to give the Germans what they asked for, _____. Our past

experience gives us confidence, and we hope our next debut into the arena of conflict will have a decisive effect on the course of the war."[27]

On Saturday, 3 June 1916, Haig, now commander in chief of the British Expeditionary Force (BEF), reviewed the brigade:

> Everybody looking as pretty as possible. He came and glanced at the first companies of each battalion and spoke to all company commanders. Behind the brigade the whole of its transport was drawn up looking awfully well, lines of lorries, box cars, motor bikes, water carts, etc. absolutely perfectly dressed in line and immaculately clean.[28]

The mortar battalion demonstrated its newest methods of frightfulness, after which each of the battalions paraded smartly past Haig, accompanied by a fife-and-drum band of the Irish Guards, borrowed for the occasion. "It was quite a good show," concluded Grantham, and Foulkes declared that Haig was satisfied. Meiron Thomas considered it a singular honor since the commander in chief usually inspected only divisions, "but we *are* an extraordinary Brigade." He thought Haig "a fine strong looking man with the most determined chin I have ever seen."[29]

On the eve of the brigade's departure for the Somme fronts, continuing army expansion necessitated yet another organizational change. Foulkes had intended that each of the four cylinder battalions should operate with one army, but the prospective creation of a Fifth Army from the Reserve would leave the Special Brigade one such battalion short. Reminiscent of his last-minute improvisations before Loos, Foulkes created an additional (fifth) cylinder "composite battalion" by temporarily withdrawing C, J, and O Companies from their respective battalions. This three-company battalion, not to be confused with Pollitt's 5th (mortar) Battalion, he designated 4A and placed under the command of Captain Garden, formerly of H Company. General Thuillier, however, had a distinctly different perception about this change. He does not appear to have been aware of Foulkes's creation of 4A and assumed instead that the mortar battalion had shed its peculiar status and had become a fifth ordinary cylinder battalion.[30] Foulkes, however, continued to refer to Pollitt's unit as the mortar battalion.

Training continued well into early June, when rumors began circulating about departure for the front. With this in mind, a rash decision to "consume all our liquid stores" resulted in a very wet night in Ronald Purves's mess. "Sergeant Potts . . . and I stepped on air groping back to our billets after midnight. 6 A.M. Reveille was just too bad. Tea helped.''[31] On 8 June Foulkes canceled all leave, and five days later the gas companies began one by one to depart Helfaut in cattle trucks and lorries for the Somme fronts.

10
White Star over the Somme

It was a foul way to kill human beings but the Germans started it.[1]

Better equipped, expanded in size, more experienced, in every way more confident, the newly restructured Special Brigade advanced to the front in mid-June 1916, anxious to contribute substantially to the preliminaries of the "big push" known today as the Somme Offensive. By this time the Germans in Picardy had dug in even more defensively, their trenches barricaded by miles of wire and breastworks, their machine-gun emplacements better protected, their dugouts deeper. Heated debate still rages over every strategic and tactical aspect of the Somme Offensive—Rawlinson's longer bombardment versus Haig's shorter, whether or not Haig's effort on the Somme was pushed forward (again) by French urging, whether it was intended to be a "wearing out" battle or a breakthrough, to what extent actual execution reflected Rawlinson's "bite and hold" tactics, the role of the cavalry. But as for Foulkes, he regarded the larger offensive that loomed in Picardy as an opportunity to vindicate his Special Companies and, at last, to fully demonstrate the awesome potential of gas.

The reorganization of the Special Companies, intended to match the five cylinder battalions each to an army, broke down almost immediately on the battlefield. The structural problem was that the dynamics of the Western Front called for a constantly changing gas capability in size—usually small clusters of gas specialists, rarely an entire company. Active divisions might temporarily require several companies, but more typically detachments of only several sections and sometimes, even fewer. Foulkes was accordingly unable to keep intact even one of his five new battalions. The sixteen cylinder companies, trained to operate in battalions of four companies each, were scattered across a British front extending about seventy-five miles. The mortar battalion split between two armies, and even gas units as small as sections separated to isolated fronts. Consequently, Foulkes lost whatever advantage

he had envisioned for the battalion organization. The gas brigade that
departed Helfaut as intact companies of five battalions was a brigade on
paper only.

Rawlinson, now in command of the Fourth Army, was to mount the
major Somme assault along a front from Hebuterne on the north to
Maricourt on the south, where the French took up the line. To support
this central battlefront of the Fourth Army, Foulkes deployed seven cylinder companies (A, B, D, E, F, G, and H) as well as three Stokes mortar
companies. Z Company would not leave England until 24 June (see
chapter 11). The men of the Special Brigade arrived in Picardy as the valley was ablaze with spring flora. Cousins, during long walks in the
cornfields surrounding Helfaut, had already observed parachute spi-
ders, nesting swallows, and ghost swifts. Arriving with H Company
along the Somme, he found the marshes at the rear of camp abounding
in lovely dragonflies.[2] John Thomas marveled at the pretty Venus'
Looking Glass (*Legousia hybrida*) blossoming in profusion at Beaumont Hamel.[3] Sid Fox wrote of marguerites and cornflowers and of the
red, white, and blue poppies that bloomed so incongruously in no
man's land.[4] Like other British soldiers quoted in Paul Fussel's *The
Great War and Modern Memory* (1975), the men of the Special Brigade
may have sought and found some solace from the horrors of war in
these bucolic reminders of nature's peace and continuity.[5]

Preparations proceeded apace. Daylight saving time went into effect
on 14 June 1916. Four days later the first steel helmets arrived. The gas
companies received and synchronized new watches.[6] Posters appeared
advertising warning signals—a gong for gas alert, whistle blasts for hostile aircraft, and so on. French civilians began to pack up and evacuate
nearby villages; a mere half dozen remained in the town of Bray.[7]

Despite the existence of the new mortar companies, the unavailabil-
ity of gas mortars meant that the bulk of the White Star gas (half chlorine and half phosgene) was to be released by cylinders. Thus, the frustrating delays and shortages that had plagued the earlier Loos action
once again compounded Foulkes's usual difficulties. As late as 10 June,
only 16,600 White Star cylinders (less than half the desired number)
had arrived, and an exasperated Foulkes discovered that most had im-
proper carrying handles or no handles at all. Thousands of leftover Red
Star (chlorine) cylinders had to be substituted. Only 6,300 of the required 26,000 pipe fittings were in hand. The gas units were also short
their full complement by over 500 men.[8]

As the cylinders arrived at the various fronts, the handlers repeated
the same arduous and monotonous routine of the past year, trudging
back and forth through the communication trenches, some over two
miles in length, to prepare the gas emplacements.[9] As earlier, it was the

portering of the cylinders that most soldiers remembered as particularly unpleasant, and this was especially onerous for the volunteer soldiers of Kitchener's New Armies coming for the first time into the lines in large numbers in 1916. Soldiers in the Pals battalions drawn from nonmanual trades not used to heavy labor, such as the Hulls Commercials, complained bitterly about this backbreaking duty.[10] No official war diaries of the various gas companies exist for 1916, but the five battalion diaries covering the month of June fully document the tedium of equipment unloading, cylinder testing, emplacement preparation, requests for telephone service, negotiations for infantry carrying parties, the carrying in of the cylinders, reconstruction of emplacements destroyed by shellfire, posting of guards, and conferences of gas personnel. Personal diaries amplify the stark factual record with human emotion. "Fatigues at all hours of the day and night." A carrying party of two hundred did "as much work as 400 men could do."[11] Operations were "fearfully tedious,"[12] and the cylinders

> were horrifying things to handle. They weighed 180 pounds and were slung on a pole between two men. Everyone had to wear his gas helmet all the time in case the cylinders leaked, and that meant most of the time we were stifled and half suffocated. . . . We tramped through the warm thundery summer rain, the shining wet cylinder swinging between every swearing group of men knocking their knees and trapping their fingers.[13]

Cousins's section made a trip to the front at Carnoy the evening of 22 June.

> Only the night voices and the rumble of the waggons! A group of officers demand the letter of our dump. "To L" we say, then advance. We run slap into a transport column who demand right of way, but our little red flags serve and we draw up near a field and wood called Dump L. Here we unload our 20 rogers with the aid of the Star shells fired off by our dear old friends the Bosch. The only inquisitive people have been our Tommies but we are sphinxes and the waggons rumble on. Arrive the R. W. Kents to transport them to the trenches with more corporals of ours as guides. Their work is just starting, ours is finished. Tomorrow, look they ever so hard, not a sign of our work will appear.[14]

Guards took up their posts, and once again the long wait to zero hour began. Henry Venables, a sergeant in H Company, spent his last few nights on earth in the trenches with the cylinders. He wrote to his mother on 26 June: "Just a line to let you know I am progressing favourably though I have had pretty well of work [in] the last week or so." Four days later, in the early hours of 30 June, Venables, twenty-seven years old, was killed by shrapnel exploding on a nearby parapet.[15]

The mortar companies worked concurrently to install their base-plates and mortars, as John Oakey in No. 1 Company explains:

> About a week's work completed the emplacements sufficiently for the mortars to be carried in. This was done by daylight and a guard left over them. Ammunition was taken in by night by a carrying party from the infantry. I remember preparing it [the ammo] at Martinsart, each shell was placed in a frame with a pointer at one end; the cartridge was put into the container, the shell into the frame and one tested the cap on the cartridge for concentricity. This was to avoid duds by not using shells with badly centered containers. Briggs and I took in our ammunition by using boxcars which came to Hamel by night from Lancashire Dump which was on the road to Albert in Aveluy Wood.

Among the many sorts of guns in Martinsart, several of them firing almost directly over Oakey's hut, was a twelve-inch howitzer called "Granny." He and the others, however, soon got so used to the bombardment din that they slept in spite of it.

Purves, posted to the front near Albert, led eight men of his subsection on a routine but harrowing nocturnal trip carrying bomb stores to the front line.

> June 20: A Bosch sniper was busy at something overhead, but at 9:45 P.M. the "Allemagnes" opened up with shell fire from whizz-bangs. . . . deliberately trying for us and our "happy home." They filled in the Communication Trench, smashed the Artillery O.P. [Observation Post], wounded one of the infantrymen & finally cut a piece out of my shrapnel helmet, which was only issued to us tonight, so mine probably saved me from a nasty one above the temples. No one else in the Section hit.

> June 23: Parade at 9 A.M. to clean up guns and at 10 A.M. to get them all up to the trenches. Marched up to the rail-head at Tramway Corner via Albert & Aveluy in tremendous heat wave. We sweated like beasts & our shrapnel helmets were like furnaces—so hot. Had to work very hard all day. At 2 P.M. a terrible thunderstorm commenced & flooded the whole place—mud instead of dust.

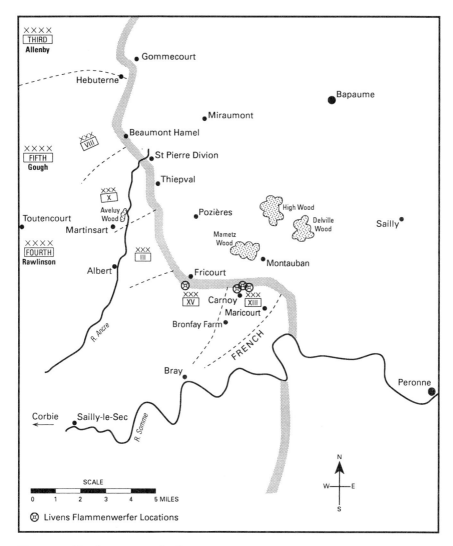

Map 10.1. Gas frontage at the Somme

However we got back by 6 P.M. in the Box Car. Found all my bed, etc. soaked, being outside under the trees.

June 24: Moved into a new billet last night about 9 P.M., where we all have beds of wire netting. The place is full of rats, but that can't be helped. Wrote a lot of letters. May not have many more chances. The bombardment commences this afternoon.

June 27: . . . up to the dump at Tramway Corner. Very heavy bombardment all afternoon, the Germans replying with heavy H.E.s and gas shells which half blinded us. When working nearly everyone wore the anti-gas goggles. Got our guns cleaned up & all ammunition ready to go over. Tied it up in sandbags—2 in each bag, and two tied together load for one man. A few splinters came round us as we worked. Couldn't hear ourselves speaking.

Following the installation of Oakey's emplacements, Robertson assigned Oakey and William Elliker of D section, a twenty-seven-year-old bank cashier from Derby, to build the observation post to be used by Foulkes on Z day. They selected a suitable spot with a commanding view in a communication trench called Jacob's Ladder, opposite Beaumont Hamel, which happened to be the same spot where Geoffrey Malins was setting up camera equipment to film his documentary, *The Battle of the Somme*, the first official cinematic record of this or any other battle.[16]

Accordingly the Skipper [Robertson], I, and Elliker reconnoitered Jacob's Ladder and fixed on a spot near the machine gun observation posts. These were well built, concealed and were connected with deep dugouts. My O.P.'s dimensions were laid down by the Skipper, and had to be built accordingly, not forgetting three layers of broken brick in bags on the top. That night I with a small party including Corporal Pritchard went to prepare the excavation which was made in a place where the trench had given way at sometime and in consequence there was a small bay. This was dug out by night no day work being possible as the place was on the brow of the hill. The next night we went up with sandbags and wood to make the frame. It was very dark and raining heavily, and work had to be given up fairly soon owing to that cause. Moreover an 18 pounder battery [British field gun] was close behind firing continuously right over our heads. The concussion made one's steel helmet ring when one was in the trench, but on top one was deafened and made silly. The third night the brick which was lying about the top having formerly paved the trench was put on, but a daylight view gave one the horrors—as it stuck, as I said it would right up on the skyline, and in consequence I had to return at dusk to lower the whole contraption.

A machine gun officer was sarcastic, saying he hoped it would remain as a ''draw-fire'' from him. When lowered, the ''higher authority'' disliked the result as the occupier would have to stoop

somewhat. Later Col. Foulkes came up and rejected the location
. . . preferring a trench behind some bushes nearer Hamel.

They finished the new observation post on 25 June. On the twenty-sixth, "not having much to do," Oakey helped toss gas and smoke candles and phosphorus bombs from Thiepval Wood. On the twenty-seventh, Oakey and Briggs conducted a tour of inspection of their lines.

As Z day approached, Foulkes gradually realized that his expectations about the major role gas was to play in the coming offensive were shared by neither Haig nor Rawlinson.[17] He also found to his continuing dismay that he lacked the freedom to adequately demonstrate the new capabilities of his reorganized units. Divisional commanders insisted on exercising discretionary authority over even such technically trivial matters as the method of cylinder installation. Some specified wooden receptacles, while others preferred sinking the cylinders directly into the ground by the firestep, dismissing Foulkes's circulars on the matter as merely advisory. Use of the more lethal phosgene only increased the resistance of field commanders to the presence of gas in their sectors, an understandable reaction considering the risk of leakage. Douglas Edwards-Ker, who joined L Company about this time, remembered "tremendous opposition to start with from the Army. They didn't like gas at all."[18] When Lt. F. G. C. Walker of E Company arrived at 30th Division headquarters with orders from XIII Corps to arrange for gas installation, its commander refused to provide carrying parties or to cooperate in any way. The next day Walker received a corps telegram canceling all plans for gas installations in the 30th Division sector.[19] It was to be an all-too-familiar scenario. Foulkes bitterly resented the curt retort of a divisional commanding officer in responding to a gas captain who had come to arrange a gas discharge: "Take your bloody gas away. I'll have nothing to do with it."[20]

Much to Foulkes's added consternation, he learned that army commanders intended to release the gas as soon as favorable winds allowed, as part of the extended preliminary bombardment rather than as a massive synchronized discharge just before zero hour.[21] Gas was not to be allowed to play the part it had played, or rather had been intended to play, at Loos—it was not to be given a second chance. The Somme schedule sacrificed both the element of gas surprise as well as any possible tactical support of the infantry assault. Even worse, army headquarters passed discretionary authority about the gas timing down the chain of command to corps headquarters and from there to divisional commanders, many of whom were either unsympathetic or unfamiliar with the gas capability. Apprehension at the presence of filled gas cylinders in front-line trenches may have led many to order the discharge

sooner than otherwise might have been the case. The plans clearly rele-
gated gas to a distinctly subsidiary role in the pre-Somme bombardment; Foulkes confessed to keen disappointment but persevered in his
characteristic enthusiasm nonetheless.

Thus on 20 June 1916 Rawlinson gave the go-ahead to his corps commanders to begin the gas discharges on Fourth Army fronts at their dis-
cretion, and permission duly passed on to divisional authorities.
Fiercely uncooperative winds prevented any consideration of gas activity for several days, but on 24 June, under only marginal conditions, the
4th (Regular) Division ordered the start of the gas discharges. In the
face of an almost dead wind, however, all but one of the gas officers stationed in this sector, following policy laid down after Loos, countermanded this order. Only 2d Lt. E. W. Jones, leading sections 22 and 24
of D Company, opposite Beaumont Hamel, allowed the order to be carried out at 10 P.M.[22] The consequence was a fairly severe gassing of the
infantrymen as well as of the gas personnel, which prompted an irate
letter of protest from the commanding officer of the 4th Division (Maj.
Gen. William Lambton) to VIII Corps headquarters. But the corps commander, Lt. Gen. Sir Aylmer Hunter-Weston, himself a Royal Engineer,
stoutly defended the actions of the gas officers.

> With regard to the letting off of gas, it is imperative for either the
> Army Commander, for me, or for you at your HQ, to decide
> whether the wind is correct for the emission of gas on any given
> portion of the front. GHQ, therefore, has rightly ordered that the
> order from a higher command for the emission of gas was permis-
> sive rather than compulsory, and that the responsibility for the
> emission of gas on any particular portion of the front must rest en-
> tirely on the Gas Officer in Charge of that section.
>
> The permissive order . . . was given by the Army Commander
> [Rawlinson], and repeated by me and by you and other Divisional
> Commanders. The gas men, other than Lieut. Jones, were of the
> opinion that the wind was not suitable. Lt. Jones, acting quite
> rightly on his own judgment, considered that in his portion of the
> front the wind was favourable, and he, therefore, turned on the gas.
> He acted according to his judgment at the time, and no blame
> whatever attaches to him for the fact that a few of his personnel got
> gassed. Even if it transpires afterwards that some of the infantry
> were gassed by our own gas, please ensure that no blame should at-
> tach to the Gas Officer. They have a difficult duty to perform, and
> they must be assured that . . . they will be backed up by superior
> authority.[23]

The winds had never been ideal, though Cousins, who took wind readings regularly during this period, reported that the strongest velocity at 12.8 mph, south-southwest, was not too bad.[24] That Rawlinson had indeed intended to release all his gas allocation on 24 June is corroborated in his diary: "Fear we did not get off all our gas."[25] On 27 June, General Allenby (Third Army), also impatient after several delays, ordered that "all gas was to be liberated as soon as a favourable opportunity presented itself whether by day or by night."[26] An increasingly exasperated Foulkes, sensing that infantry commanders wanted to "get the stuff off" as soon as possible, compared their apprehension of gas to an irrational fear of snakes.[27]

Why did General Rawlinson, no stranger to gas, allow it to be wasted so far in advance of Z day in this way? The evolution of Rawlinson's thinking about gas is enlightening. Although not directly involved in the first German gas attacks at Ypres, he was scandalized by the news: "What is war coming to?" he wrote to Kitchener.[28] But only five days later, 29 April 1915, he was conjecturing that given proper weather conditions chlorine gas might make an effective weapon. "Personally I would like to use something far worse on the Germans."[29] However on 8 May, in a letter to Col. Clive Wigram, he expressed doubts about its usefulness given the unbending wind requirements without which the user may suffer more than the enemy.[30] On 24 May he wrote to the War Office, "I hope you are sending us out plenty of big cylinders with chlorine gas in them for when the west wind commences, we shall want them badly."[31] Again in June, at La Bassée, facing some deep German strongpoints and supplied only with Jackson's defective gas grenades, "Rawly" complained:

If we had some 1000s of gas cylinders we could get a move on them, for our trenches are close enough together to use gas on quite a wide front but it must be heavy and the more poisonous the better so as to reach the deep dugouts. Are you not going to send us out some proper gas? These stink bombs that have arrived are perfectly useless, they only leak and poison our own men. Until we get something effective in this direction we shall not get the Germans out of France.[32]

But such gas was unavailable at the time. The following month Rawlinson was present at Foulkes's 22 August 1915 gas demonstration and concluded: "Many cylinders wanted—one to every two yards gassed." Throughout the weeks leading up to Loos, Rawlinson's diaries contain almost daily sanguine references to the potential of gas.[33] He expressed the hope that "the Smell" would prove as disastrous for its victims as at Second Ypres and wrote, "I watch the glass [barometer] every day."[34] From 20 September: "I am very anxious about the weather as without gas we shant do much." From 22 September: "I am getting very anxious about the weather as it means so much to us in our attack on the 25th. If we cannot use gas we shall not I fear get far."[35] He held the highest hopes for gas and was keenly disappointed that the attack was not to wait for the required wind. Hearing early reports of its success he wrote in his diary for 25 September, prematurely as it turned out, "A great day! Gas attack at 5:30 A.M. succeeded! Took Loos and captured Hulluch." When it later became apparent how disappointing and ineffective a role gas had really played at Loos, the previous enthusiasm and optimism evaporated quickly.

By the spring of 1916 gas had become for him just another ancillary weapon. In the months leading up to the pre-Somme, Rawlinson's diary contains only casual, offhand references to the weapon which had gripped his attention so decisively the year before. Both he and Haig relied exclusively on gas shell (delivered by the artillery) to reach the enemy's deep dugouts.[36] A few days before the pre-Somme bombardment, Rawlinson seemed confident that the 150,000 rounds per day and 50,000 per night of high explosives would be sufficient to demolish strong enemy resistance. "There should not be much left of his defenses at the end of it."[37] Even when raiding reports disclosed that, astonishingly, these deep dugouts housing the machine-gun crews had survived the heavy artillery pounding, there is no mention of cloud gas as the appropriate weapon to deal with them. A wave of concentrated heavy gas released just before zero hour might have sunk down into some of these enemy dugouts and neutralized at least temporarily their machine-gun crews. By contrast, Rawlinson's early release, a full four days in advance even of the beginning of the heavy artillery bombardment, could have had no possible effect on the later infantry assault. Its effect on the enemy would have been no more than that of a temporary irritant. The only plausible explanation seems to be that Rawlinson had taken to heart the sad lesson of gas failure at Loos. On 26 June he writes, "We have got rid of most of the gas and the bombardment proceeds."[38] His choice of words betrays a lack of confidence in gas, an attitude shared by many British commanders at this time. Thus it was that Rawlinson's Fourth Army expended the last of its gas during the night of 27/28 June, a full four days before zero hour.

In reporting the gas releases of the pre-Somme bombardment, the war diaries of all five gas battalions show days and nights of feverish and concentrated activity, punctuated by shrapnel injuries, shattered emplacements, gas-related accidents, and so on. "On first night cylinders carried into trenches but after cylinders covered with sandbags a large trench mortar bomb (oil can) burst on the parapet and buried cylinders—one burst. 22 infantry gassed. 9 died. one R.E. corporal gassed.''[39] As at Loos and in spite of improvements, the gas equipment still performed imperfectly. Gas leaked from piping joints. Contrary wind eddies blew gas back into British trenches. Enemy shells and shell fragments ruptured gas pipes. Human error or human carelessness generated additional problems. Parkes admitted that in the heat and excitement of the moment he inadvertently turned on one of his cylinders before throwing out the parapet pipe.[40] And as before, discomforts associated with wearing gas helmets induced men to remove them too soon. The new box respirators were unwieldy, and if the nose-clip caught on anything during operations, the helmet was easily misadjusted.[41]

The mortar companies, still without gas shells, used their mortars to lay down smoke screens. Four typed pages of meticulously drafted instructions of Capt. A. E. Kent, commanding officer of No. 4 Special (Mortar) Company, including detailed alternatives for various wind conditions, illustrate the care and deliberation that went into the planning of a smoke screen.[42] John Oakey was at Martinsart with No. 1 Mortar Company on the opening of the Somme assault.

The night June 30-July 1 was one of bustle and we were able to help the infantry manning the line for the next day quite a lot, owing to our detailed knowledge of the trenches in the neighborhood. At 5 A.M. I went into the mortar emplacements to prepare for zero. I had not slept much owing to people coming in and out of the dugout so I spent most of my time reading "Dracula," a copy of which I found in the dugout.

The morning broke very still and misty with the wind at "nil." The frogs in the Ancre had been croaking loudly all night. The bombardment which had continued all day and night for six or seven days at Zero less 60 minutes, i.e. 6:30 A.M. suddenly intensified itself many times.

According to orders each mortar had a pit dug in front of it into which dud shells with lighted fuses were to be put by up-ending the mortar, with the idea of not giving away the emplacements by smoke from shells burst in the barrels arising from them. Unfortunately it had rained two or three nights previously and the soil on the floor of the emplacement in the "Minnie" hole gave way and the base plates sank out of sight. The mortar in the dug-out had a round jammed in the bore, and Corporal Leigh on the left alone kept going. Briggs seeing my thin smoke that I was in difficulties got going and between us we kept up the 80 minutes barrage which was to screen the high land above St Pierre Divion from Beaumont

Hamel, and so hide the left flank of the 36th (Ulster) Division on their attack out of Thiepval Wood on to the Bosch line.

The previous week's bombardment had sadly disfigured the trees about Thiepval village and the Bosch trenches which had lain between Thiepval and St Pierre Divion like straight white marks across and along the green hillside, were now just a confused mass of grey rubbish and upturned earth and chalk; every speck of turf seemed to have been torn up.

Oakey's C section assignment on the morning of 1 July was to establish mortar positions at the enemy side of no man's land at zero hour plus thirty minutes, one of the few times any units of the Special Companies were ever called upon to go over the top in infantry fashion:

When C's turn came to go over, Hardman and Sutton were killed as soon as they were "over the top." Thus two officers out of three were down before the start, but Sgt. Potts and Corporal Gavin for their efforts to get the men on, were awarded the D.C.M. [Distinguished Conduct Medal]. Swann, left with a couple of mortars and a few rounds of ammunition, managed to cross No Man's Land and got some way into the trenches, but his party was so thinned [from] so doing that all he could do was to fire a few rounds using a helmet as a base plate. The rest of the shells were thrown into dugouts and Bosch smoked out and taken prisoner. He took some 30 prisoners.

The cylinder companies, having discharged their cylinders in advance, were nevertheless not idle on this extraordinarily memorable day, the first day of the Somme, 1 July 1916. Purves, opposite Thiepval with the 32d Division, writes of fierce fighting and streams of wounded and notes the lack of food and drink which sapped the energies of men in both the infantry and the Special Companies. Much of Purves's work involved carrying duties and care of the wounded.

July 1: I had a few minutes sleep at the most. Got our breakfast—a drop of tea, bacon and biscuit at 5 A.M. & moved up to "Blighty Wood." Got guns and ammunition up No. 1 Dumbarton Track & waited for the 1st Dorsets. The XI Borders came up and went over, & got wiped out by machine gun fire, never reached the German front line. Wounded were coming back thickly, at least 2 out of every 6 wounded & 1 knocked over—killed. We waited for orders to go over & get our chance of being wiped out, but it never came—luckily. It was a near thing for us as the Brigadier came up and asked us who we were & what our orders were, and then, why we were hanging back.

About 9 P.M. . . . we put up a smoke screen as the Dorsets were going over, which helped them a bit. Five of us worked the guns. I think I put over 50 rounds out of No. 1 gun. A Lewis gun 5 yards away on our right was put out of action but we managed to miss everything. Pioneer Morris got hit by shrapnel on the way up, & about 7 or 8 of my carriers. I worked on till about 3 P.M. bandaging up the wounded. Then about 3:30 P.M. we were ordered to go to the 36th Division Ammunition Reserves to bring up 60 bombs. Took 30 men down—took us about 2 1/2 hours to get there—only 2 1/2 miles or so—. . . . everyone knocked up—no rations of any kind since 5 A.M. Managed to get a dixie of tea & a few biscuits from C Section. They had gone "over the top" at Thiepval. 2nd Lt. Hardman & 2nd Lt. Sutton, two of the best sorts, were killed about 25 yards over & 7 men went down also. Sergt. W. W. Potts crawled back . . . safely—and that finished them off for any further work. We started off at 7 P.M. for Blighty Wood after getting my bombs. Gas shells were plumped-in all day into Blighty Wood & we have had to wear gas goggles nearly all day. We got up to Divisional Dump at the foot of "Dumbarton Track" about 9 P.M. All the men absolutely done-up. Two had fainted—and had fits (one turned out to be epileptic later). A few others were nearly as bad & I was ready to fall asleep at any moment. My equipment cut into my shoulders like irons. Put our bombs into Ammunition store & then got orders to take them up to Rock Street Store. Got up there about 10 P.M. with a struggle. Dumbarton Track was full of shell holes, littered with dead men, rifles, equipment, bombs, Bangalore torpedoes & all sorts of materials lying around—broken trees and branches. The whole place was full of lachrymatory gas, & our eyes ran nearly all the night with tears, very painful too.[43]

Once the infantry assaults commenced on 1 July, especially along the main battlefront of Rawlinson's Fourth Army, the heavy and constant fighting precluded much immediate gas activity. Geoffrey Higson, now in D Company, enjoyed a nap and on the next day slept in until 9 A.M. and after tea "settled down for a quiet game of auction [bridge]."[44] According to Foulkes this Fourth Army front afforded virtually no opportunity to install any cylinders for a long time after 1 July.[45] But the war diaries of the gas battalions show sporadic cylinder activity throughout July and August.

Foulkes had distributed several Special Companies among the First, Second, and Third Armies in Flanders and Artois, north of the Somme

battlefields. C, J, and O Companies occupied a part of the front line opposite Hulluch, familiar terrain holding painful memories of the autumn of 1915. The men found billets in a coal mine at Minx, just to the
west of Vermelles where the communication trench began. Minx, an
abbreviation for "MINes de NoeuX," was halfway between Noeux and
Bethune. Operating in the Loos area, C Company lost a corporal and a
pioneer, killed while helping to rescue wounded 10th Gordons. Parkes,
with O Company on the same front, recalled the intensity of an artillery barrage intended to mask the gas discharge, "a noise sufficient to
deafen anyone." After the gas release, Parkes counted eleven dead,
eleven wounded, and ten gassed. "At least five deaths were caused by
not using respirators and the ten gassed were of course through this neglect."[46] Several years later J. B. Platnauer, in the same company, recalled the incident somewhat differently:

> Machine guns started firing and we heard shells begin to explode in
> front of us. The noise seemed to increase and they brought a lot of
> gas casualties along the trench . . . yellow-faced men coughing
> their lungs up, their buttons tarnished as though with Lyddite.
> Most of them were wearing the red, green and white brassards of
> the Gas units of the Royal Engineers. The German shells had
> thrown the gas pipes back into the trench and smashed the gas cyl-
> inders that had been dug into the parapet. Instead of gassing the
> Germans they had gassed themselves. They had lost 58 men out of
> 64.[47]

Platnauer suffered gassing too, vomited, and was taken by stretcher to a
field dressing station and attended to by the Duchess of Westminster.
Surgeons also removed from his hand three pieces of shrapnel, the largest of which, "about the size of a runner bean," he mounted as a nov-
elty tiepin and sent to his father as a present.[48]

On 19 July, at Fromelles, in front of Lille, the Australian 5th Division
and the British 61st Division launched one of the most futile and poorly
thought-out attacks of the war—a diversionary assault uphill against
the heavily fortified Aubers Ridge.[49] In preparation for this assault, J
Company, which had been operating since June on the 61st Division
front and standing by for three successive nights awaiting favorable
weather, discharged 549 cylinders during the night of 16 July.[50] Among
those infantry involuntarily sharing the front-line trenches with the
personnel and apparatus of the gas companies on this occasion was a
company commander of the Royal Warwickshire Regiment, Geoffrey
Boles Donaldson, a twenty-three-year-old Cambridge botanist. In a letter to his mother, his last, written immediately after the gas discharge

Going over the top amid bursting gas and tear shells to storm the fortified villages of the Somme. (Courtesy of Liddell Hart Centre for Military Archives)

of 16 July, he illustrates the feelings of one such infantry commander who faced chemical warfare for the first time:

> I met streams of men making their way into our trenches carrying weird pipes and great round trench mortar bombs like footballs. The CT crawled with men. Then I realized what was going to happen. You will remember, some weeks ago I described how we had to carry certain stores into the trenches about here when we were in rest billets. I am now free to tell you, that those stores were heavy iron cylinders of GAS and the weird pipes and the crowds of men that I met yesterday showed that a gas attack was intended. This was confirmed when I reached Battalion HQ. There was only an hour or two to complete arrangements before it was to start as they were afraid the wind would change. I can tell you that, in that 1/2 hour before the gas attack started, I came nearer to ''having the wind up'' or in other words, losing my nerve than has ever been the case before. This was more especially the case as the R.E. officer responsible for letting off the gas on my frontage told me, he had

done several such stunts, but he thought the wind rather weak and he did not like doing it in daylight as the Bosch could shell more accurately. At 8:30 P.M. the show started. I had all the men in the trench out of dug-outs and we all had our gas helmets on. It was like an appalling night-mare as you look like some horrible kind of demon or goblin in these masks. There were words of command along the line from the R.E. and then a loud hissing sound as the taps were turned on and the deadly greenish white vapour poured out of the jets and slowly blew in a great rolling cloud towards the opposite line of trenches.

In the next fire-bay to me, one idiot of a sapper turned the jets in the wrong direction, and filled our trenches with gas in slewing it round over the parapet. My buttons became quite tarnished, but I felt no ill effects, but four men in the fire-bay where this happened were slightly gassed.

Three days later, 19 July, infantryman Donaldson led his company over the top. For both attacking divisions, the effort proved a total fiasco and casualties were severe: The Australians lost 5,355; the 61st Division lost 1,547; the two attacking companies of Donaldson's battalion lost thirteen officers and 305 men. In C Company, three were killed, among them Geoffrey Boles Donaldson.[51]

The greater toxicity of the phosgene component of the White Star, more insidious because of its delayed effects, meant more serious injuries among the complacent. Even the Specials themselves underestimated the new gas, having worked so long with the relatively milder Red Star (chlorine). A sergeant with K Company, deployed around Ypres, received a slight dose of White Star in disconnecting a four-way pipe: "He paid no attention to it, did not even report it and carried on with his work. He returned to billet, slept well, collapsed while taking breakfast the following morning and was dead within 24 hours." On the same occasion a shell bursting on a trench parapet sent billows of gas into one of the bays. Though a gas corporal and two pioneers stationed there reported only slight irritation, their section commander sent them to a dressing station at once. The corporal, protesting that he felt "quite well," returned to the line, but was again ordered back. All three men were dead in the morning.[52]

Although by mid-1916 White Star had become the chemical mixture of choice—the "workhorse" gas—Foulkes encouraged the gas companies to experiment from time to time with a wide variety of gases for both cylinders and mortar fillings in order to keep the enemy off balance. On 12 July at an operation at Monchy (Third Army front), several companies experimented with another gas combination—sulfurated hydrogen with 12 percent carbon disulfide, called Double Red Star, and highly inflammable. "As soon as enemy shelling began, the whole line became a blazing inferno and 2 sections of Q Company assisted by another Special Company sustained heavy casualties."[53] The 4th Battalion war diary corroborates experimental use of Double Red Star at this time, but, like Blue Star, the mixture saw no further use.[54]

On 13 July Foulkes noticed an anonymous article in the *Evening Standard* under the sensational headlines:

BATTLE OF THE CYLINDERS

DOSING THE HUN WITH HIS OWN MEDICINE

THRILLING STORY OF A BRITISH GAS ATTACK

by A BRITISH "GASMAN"

The two-thousand-word article disclosed specific inside information about the activities of the Special Brigade. Convinced that the source must have been a member of his unit, an outraged Foulkes circulated an angry memorandum of warning and censure. "The writer has betrayed his country and has broken trust," he wrote, and threatened trial by court martial "with the severest penalties in the event of conviction."[55] The culprit, if indeed within the brigade, was never identified.[56]

The summer heat and Somme casualties exacerbated the problem of the trench rats. Oakey described the Thiepval trenches as "far from pleasant as the dead were still unburied from the 1st and the hot sun and damp had done their share to make things beastly."[57] The dead and decomposing bodies left in no man's land by the carnage of the Somme fighting provided grisly feed for the ravenous scavengers, from the description of one soldier, as large as rabbits.[58] The sudden presence of gas in the trenches created near panic in the rodent population. A lieutenant colonel in the London Regiment painted a macabre picture of a trench scene following a gas attack:

> The trench swarmed with rats, "big rats, small rats, grey rats, tall rats" in every stage of gas poisoning! Some were scurrying along scarcely affected while others were slowly dragging themselves about trying to find a corner in which to die. A most horrid sight— but a very good riddance![59]

In his last letter home Donaldson had written with deadpan humor of great numbers of dead rats lying about, killed by the gas, "as they have no gas helmets."[60] The lethal effect of the gas on the rats was one of its oddly incidental blessings but did not seem in the end to affect adversely the total rat population.

Gas leakage was, naturally, also deleterious to pets. Though officially forbidden to do so, many infantry units harbored dogs and cats in the trenches, and the gas units were no different. A 2d Battalion (Special Brigade) order in February 1916 directed that all dogs in possession of men in the battalion be destroyed or handed over to civilians, but group pictures of gas units with dog mascots show how little the directive was obeyed.[61] C Company's section 14 group picture in 1917 features Marquis, the section mascot, front and center. Sadly, Marquis succumbed to gas poisoning early in 1918 when he broke loose from his chain during a practice gas discharge and ran into the cloud.[62] K Company kept a dog named Madame Spigot.[63] Frequently dogs sensed the presence of gas in the trenches before their human occupants did, their sickness providing early warning.[64] A major with the Royal Engineers writes of a company cat that got slightly gassed in 1916 and "wheezed very much" but recovered.[65] The effect of gas on horses was particularly tragic, and in spite of ill-fitting horse gas masks, gas "killed off the horses like flies."[66] A lieutenant with the 5th Worcesters discovered that mules, also used extensively for transport, were terrified by the sight of anyone wearing a gas mask, and therefore prone to panic during gas attacks.[67]

The brigade was not immune from occasional grousing about both minor and major complaints. Repeated cancellations following the most arduous preparations caused understandable frustration and exasperation: "Everything connected up by 9:15 and all nuts tightened. Zero announced at 10. A very anxious slow wait from 9:30 to 10. Respirators fixed up, spanners in hand, when at 9:58 zero was cancelled."[68]

August 4: 2 years of war today. Our strafe was *not* of much use. Wind against us, smoke coming back over the "Nub," and range was too short. None of the bombs would reach even their barbed wire, so, in my opinion, the night's show was a successful damned failure & waste of time and bombs. . . . It makes me thoroughly fed-up to make a useless job like this, as we didn't even draw their fire, as we were supposed to do.[69]

Cylinders left in the front lines for long periods required constant surveillance, a particularly unwelcome guard duty. The party typically consisted of one corporal and two pioneers who were responsible for dealing with any leaks that occurred by either burying or carrying off faulty cylinders.

After inspecting the cylinder emplacements the Corporal would make a list of the duty hours to ensure that there was always one man on duty in the front line during the night. The relief was made every two hours. During daylight we were more relaxed and had time to spare. Apart from reading, writing or a game of cards, there were various other entertainments such as chats with the infantry, modelling with clay or carving from chalk, ratting and souvenir hunting. . . . In summer it was pleasant to explore some of the abandoned trenches which intersected those still in use. Most of us developed the collector's instinct, and accumulated such treasures as British, French and German cartridge cases, shell fragments, . . . buttons and cap badges.[70]

It was during the summer and autumn of 1916 that Foulkes encountered the greatest resistance to gas—even obstructionism—from infantry commanders: A division was leaving the front in four days, therefore no gas; a front had no breastworks, therefore no gas; a divisional commander simply did not like gas, therefore no gas; a division was new to the line, required time to familiarize itself with the front, therefore no gas. Excuses seemed unlimited. Capt. Norman Campbell, a thirty-year-old schoolteacher commanding N Company, about this time encountered a general who "turned on him, abusing him like a pickpocket, telling him that all their difficulties arose from the gas people, and ending up by telling him to take his messes elsewhere." Campbell wrote to his wife that "the infantry had no cause to love the Special Brigade; in fact their advent in the trenches was a sign for much bad language on the part of the former."[71]

In addition to obstructionism, the gasmen from the first had suffered a good deal of ridicule. Quips and wisecracks circulated widely about the ineffectiveness of British gas. Adrian E. Hodgkin, a technical chemist from London, recounted a story making the rounds in which "we gassed about 300 of our own men and killed one German who laughed so much that he blew his gas mask off!"[72] Foulkes heard a story about experiments in which a chlorine-gassed rabbit suffered no ill effects whatever.[73] Many infantrymen ridiculed the toxicity of British gas, especially the earlier Red Star:

I don't know much about smells, but this one had none on the Bosche. They fairly snuffed it up and loved it! If we are going to descend to using that sort of thing, there is no point in making ourselves ridiculous by having a sort of sneezing mixture. What we want is something to lay out the Blighters, not fill them with beans.[74]

Foulkes strove to counter such resistance with a program of gas presentations at Helfaut for officers and visiting dignitaries. The carefully or-

British troops in antiphosgene masks manning a Vickers machine gun on the Somme front, July 1916. (Courtesy of Imperial War Museum)

chestrated shows included demonstrations of a variety of chemical weaponry—cylinders, projectors, and flame-throwers—"putting the hell into Helfaut," according to one soldier.[75] Throughout the war Foulkes also attempted to tally enemy casualties attributable to gas. The campaign to claim credit for casualties sometimes reached comic proportions. In November 1916, following a dispute over eight German bodies discovered in a dugout at Beaumont Hamel, Z Company asked the Royal Army Medical Corps to corroborate death by gas. With questions still remaining after a preliminary finding in the affirmative, Capt. Claude Douglas agreed to perform autopsies on several rats lying nearby. Unfortunately for the Special Brigade "count," the autopsies revealed cause of death to be carbon monoxide poisoning from underground fires rather than gas.[76]

From a plethora of anecdotal evidence Foulkes carefully selected those accounts most favorable to the gas effort. Some of his own more candid company and section reports in the battalion war diaries, however, indicate less positive results. In support of an infantry raid in early July, L Company successfully got off 387 cylinders of White Star, but according to its own commander, the effect of the gas seemed negligible: "The volume of hostile rifle and machine-gun fire was not diminished by the gas cloud, doubtless owing to the fact that warning had been inadvertently given. The raiders also met with considerable opposition."[77] Interrogation of German prisoners by the 3d Battalion revealed "practically no casualties inflicted" during a June gas attack at Armentières, but fifty-two men were killed in two battalions in a smaller attack. "There were practically no cases of slight poisoning. If men put their masks on quickly enough and in the right way they were unharmed. If a mistake was made it cost a man his life."[78] A detailed report by I Corps characterized two gas attacks by C Company in support of the 15th and 16th Divisions on the Loos front as professionally carried out "without a hitch" but judged that the tactical results were very disappointing. In both instances, raiders attempting penetration of enemy trenches thirty minutes after the gas release met heavy rifle and machine-gun fire. Prisoners taken on this front would "in no case own to any serious casualties from our gas."

> Probably if gas could be quickly followed up at night by an attack on the trenches successful results might be obtained, but this is not possible owing to the danger of advancing troops being injured by their own gas. If however, an interval of 30 minutes has to be waited for before it is safe to advance, well disciplined hostile troops provided with good gas helmets have time to get over the first surprise and make preparations to meet the attack of which the liberation of gas by our side has warned them, and as a rule, in my opinion, great results cannot be expected.[79]

On both sides, gas defense was more than keeping up with gas offense.

Throughout the summer and on into the autumn the Somme Offensive wore on, foray after foray, with meager gain and enormous casualties. Haig nevertheless pressed on, and the Special Companies continued their now routine chores, working primarily at night, sleeping by day. The mortar companies were to wait until mid-1917 for proper gas bombs and in the meantime, in addition to their smoke screen discharges, extemporized by firing off mortar bombs emptied of high explosive and refilled with White Star from cylinders.[80] The cylinder and projector companies kept busy as much as weather permitted. In late August, Malins and McDowell completed their filming of *The Battle of the Somme*, which opened in London to universal acclaim and was soon showing simultaneously in about thirty London cinemas and throughout France. In mid-September, some of the sergeants and officers of the Special Brigade viewed the film. Sgt. R. Dawson, with extraordinary understatement, pronounced it "very good."[81]

The life of the Special Company motorcycle dispatch riders is illustrated in the reminiscences of L. W. White. On one occasion he acted as

Small box respirator. (Courtesy of Royal Engineers Museum)

cycle guide for a convoy of 3 ten-ton lorries carrying gas cylinders to the front.

Unfortunately I chose from the map what proved to be one of the worst roads out of the village and a couple of the lorries slid off the steeply cambered road into the gutter. With a good deal of wheel-spinning (solid tyred in those days) and pushing by the other drivers both got going again and we all reached the main road where they waved me a cheery good-by. Wailly suffered from long-range machine-gun fire and I remember on another occasion bending low over the handlebars while bullets crashed through the branches of the roadside trees. Our other D. R. assured me that on another exposed stretch of road he heard machine-gun bullets hitting the spokes of his wheels but I think it must have been gravel from the road!

From Berles au bois we went to Achicourt just south of Arras where we spent the winter of 1916-1917. We had some very cold weather and in the outskirts of Arras a burst pipe covered the road with a quite extensive glacier. I had one very pleasant trip in bright moonlight over roads covered with packed snow and another not so pleasant through Beaumetz les Loges where the Pavé had lifted with the frost and then in the thaw lorries had made ruts and pot-holes so that motor-cycling was almost impossible. Later I had to go to Divisional HQ at Gouy en Artois on a pouring wet night, and getting water in the magneto, only just managed to get there. The Signal Service D.R.s found me a bunk for the night and after an early breakfast I was able to coax the bike back to my own unit. I don't believe that I had been missed! I suppose that what I most enjoyed was the regular trip to Avesnes le Compte to meet D.R.s from the other Special Companies. We forgathered in the Expeditionary Force Canteen and exchanged Dispatches over cups of tea and buns.[82]

White remained with the Special Companies as a dispatch rider until 1918 when he won a commission in the artillery.

On the night of 4/5 October 1916, opposite Hulluch, C Company carried out the largest gas attack by a single gas company to date.[83] In command was thirty-five-year-old Capt. Thomas Henry Davies, Foulkes's favorite company commander, sharing the latter's preference for cloud attack. Davies arranged for the attack in three waves—the first at 8 P.M. in which 917 cylinders were to be released; then 555 cylinders at 8:45 P.M.; and, finally, 1,055 cylinders at 10:30 P.M.. In a perfect westerly wind blowing at four mph, the company discharged eighty tons of the usual White Star and large numbers of smoke candles. According to Sid Fox the gas attack was the most flawless and successful he could remember.

The whole experience was quite an eerie one for us. The absence of enemy fire, the weird silence over No Man's Land, and the over-awing sight of dense billowing clouds of gas drifting slowly over a vast extent of country made it an unforgettable experience. Never before had we been free to climb out of our trenches and look around; there was not even the crack of an enemy rifle.[84]

Foulkes, too, considered it one of the most successful of all cloud gas attacks of the entire war:[85] "Everything seemed to favour us that night.

The wind was right and I believe we had a 100 percent discharge of cylinders. I distinctly remember the intense silence on the enemy's part the following days and it seems difficult to imagine that they escaped without very heavy casualties."[86]

Although a technical success, the operation was not without cost. Eleven men of C Company were slightly gassed, and five were killed, including Sam Naylor who volunteered to accompany the infantry raiders. Heavy trench mortarfire struck bays 70 to 73, destroying 130 cylinders, and heavy shellfire wrecked nine pipes. Moreover, the subsequent raid was a total failure. The raiding party ran into surviving enemy machine-gun fire, although Fox blamed this on mistakes the raiders themselves made.[87] The report of the 8th Division Commanding Officer, Maj. Gen. Henry Hudson, complimented the work of the Special Brigade, but Foulkes bristled at the words: "no very direct evidence was gained as to the effect produced."[88] Even worse, I Corps commander, Lt. Gen. C. A. Anderson, branded as "far-fetched" the notion that there were heavy enemy casualties from gas.[89] Foulkes took it as a personal insult, again citing the "disinclination of our commanders to believe in the success of this method of attack."[90] Foulkes makes no mention of the five killed in C Company, but devotes the better part of twenty pages to testimonials from captured German sources to the ostensible effectiveness of British gas on this occasion.[91]

During this same battle an officer of C Company, Lt. E. S. Armstrong, reported a bizarre experience:

While leading a cylinder fatigue party, a shell dropped into Posen Alley, a few feet in front of me. It smashed the duckboards but did not explode. A little later, I heard one of the carrying party coughing and sputtering. I told him he should have reported sick, and offered to take his turn at humping. It was while I was doing this that a shell burst near us. The man in front of me with whom I had changed was killed outright, the one carrying with me was also killed, and the man behind me so badly wounded that he died in a few minutes. I received only the blast and was unhurt.

On three separate occasions I had had a most vivid dream. In it I saw a corporal and two pioneers lying dead in a trench. . . . This was to have been the largest attack yet, with over 1,000 cylinders, and so we had to draw upon some extra help. Some men of E Company arrived, and a Section was attached to mine. It was decided that the men from E Company should be on the right half of my line under their own sergeant, and we would be on the left. On taking up positions one night I went along the right half, and at the extreme end I met the corporal and two pioneers of my dream, detailed to the very trench in which my dream had seen them killed. This worried me greatly, but I was much relieved two days later when I heard that these three men had gone on leave. . . . But I was amazed when later touring our front to come across the three actually in the trench where I had first met them before. They explained that the Sgt. Maj. had given them permission to come with us, since they were keen to take part in a big show. I was convinced that harm was coming to them, so that when zero hour drew near I decided to be at that spot before going along the line. At zero, I gave them the signal to turn on, and moved to the next bay. As I went a shell landed in their bay and killed all three instantly.[92]

Always on the alert for the opportunity to surprise, Foulkes, in September 1916, suggested to the French a gas attack at Nieuport, along the Yser River.[93] Unfavorable Channel breezes in this part of Belgium, it was thought, had made the Germans complacent about gas in this sector, and reports indicated that the German marines stationed there were not equipped with gas masks. French XXXVI Corps agreed to cooperate. In mid-September, under the joint command of Captain Lefebure, who spoke fluent French, H and J Companies installed somewhat over 2,000 cylinders of White Star gas. A spate of unfavorable weather, however, postponed the attack for two weeks, during which time the Germans overheard the sound of hammering on metal, and on 2 October a German raiding party penetrated the lines and discovered the cylinders. The element of surprise gone, Lefebure decided, in view of the work already undertaken, to carry on nevertheless. On the night of 5 October, coincidentally the same night as the Hulluch operation, at 11 P.M. in a southwest wind blowing at five mph, the Specials discharged 1,800 cylinders (fifty-four tons) of gas, roughly six times the average discharge. A German deserter from the 1st Matrosen Regiment reported 1,500 casualties in his division and said that after the gas attack his company could no longer operate their rifle bolts due to chlorine damage. Foulkes devoted the better part of eight pages of his book to this incident, once more quoting extensively from this deserter and other captured German documents supporting the effectiveness of this attack.[94] T. Evans in J Company, however, countered that although the attack was supposedly successful, "unfortunately, very many Belgian civilians became casualties."[95]

In late summer Lloyd George began to recruit chemists away from the Special Brigade for more appropriate service in chemical laboratories in England. Dr. D. A. Clibbens and the other members of his overqualified broom squad from Helfaut left the Special Brigade for reassignment to

H.M. Cordite Factory in Gretna, one of the 220 national munitions factories which were now functioning.[96] Later, in January 1917, the director
of the Woolwich Research Laboratories interviewed another twenty-
eight officers and ninety-four men for chemical and munitions research
at Woolwich.[97]

Foulkes continued his fast pace throughout the remainder of 1916.
While driving in late July near Cassel in France, he struck and knocked
over an Army Signal Corps motorcyclist. He took the injured soldier to
the hospital—fortunately the victim suffered only hand and eye cuts.[98]
In August Foulkes visited Versailles, strolled in the gardens, and viewed
some newly opened rooms in the palace. In September he managed a
week's visit to London, and in October he made three Channel trips.
On 2 December he received the Distinguished Service Order from King
George at Buckingham Palace and in the evening saw "Chu Chin
Chow." Following a concert at the Coliseum, he spent a week in
France. Back in England at Porton, he watched projector experiments
until dark, then played billiards with Thorpe in the evening. He saw
the play "High Jinks" before sailing again for France on 22 December.
During the year Foulkes visited Paris four times, England thirteen
times, took in two cinemas, two concerts, and fifteen plays. Except for
the three summer months, Foulkes crossed to England at least once
during every month of the year.[99]

As the fury of the Somme Offensive subsided, leave was again possible. Unlike their commander, the men of the Special Brigade were for-
tunate to obtain one eight-day leave per year, nine days if home was
Scotland. "It was a time for which all men craved and for which they
hoped to live, . . . once, surely, for fear the chance would never come
again."[100] Like all Tommies, however, no matter how enthusiastically
they sang "I Want to go Home" or "Show Me the Way to go Home,"
the gas Specials remembered furlough as a surreal time, and Blighty
(England) as a place apart. Though civilians in southern England were
close enough to the battlefields to hear the roar of the heavier artillery,
their lives seemed thousands of miles distant. A policeman asked Fox
what it was like: "Yet of course it was all unreal to him, and one did
not try to explain things to anyone while on Leave. Blighty and the
trenches were of different worlds." But after Fox returned from his
seven-day leave, he found it just as impossible to tell his comrades in
the line "what Blighty was like and what he had done."[101]

The Special Brigade, like any other unit, had its share of those who
did not easily accommodate to the roughness of army life, among them
Parkes, who was deeply religious and who experienced great loneliness
and unhappiness in the brigade. His lecture notes reveal a scrupulous
seriousness, his diary a devout puritanism. After attending evening

church service at La Mairie he wrote: "Thoroughly enjoyed the service because the drunkenness, language, and gambling was having some effect on me and this pulled me back again." In September 1916, he was gassed slightly when disconnecting pipes, and although he completed the routine cleaning up the next morning, he spent the next two free afternoons lying in a bunk to avoid unnecessary exertion. But within forty-eight hours he was back at work, making three trips carrying full cylinders out of the front lines. Three weeks later he sprained his ankle while portering lumber for constructing sheds. Lying alone in a barn, miserable and gnawed by loneliness, he wrote, "Loneliness greatly relieved by thoughts of darling Gert," and three days later, "Wished beyond measure to have G. in my arms for consolation and love." Parkes's diary ends abruptly on 9 January 1917. The last entry reads simply, "Wrote to Gert."[102]

Loneliness and homesickness, the ever-present fear of injury, physical discomforts, these were the constants in soldiers' lives as Christmas 1916 approached. The winter of 1916/17, Germany's "turnip winter," was the coldest since 1880.[103] Fox complained of digging in ground hard as iron.[104] The water in the trenches rose in places to the armpits and froze along the top. Soldiers wrote of having to break the ice as they went along.[105] Eden and his buddies in K Company, housed in their inadequately heated Wakefield huts with corrugated iron roofs and gaping holes in the floors, complained of the severe cold and of insufficient blankets and fuel. "Our water came from a pond which had a hole kept open in the foot or more of ice on top."[106]

The overall effectiveness of the cylinder gas released during the various 1916 operations is hard to assess. Anecdotal evidence points in both directions. Lt. Gen. Sir Henry Wilson, in command of IV Corps at the Somme, found the evidence for and against gas so contradictory and confusing that he changed his mind about the utility of gas several times before concluding that under favorable circumstances gas might serve an effective role as an adjunct to raids.[107] If not after Loos, certainly by the end of 1916, army command had all but given up on attempts to synchronize massive gas discharges with large-scale infantry assaults. Gas was fast becoming a weapon of opportunity, an ancillary to small-scale raids, a supplement to the general discomfiture and harassment of the enemy. As such, gas was occasionally effective, never decisive.

II

Livens and the Flammenwerfer

All things bright and beautiful
Gadgets great and small
Bombs, grenades and duckboards
The Sapper makes them all.

Belching spectacular streams of flaming oil a hundred yards from its underground reservoirs, the British *Flammenwerfer* made its fearsome battle debut the first morning of the Somme Offensive. Developed by one of the most innovative and resourceful men in the Special Brigade, William Howard Livens, the flame-thrower was the most frightful of the experimental weapons of the Special Brigade.

Livens was an exceptional individual. Born in 1889, educated at public school (Oundle) and Christ Church, where he was captain of the Cambridge rifle team, Livens was a civil engineer like his father, with whom he enjoyed a close relationship. The elder Livens was shareholder, chief engineer, and one of the directors of Ruston and Proctor, a large publicly owned engineering company in Lincoln with 5,000 to 6,000 employees. The younger Livens joined the army in September of 1914 as an officer in the Royal Engineers and took up clerical duties in the motorcycle signalling section at Chatham.

Following the German gas attack on 22 April 1915, Livens initiated a series of private experiments in appropriate methods of gas retaliation. He fitted out makeshift laboratories both in his Chatham barracks bedroom and also in the officers' garage. For a firing range he used vacant land near one of the old forts which overlooked the Thames estuary. Livens later maintained that he did not know Foulkes while at Chatham, but that his gas experiments were common knowledge around the camp and that the brigade major did suggest he look into Foulkes's unit.[1]

In late August 1915, Livens left Chatham to enlist in the Special Companies, one of the few original members trained as an engineer rather

148

William Howard Livens. (Courtesy of Chemical and Biological Defence Establishment, Ministry of Defence, Porton Down)

than a chemist. He arrived at Helfaut in time to join Company 186. Not by nature a timid man, Livens immediately pointed out the defects he saw in the crude apparatus initially provided. Foulkes, somewhat taken aback by the brash manner of the new recruit, was nevertheless impressed by his undeniable competence. As described earlier, the outspoken Livens experimented with and brought to Foulkes's attention several equipment modifications and improvements which were incorporated into the Special Companies' routine in the days after Loos. An amusing incident that occurred about this same time illustrates Livens's ingenuity and resourcefulness. Foulkes, Livens, and Gold had departed from Helfaut early one morning to catch a Channel boat at Boulogne when their car broke down in mid-journey. Foulkes managed to catch another ride, but Livens repaired the broken mechanism with a rubber band, and he and Gold caught up with Foulkes in time to catch the 10:20 A.M. boat.[2] Years later Foulkes admitted somewhat grudgingly that although Livens was potentially troublesome, he was a "go-getter" and most energetic both in obtaining supplies and in implementing improvements.[3]

Livens was not a man of innate caution. Like Foulkes he took repeated risks while developing and testing a whole variety of gas-related contraptions. On one occasion when he was testing a gas mask for protection against sulfurated hydrogen, he fell unconscious and had to be physically dragged out of the cloud. Fortunately he suffered no lasting effects.[4] Foulkes later wrote that Livens displayed "little use for factors of safety or correct official procedure."[5]

Throughout the autumn of 1915 Livens continued his experiments with flame-throwing devices, one of the projects he had started at Chatham. He later claimed to have shown to Foulkes in August 1915 a portable thirty-inch model which had a range of thirty feet, but Foulkes did not remember having seen it. Since April 1915, Col. Lucius Jackson, under the sponsorship of the Ministry of Munitions, had been supervising simultaneous experiments with approximately twelve semiportable (knapsack-type) flame-throwers, as well as a lesser number of large flame-throwers called *Flammenwerfer.*[6] In December 1915, Livens accompanied Foulkes to the Wembley sports grounds to witness demonstrations of several flame-throwers developed by the ministry. One of the portable flame-throwers under consideration employed oxygen as the pressurizing gas, and on this occasion the apparatus exploded, setting on fire its hapless American inventor. Foulkes helped extinguish the fire with the man's overcoat, but not before he and Captain Hay had been seriously burned on the hands and face.[7] Captain Hay had collaborated with Jackson in the development of a larger flame-thrower called the Hay flame gun, which proved unsuccessful in the trenches but was eventually put to use by the navy.

Initially, Foulkes favored one of the larger models demonstrated, a cumbersome gallery-type machine designed by Capt. F. C. Vincent of the Ministry of Munitions. Livens, however, persuaded Foulkes that he could devise a much superior one and obtained permission to work independently in England on the flame-thrower project, with authorization to spend £450. "It was a somewhat delicate matter," admitted Foulkes, "and I arranged that he should be given a free hand from the Trench Warfare Department in order to employ himself upon the production of the *Flammenwerfer* which he had suggested to me."[8]

Livens began his work by modifying Vincent's contrivance but was slightly injured when it exploded during experiments. "This would never do at all," he wrote to Vincent. The apparatus was too heavy for use in trenches, it presented too large a target, and the use of an oxy-

genated fuel was too dangerous.[9] Rejecting the Vincent version altogether, Livens returned to Lincoln, where he and his father set about
designing their own device, a machine that could be sunk in a mine
gallery sap leading out into no man's land.

Livens was aware that he had to sell his design not only to Foulkes
but also to Thuillier. At some point in the first half of 1916 Livens heard
that Thuillier had witnessed Vincent's flame-thrower and was not impressed. Livens promptly went unannounced to Thuillier's hotel and
persuaded him to evaluate his own model. "I went with reluctance,"
Thuillier later recalled, "but was surprised to find it quite suitable."[10]
Livens had an uncanny way of overcoming objections and wangling his
own way through persuasion and persistence. The army placed an order
with the Ruston firm for thirty-four of the Livens *Flammenwerfer*, but
only five were ever delivered.

To deploy and operate both large and small flame-throwers, Foulkes
placed four gas sections under Livens's command as part of the restructuring of the Special Companies implemented at the beginning of 1916.
At first called simply Special Sections, Foulkes later designated the
unit Z Company. J. B. Ventham, a charter member and transfer from a
Guards division, remembers a unit of about one hundred men and the
mission as the development of "Liquid Fire."[11] Livens recruited as
many engineers as possible to staff his sections, as distinct from the
chemists whose expertise he regarded as wasted in the other gas companies. For his second in command he chose J. W. Bansall, a Scotsman
and also an engineer at Ruston's, who had been invalided out of the
Royal Engineers 105th Field Company. Another recruit was Harry
Strange, an adventurous young man just arrived from Honolulu.
Strange had tended bar for a time in the Klondike, was a friend of Jack
London, and may have been the bartender in *Smoke Bellew* (1912).[12] He
joined Z Company as a section commander and quickly became a close
friend and confidant of Livens. Training headquarters of the secret mission was a large house called "The Beeches," situated near Greenwich
between Lewisham and Blackheath in southern England. Livens obtained permission for the company also to train and experiment on the
stately grounds of Hatfield, in north London. Acting in concert with
the Ruston firm, Z Company developed two kinds of flame-throwers,
the large Livens *Flammenwerfer* and a smaller semiportable model.

Ventham compared the smaller flame-thrower to a large milk churn.
It was made of galvanized steel, stood about four feet six inches high,
and weighed over 150 pounds when filled with ten gallons of enriched
Persian crude oil and an equal measure of nitrogen at 250 pounds pressure. To fire the mechanism, its crew of two attached a separate pipe
and nozzle apparatus, opened a valve, and ignited the escaping jet of oil

A Livens large gallery Flammenwerfer *at rail siding. (Courtesy of Imperial War Museum)*

with a match. Ventham's description of practice firings suggests genuine skepticism as to its safety. "When it was fired, the two men had to stand behind it and press it forward at the top, holding on like grim Death to overcome its tendency to turn over on its back."[13]

The *Flammenwerfer*, the large, nonportable flame-thrower, consisted of a huge tube, which had to be placed on the floor of a trench or mine gallery, on top of which lay the series of drums containing the combustible material. The apparatus required a trench at least forty-five feet long, ten to twenty feet deep, and three feet wide. To avoid working with highly pressurized fuel in the large tube and drums, a separate smaller tube running alongside the large one provided the reservoir of pressure. At the front end of the tube was a vertical shaft, called the monitor, which carried the fuel to the surface. The crew fired the "gun" by releasing pressure from the small tube into the large tube, forcing the fuel into the monitor and simultaneously forcing the monitor up through the remaining soil to the surface, at which point a pressure-sensitive valve automatically opened, and, in Livens's words, "Then it bobs out its dragon head and begins to start its firing." A fire below ignited the pressurized fuel as it spewed forth from the monitor in a jet stream. When all the fuel had been expended, the lessening pressure automatically allowed the monitor to fall back down the shaft into the ground. Engineers had to design the bulky, two-ton machine so that it could be disassembled into parts light enough to be carried into the trenches by only two men. The elder Livens contributed substantially to the engineering involved, most notably the idea of a floating piston in the long tube to expel the oil. The gun had an impressive range of up to one hundred feet, the longest of any flame-thrower used in the war. For each ten-second shot, the gun required a ton of fuel. Following experiments with a variety of fuels, the Ruston engineers decided on a mixture of one part light to two parts heavy of Persian oil distillate, and for the propellant, deoxygenated compressed air. A prodigious amount of time and effort went into practice in transport of disassembled parts and precision assembly in simulated combat conditions. Secrecy remained a high priority, and Bansall described the operation as "frightfully hush hush."[14]

On 24 June 1916, Livens and his strange entourage departed Southampton on two steamers headed for Le Havre.[15] The Special Sections brought with them four disassembled large flame-throwers and sixteen semiportables.[16] From Le Havre, the men transported their heavy equipment on trains to Corbie, a village southwest of Albert at the junction of the Ancre and the Somme rivers about twelve miles from the front lines. Four of their own three-ton lorries brought their heavy equipment the rest of the way to Rawlinson's Fourth Army area, where they established a small depot at Bronfay Farm, a few miles from the front lines (see Map 10.1, p. 125).

Livens gave the semiportable flame-throwers to section 2 and sent them to the various front lines of X, XV, and XIII Corps. Burdened with these cumbersome weapons and impeded by muddy trenches already strewn with obstacles of every description, the men wrestled their machines forward. The limited range of the semiportables, thirty-two to forty yards, meant that their crews would have to advance deep into no man's land in order to use them effectively. Although several detachments struggled some distance beyond British lines on 1 July, in no case did any of them succeed in achieving the required close range, and consequently not one of the sixteen semiportables was fired.[17] Ventham claimed that the semiportables were so cumbersome that their handlers were unable to keep pace with advancing infantry. The same problems of bulk and unwieldiness, combined with their short range, frustrated several subsequent attempts to use them. They were also extremely dangerous to the user. On several occasions the tube came apart at the Morris coupling, and following one such incident in which a man in the Special Sections was seriously injured, a court of inquiry declared the weapon unsafe for use as then designed. It was clear that the weight had to be at least halved to make it practical, and it would have to be more easily assembled from smaller parts. Following repeated failures during the first two months of the Somme, the Special Brigade abandoned offensive use of the semiportable altogether. Since the Germans continued to employ a better designed semiportable flame-thrower throughout the remainder of the war, Livens consigned the British version to defensive demonstrations, but not one was ever fired successfully against the enemy during the entire war.

As for the large flame-throwers, the *Flammenwerfer* proper, they were of course far less mobile than the semiportable models. Each one required a team of about one hundred men just to transport its disassembled parts to the front. At 8 P.M. on the evening of 27 June 1916, Bansall and section 1 left Corbie, picked up one large *Flammenwerfer* at Bronfay Farm, and started for the front lines of the 7th Division (XV Corps) opposite Fricourt. Bansall later recalled the formidable difficulty of the task and the improbability of success:

> Our equipment was complicated machines to be assembled in saps under the Boches front line and then at zero hour pooped off when theoretically a ram would rise through the enemy trench and enfilade it with a vast volume of burning oil. Imagine the business of carrying up the gear through the toughest barrage of all time and assembling it in the remains of the sap![18]

By 11 P.M. they reached Ludgate Circus via Waterloo Junction where the road became impassable for further lorry transport. The men unloaded the huge gun and requested additional carrying help from the Devonshires of the 20th Infantry Brigade. After a delay of several hours, the heavily loaded party of Devons and Royal Engineers slowly inched its way up the communication trenches toward the front line. Upon encountering sudden and severe enemy bombardment at 71st Street, the party dropped the *Flammenwerfer* parts and dived for cover. Not until 5:30 A.M. on 28 June was Bansall's section able to collect most of the crucial parts and secure them in a shallow mine-shaft. But persistent enemy shelling quickly sealed up the end of the gallery for a length of twenty feet, burying vital parts of the gun beyond recovery. Bansall's party thereupon salvaged what parts it could, abandoned the remainder, and returned to billets at Maricourt.

Only with the most herculean effort were the men of Z Company able to deploy the remaining three of Livens's machines in three saps (7, 10, and 13) between the Carnoy-Montauban Road and Kasino Point, along the 18th Division front and on the left side of XIII Corps. Here several suitable galleries, actually mine-tunnels, extended into no man's land from the British trenches. The width of no man's land at this point was about two hundred yards, so that advance galleries were necessary to bring the guns forward to within the one-hundred-yard range. Under constant bombardment, Strange and section 3 wrestled the three flame-throwers into position and began the assembly and installation. In the midst of this harrowing job, enemy shelling demolished one of the galleries and eight men had to be dug out by Tunneling Company 183.

It was very difficult because of the way the roofs of the galleries were continually blown in; the deepest gallery, 17' 6'' below ground was blocked by one of our 12'' shells in front and a Bosch 10'' behind within about 20 hours of when we had to perform, and eight of my men entombed. It was an awful job to clear up the mess and reconstruct the apparatus in time.[19]

Though Strange's men succeeded in completing the installation of all three of their machines, further artillery hits near and on the galleries forced continual clearing by the tunneling companies. Ventham endured a nightmarish several hours in the tunnel surrounded by a German attack but, fortunately, was not discovered. Artillery fire so completely wrecked the mechanism of the flame-thrower in sap 13 (the one farthest to the left) that it also had to be abandoned, except for salvaged parts. When the signal to fire came at 7:15 A.M. on the morning of 1 July, only two flame-throwers (in saps 7 and 10) remained intact and operational.

According to Livens, there had not been sufficient time to cut all the holes through to the surface for the monitors, and so at zero hour "we just turned on the pressure and ripped through the last four inches of ground, making use of the steel cutting edge on the protecting hood and the one ton thrust the ram gives."[20] Mechanically everything worked perfectly. As the monitors traversed back and forth, spewing out the pressurized oil from their two jets, automatic lighters ignited the oil with a stupendous roar. Amid dense belching smoke the streams of flame reached well over the enemy trenches. The shots lasted only ten seconds each.

When the infantry of the 18th Division (1st Brigade) went over, they suffered far fewer casualties in the swath of ground covered by the flame-throwers. Reconnoitering shortly afterward, 2d Lt. R. W. Stewart brought in about fifty German prisoners and told of seeing several charred bodies lying in trenches in the direct line of fire. Only two men of Z Company suffered wounds. Immediately after the Saturday morning firing, Livens, who had not slept properly for a week, went to bed for twenty-four hours.

On Sunday morning, 2 July, Livens, Strange, and several other men of Z Company reentered no man's land to further gauge the effect of the *Flammenwerfer* firing. Livens later estimated that the two machines actually fired had "netted about 40 Bosches in actual slain and put the

Flaming discharge of the Livens Flammenwerfer. *(Courtesy of Imperial War Museum)*

wind up lots more."[21] Close examination of the burned ground indicated that the two guns had achieved ranges of ninety-four and eighty-seven yards, respectively.

That same Sunday, Z Company began the task of salvaging and repairing the various parts of the four large flame-throwers, with a view to improvements and possible redeployment. For this purpose Livens set up a permanent base, first at Sailly-le-Sec, then moved in late July to Toutencourt. A representative from the Trench Warfare Department, Lieutenant Tribe, joined the unit toward the end of the month, bringing with him one of the Vincent *Flammenwerfer*; in mid-August the fifth and last large Livens *Flammenwerfer* arrived from England.

General Gough, now commanding the Fifth Army and having taken a liking to the enterprising Livens, ordered a *Flammenwerfer* attack for his sector in the neighborhood of High Wood as part of the continuing Somme Offensive. With the usual great difficulty, Z Company, now working closely with F Company, installed both the Livens and the Vincent machines near High Wood in mid-August. Shellfire almost immediately damaged both before they could be fired, but the two companies managed by early September to repair and reinstall them. Shots on 3 September produced "a good moral effect" on the enemy, and Capt. R. H. Thomas, F Company, contributed a synchronized oil bombing.[22] Five days later, another firing of the large *Flammenwerfer* succeeded in putting out of action a German machine gun in the direct line of fire. One of the Livens machines achieved a traverse of eighty degrees. The infantry reported finding no burned bodies afterward but claimed they were "helped materially." Additional shoots were attempted at Mametz Wood.

Following these operations, Thomas prepared a report on the comparative value of the two large flame-throwers.[23] Though the Vincent machine was more easily and more quickly installed, the Livens *Flammenwerfer* was superior on all other points. It was more easily carried, had a slightly greater range, boasted a possible traverse of ninety degrees versus only half that for the Vincent, achieved a steadier flow, and involved less exposure of its operating team. Throughout the next months members of Z Company continued experiments, both at Toutencourt and in actual battle conditions, but it was dangerous work. At a demonstration in late October, a premature explosion drenched the area with concentrated gas. Fortunately there were no serious injuries.

The actual military advantages gained by these initial shoots were uniformly disappointing. Although the mechanism frequently operated flawlessly in a technical sense, the enormous effort of deployment both in terms of technology and manpower was out of all proportion to its limited and purely localized benefit. Because of its size and complexity, the time and space required for installation rendered it particularly vulnerable to enemy shelling, and even close hits caused costly damage. The *Flammenwerfer* was clearly not a cost-effective weapon. Ventham considered both the large and semiportable models more or less a flop. Bansall thought the entire scheme quite hopeless, and even the perennially sanguine Foulkes expressed disappointment.[24] Never overly enthusiastic about it, he was quick to abandon the large *Flammenwerfer*, on grounds of vulnerability and manpower requirements.[25]

For the time being Z Company placed all existing machines in "mothball" storage at Toutencourt, where they remained to rust and deteriorate for the better part of a year. In October 1917, Davies, then second in command of Z Company, conducted an examination of the stored parts, reported that it was impossible to maintain the parts in working order owing to lack of any protection from the elements, and recommended that either they be moved to proper indoor storage or, if there were no plans to use them again, they be scrapped.

On the day following Davies's report, Foulkes gave orders to retrieve a few *Flammenwerfer* from storage and prepare them for another firing on the Belgian front. Two weeks later, together with N and P Companies, Fraser's section 2 of Z Company entrained for Belgium for both projector and *Flammenwerfer* work with Belgian 2d Division. Fraser and his section set up the large flame-thrower at Dixmude while the cylinder companies prepared both projector and cylinder attacks. On the night of 26/27 October, Fraser's team successfully fired two shots. During the first shot, the spray from a bursting shell nearby extinguished the ignition fire, resulting in the spouting oil merely spilling on the ground and into the trench where it caught fire. Fortunately the Specials suffered no casualties. The second shot was more successful, but no specifics were available on the damage inflicted on the enemy. This rather lackluster performance put the final nail in the coffin of the *Flammenwerfer*, and it was never used again.[26] Z Company had fired the large *Flammenwerfer* a total of only ten times.

12
Somme Strange Guns

Gases to the right of them
Gases to the left of them
Gases in front of them
    Chemic'ly thundered
Nix on the shot and shell
War has a newer hell—
Into an acid bath
Into a poison smell
    Rode the six hundred.[1]

With the gradual demise of *Flammenwerfer* operations, Z Company lost its original raison d'etre and Foulkes seems to have paid little attention to its subsequent activities. The inventive Livens, however, had already turned his quicksilver mind to another favorite project—delivering gas to the enemy lines in a container instead of a flaming airborne discharge—which promised to be a laborsaving and safer system and, in addition, more independent of the weather than cylinder releases. Though called the Livens projector, the weapon was clearly the result of brainstorming and experimentation by several Z Company engineers, Harry Strange in particular.

Livens later asserted that his experiments at Chatham in 1915 had anticipated the basic idea of the projector, but even if this were so, projector experimentation took a back seat until the summer of 1916.[2] In thinking of ways to avoid the *Flammenwerfer's* worst features, members of Z Company hit upon the idea of projecting oil onto enemy positions in a container which would ignite upon impact rather than projecting already-burning oil. Most accounts traced the idea to an incident that took place during a reconnoiter on the second day of the Somme attack. Livens, Strange, and Stewart, another Z Company officer, had on that occasion come upon an undisturbed dugout still sheltering an unknown number of Germans. On being told that there was hostile fire originating in the area and that one man had already been shot, Strange tossed a few Mills grenades into the dugout. When that seemed not to have the desired effect, Livens filled two five-gallon oil tins with the highly flammable distillate used in the flame-throwers, covered them with some sacking, ignited the sacking, and threw the tins down into the dugout, with instant and spectacular success.[3]

> The effect was so good that Strange thought it would be a better plan to throw the oil over to the Bosch in the original packages in preference to the labourious method of discharging it from the elaborate flame-thrower. When we got back to Sailly-le-Sec we first tried several tins of petrol to make sure they would always explode with the Mills bombs attached.[4]

Z Company had no shortage of ingenious officers, for Livens had as much as possible packed his company with inventive sorts. Infantryman J. B. K. Crawford, after visiting Z Company later the next year, appraised the officers of Z Company as "unorthodox types" with lots of originality.[5] Livens spent most of the late summer and autumn in England, as liaison with the Ministry of Munitions. Bansall commanded the company during his extended absences. Bansall, Ventham, and Thomas, whose F Company collaborated closely with Z Company engineers during this period, all credited Strange with the primary development of the projector.[6]

Regardless of who deserved credit for the original idea, Z Company initiated projector experiments in early July. The earliest devices tested at Toutencourt were extremely crude—simply five-gallon tin cans stuck in the ground, out of which the engineers fired ordinary two-gallon cans of oil in mortar fashion. Oily sacking wrapped around the can and set aflame just prior to firing ignited the oil when the can burst upon landing. Initial range was a mere few hundred yards.

> When we tried them out, they were a truly comical sight as they hurtled through the air followed by the wooden block with the sacking well alight.
> We thought of filling our projectiles with old door knobs, razor blades, steel punchings, etc., but there were difficulties about getting them small enough to go neatly into the canisters.[7]

The company even tried to hurl ordinary gas cylinders over enemy lines by this same method. Some of Strange's friends labeled primitive models with a double pun: Somme Strange Gun. Subsequent improvements replaced the five-gallon tins with steel mortars made from pipes welded at one end. The addition of a base-plate increased thrust. Time

Complete Livens projector equipment—bomb, exploder, coiled leads, charges, and, in foreground, Livens projector and base-plate (propped at a forty-five-degree angle). (Courtesy of Imperial War Museum)

fuses replaced the oily sacking and permitted automatic ignition.[8] It appears that the ultimate employment of Strange's contraption for the projection of gas rather than oil evolved as an afterthought to the preceding experimental uses.

As improved, the Livens projector, ingeniously simple and effective, resembled an ordinary mortar. Cpl. Leonard E. S. Eastham, J Company, described it as "a mild steel tube shaped like an enlarged chemist's test tube."[9] The base-plate provided a foundation platform to absorb the firing impact, and the three-foot-long tube, the actual projector or mortar gun, was positioned on the base-plate at an appropriate angle. Electrical firing by means of a wire threaded through the projector allowed remote detonation by the crew. Strange and his men achieved some measure of range and direction through the crudest calibration, as described by a soldier from H Company:[10]

When testing the range of the missiles with the Projector tube at 45 degrees, the charge being in small separate bags [made] it easy to add or take away explosive and measure the distance. . . . Standing at the target, it was a little bit frightening to see three or four "wooden" bombs coming toward you. Marking the position where the bomb dropped was like being at an Athletics Meeting and facing the throwing of the Discus or Javelin.

An abominably parsed ditty found in Frank Winn's notebook, titled appropriately "Pooping Off," illustrates the handling of the projector by a zany company comedian:

> I connect up one lead
> Ha Ha Ha Ha
> I connect up the other one
> Ho Ho Ho Ho!
> What care I if the zero pass
> So long as I can give the Bosche a dose of gas
> Then it's over the top and camouflage
> No R.E. could be bolder.
> But when they shell, we run like hell
> And dump the old exploder.[11]

Although its range and direction of firing were clearly not very accurate, the projector was easy to fire in large numbers and fairly safe for its crew because of the lengthy leads. Normally the filling consisted of thirty pounds of pure phosgene, but if unavailable in the required quantities, almost any combination of gases might be used. Improved still further, the Livens projector was capable of dousing large areas with heavy concentrations of gas and was to become one of the most effective gas delivery systems devised by the Special Brigade.

Livens shrewdly considered that Z Company's unauthorized shift to aerial experiments had best be kept secret from the artillery, who might interpret such activity as poaching. Bansall later wrote that the artillery was "jealous of our encroachment" on its terrain; high-ranking gunners constantly sought to obstruct the projector work for this reason.[12] Thus Livens obtained materials for Z Company's projector experiments on the sly—"by false pretenses."[13] He felt he could not simply place orders for mortars—he had either to call them something else or camouflage the request in some way. But Livens, cavalierly contemptuous of procedural niceties, never worried about exceeding his authority, confident in his ability to set matters right afterward: "I saw Col. Matheson in General Thuillier's office today when I was getting the orders for spare parts and oil drums cleared up. Both were extremely amused by the ultimate use certain apparently innocent articles are put to."[14]

Livens knew well the value of army contacts and how to exploit them. In the opening hours of the Somme battle Haig had created a Fifth Army out of the Reserve and two corps (VIII and X) from Rawlinson's Fourth Army, and this army had taken over the line from Thiepval Ridge northwards to Serre. One of Livens's early converts was the new Fifth Army commander, General Gough, who first noticed Livens and Z Company at the Somme: "I [General Gough] applied to HQ and asked that he [Livens] be attached to my Army. . . . I had him placed quite close to me. I lived in a village called Toutencourt and he was just beside it, and I went very often and inspected his experiments and took an interest in how things were getting on."[15] Actually General Gough took the Livens team fully under his wing and afforded the engineers all the covering protection they needed. After the war the Royal Commission on Awards to Inventors, to whom Livens had applied for remuneration for the projector, questioned General Gough about the nature of the sponsorship he had extended to Livens:

Q. Can you say whether or not he had any difficulty in being able to carry out his experiments, having regard to the fact that he was a *Flammenwerfer* officer?
A. Of course he had this difficulty, that he had no legal status, and therefore he could not apply through his own branch for any stores of any sort or kind, or any materials. Everything had to be done sub rosa.
Q. Camouflaged?
A. Yes.
Q. In fact, it was really only by reason of your special interest that he was able to get through this matter?
A. Yes, as things were, certainly. . . . If somebody had not protected him he could not have done it.
Q. So after you met him, you wanted him to be attached to your Army so he could experiment?
A. As far as I was concerned that was what I wanted him to do.
Q. You wangled it for him.
A. Yes, I suppose I did.[16]

Bansall considered the activities of the company sufficiently borderline that he thought it prudent to obtain explicit written authorization from General Gough: "Special Brigade consider that it would be advisable to have this covering authority in case of subsequent accident or trouble of any other nature."[17]

Why did Livens not take the more logical course and seek covering authority from Foulkes? Based on prior experience, he apparently anticipated some resistance. Perhaps he feared that Foulkes's widely known

*Livens projector deployed, showing placement of the propellant charges.
(Courtesy of Imperial War Museum)*

enthusiasm for cylinders would incline him to convert Z Company to an ordinary cylinder company. When asked later what work its engineers were doing during that summer of 1916 Foulkes acknowledged: ''I knew that they were making experiments at various times and I left them to it. . . . they were doing various experimental work in a field at Toutencourt.'' When asked to identify the method of ignition used on the first projectors, he had to reply, ''I could not tell you.''[18] Apparently Livens had succeeded only too well in keeping Foulkes completely in the dark as to the activities of Z Company.

Livens's reticence about divulging Z Company's projector work to Foulkes seems justified. Eventually, of course, Foulkes found out, and Livens, on 18 August, provided a full demonstration of all Z Company's experimental weapons. Though professing to promote inventiveness within the various companies of his unit and publicly applauding Livens's various devices, Foulkes from the first opposed the introduction of the projector, especially for hurling oil bombs. Livens was later to testify before the Royal Commission on Awards to Inventors. ''I remember Col. Foulkes said he did not like the idea of these oil cans being used.''[19] While Bansall considered the projector an extremely effective weapon, he too was keenly aware of Foulkes's well-known preference for cylinder discharge: "Perhaps that is why Foulkes did not always like us."[20] Additionally, the projector would compete with the Stokes mortar, another favorite weapon of Foulkes, who freely admitted that the Livens projector and the Stokes mortar were great rivals.[21] After the war, however, Foulkes would claim he had expressly given Z Company officers "carte-blanche" permission to develop the projectors.[22]

General Gough first employed Livens's Z Company to fire a primitive version of the projector in support of the 48th Division during the battle of Pozières in late July of 1916. The war diary of Z Company records Strange firing six "oil-throwing minenwerfers," as some of the experimental projectors were called, and Bansall, fourteen. Throughout August and September the company fired, though not without accidents, increasing numbers of the devices filled with a variety of substances. On the day he was promoted to lieutenant, 2 September, Strange received a flesh wound in the arm from a trench mortar fragment and was hospitalized in England. His replacement, Lt. D. Malloch, was killed the very next day in an accident at Toutencourt. He was bending over a fuse tube while a pioneer scraped powder out of the tube with a piece of tin when the spark exploded the remaining powder, killing Malloch instantly and wounding four others. As for Strange, he recovered quickly and after accepting the Military Cross, returned to the unit in late November 1916. Strange later won another Military Cross for his action in the Arras battle, and in mid-1918 he joined the officer complement of C Company.

On 3 September in the environs of High Wood and in conjunction with one of the rare *Flammenwerfer* shoots, Z Company fired twenty most unconventional "mortars."

> These were cans containing 30 pounds ammonal. Fired electrically. Ranges varied 180–250 yards. Mortars were 9" steel pipes 4'0" long and the "shells" were standard gas cylinders (Red Star) suitably fuzed and detonated to explode on landing. The gas cylinders were clearly visible in their flight. Range was 450 yards for the heavy mortar battery and 200 for the light. No wind. Hostile machine gun fire gradually ceased.[23]

But British trench mortar fire destroyed several of the oil mortars and a company sergeant was killed.[24]

As Z Company perfected its apparatus and methods, the effectiveness of its weapons became more and more evident. The company's successful projector attacks contributed prominently to the taking of Beaumont Hamel on 13 November, a town which, according to Thomas, had been fortified by the Germans into a "miniature Gibraltar.'' Gradually word circulated of the development of a new and improved means of discharging gas that virtually eliminated the arduous cylinder transport and that was feasible under wind conditions that precluded cylinder discharges. From that time on, commanders acquiescing to gas support increasingly tended to specify gas by projector, much to the dismay of Foulkes.

Whether Foulkes liked it or not, the projector was to come into its own during the many operations of 1917 and 1918. It was clearly a far more efficient and less vulnerable weapon than any other developed by the Special Brigade and, according to Haber, the most cost-effective Allied weapon developed during the war.[25]

13
Another Brigade Reorganization

The reorganization of the Special Companies into the Special Brigade in early 1916 had solved none of the chain-of-command problems associated with a large unit deployed customarily in small detachments. Operations during the summer dictated the need for further modification. Not once had one of the gas battalions operated in the field as a battalion. With their companies deployed so randomly over the entire front, battalion commanders could exercise little supervisory role. Since the beginning of the Somme operations a more practical and sensible grouping of gas companies began to take de facto form, consisting of those clusters of units operating within the various individual army sectors. Though temporary, such army groupings gradually replaced the battalion structure both in name and practice. By the end of August 1916, the battalion formation had fallen into virtual abeyance, and though its official demise did not occur until March 1917, for all practical purposes the Special Company by itself became the basic offensive gas unit. Foulkes's five former gas battalion commanders, attached in the new system to the staffs of the five armies, served as supervisors of any and all gas units which came into their army area, regardless of gas battalion. A new nomenclature for both companies and officers reflected these changes. What had been called battalion headquarters now came to be called headquarters Special Companies. The five former gas battalion commanders came to be called "O.C. Sp. C'oys," or, more commonly, "C.S.C., R.E., 3d Army," that is, "Commanding Special Companies, Royal Engineers, (attached to) 3d Army.'"[1] These officers now acted as liaison officers between the army and as many of the gas sections (or companies) as happened to be assigned to the area of their army at any given time.

During the winter lull Foulkes set out to deal with the restructuring of his forces on a more permanent basis. First he formalized the de facto modifications which had become common practice during the summer of 1916, discarding altogether the battalion formation. Each of the gas companies became a virtually self-contained administrative unit, responsible for its own war diary, for example. The sixteen cylinder companies, the four mortar companies, and Z Company now shuffled in any combination among the five armies as circumstances demanded. The new structure promised a far greater elasticity for the gas mission (see Appendix A).

The size of the individual cylinder companies remained about the same, but Foulkes ordered a reorganization of each of their former six sections into five. D Company, for instance, reconstituted itself by redistributing the members of old section 19 among the others and then renumbering the remaining five sections.[2] Since the former section numbers had run consecutively from 1 to 96, six sections to a company, the new numbers again ran consecutively, but from 1 to 80, five sections to a company. Every company's section numbers changed (except those of A Company, which simply dropped number 6). To illustrate, the reconstituted P Company consisted of sections 71-75 instead of 85-90. Finally, the company designation changed slightly. P Company, 4th Special Battalion became simply P Special Company. The mortar companies and Z Company remained unchanged. Foulkes claimed, both in his book and in his personal diary, that he had to make a "reduction" in the Special Brigade specifically to accommodate increases in the defensive branch, but all other evidence points conclusively to a regrouping rather than a reduction.[3]

At full strength the normal size of a reconstituted cylinder company at this time totaled about 225 men and officers: 1 captain in command, 1 captain or second lieutenant as second in command, 5 lieutenants or second lieutenants, 1 company sergeant-major, 11 sergeants, 200 O.R.s (other ranks), and 6 drivers. The mortar companies were somewhat larger at a normal authorized strength of 329: 1 captain, 1 lieutenant, 4 section commanders (usually also lieutenants), 12 subsection commanders (NCOs), 1 company sergeant-major, 1 clerk, 13 sergeants, 288 O.R.s, and 8 drivers. Z Company was even larger at just over 350.[4] Grouped in only four sections, these were the strongest in the brigade organization. The Calais Special Factory Section numbered 221. Normal personnel at Special Brigade headquarters numbered 14. Forty-seven men and officers staffed each of the five "HQ with the Armies," 5 at each corps headquarters and 8 at divisional headquarters. The 46 permanent staff at the Helfaut depot brought the total strength of the brigade to just under 6,000.[5]

The newly formalized arrangements, moreover, entailed a different and unfamiliar chain of command. Gas units allotted to one of the armies entered a potentially ambiguous administrative no man's land. Dependent on its respective army command for operations, instructions, rations, billeting, and occasional heavy-duty transport,[6] the gas company received reinforcements, drafts, promotions, officer postings, and other internal administrative orders through the headquarters Special Companies. Foulkes candidly admitted that the position might at times "be rather delicate and will require tact in order to prevent friction."[7] While the five headquarters Special companies remained permanently attached to an army staff, the individual companies passed among armies, corps, and divisions as the military situation required.[8]

Each of the five new headquarters Special Companies set up its own workshop, supplied where practicable from the army to which it was attached, otherwise supplied from the central gas depot at Les Attaques or other depots and establishments of the Special Brigade. The gas companies obtained all specialized gas stores—supplies and equipment—from these workshops.

The new arrangements further decentralized gas authority, already seriously eroded in 1916. Gas companies found themselves increasingly under more direct control of divisional and corps officers who might or might not be sympathetic to the gas mission. In effect Foulkes surrendered a significant degree of direct operational control of his unit. It was a brigade under his command in name only. Under the new structure, army commanders increasingly viewed gas companies "allotted" to them as "at their disposal"—phrases not calculated to foster uniformity or unanimity of gas policy.

Another dilemma which had bothered Foulkes throughout the last half of 1916 was the increasing popularity of projectors over cylinders. While the four mortar companies continued to operate the Stokes mortars, the two most conspicuous methods of gas delivery were cylinders and projectors. To the last Foulkes remained convinced of the superiority of cylinders. An amusing illustration of this well-known preference comes from the diary of John Thomas who describes a typical interview with Foulkes required of officers being commissioned:

> Every man had to march the whole length of the wooden floor of the hut, salute the General, and give his name, Section and Company, after which the General asked his favourite question—cylinders versus projectors. He was still a cylinder man in spite of all the disappointments we were getting with unfavourable winds, whilst most of the companies preferred the projector since the wind conditions were much less complicated.[9]

Foulkes felt that infantry commanders preferred the projector simply out of self-interest rather than on its merits, that is, because its use made fewer demands on infantry labor since the guns were dug in between rather than in the trench lines.[10]

Foulkes, however, found himself virtually alone in clinging to cylinder-discharged cloud gas attacks. Given the choice, most everyone else outside the Special Brigade, and many inside, preferred projectors. The Germans had long since concluded cloud gas to be inferior to gas delivered by shell. By the end of 1916 Foulkes had partially acquiesced and reluctantly approved projector training for all Special Companies. Under Strange's supervision, Z Company inaugurated a program of projector indoctrination for other gas units. The Livens projector is "to be used on a big scale," noted a war diary in December.[11] Thomas, now in command of A Company, reported being extremely busy the whole of January and February of 1917 mastering the new projector system through practice with dummy bombs. The range used by the company for these dummy shoots served also as Haig's daily exercise ground, and Thomas personally and very thoroughly scanned the range before each shoot.[12] Rumors circulated that the brigade was to give up cylinder gas altogether in favor of projectors.[13]

In December 1916, Haig had directed that the supply of gas cylinders be halved, and Thuillier, the Director of Gas Services, had recommended transfer of Foulkes's mortar companies to the artillery, a reduction of the cylinder companies, and eradication of all distinctions among the remaining Special Companies.[14] Foulkes stubbornly rejected each of these recommendations. He continued to refer to the first sixteen lettered companies (A to Q) as cylinder companies and the four numbered companies as the mortar companies. Z Company also retained its unique distinction in Foulkes's mind, even though in actual practice, since the discarding of the *Flammenwerfer*, Z Company had shifted its focus almost exclusively to projectors. Far from reducing the cylinder component of his force, Foulkes envisioned an even larger piece of the gas action for the cylinder companies. Thuillier, anxious to avoid a confrontation, allowed Foulkes a relatively free hand, while quietly promoting the projector effort whenever he could.[15]

As hostilities began again in earnest early in 1917, Foulkes was determined that his companies find opportunities to demonstrate gas effectiveness in its various forms. He arranged a series of lectures and demonstrations for each of the five army staffs. Addressing Fifth Army officers, an uncharacteristically deferential and diplomatic Foulkes attempted to advance an appreciation of the advantages of cylinder attacks: "I believe the present exclusive use of projectors is reducing the utility of the Special Brigade very much."[16] It seemed a losing battle, and in a speech to the Second Army, a frustrated Foulkes fumed that "it is one of the ironies of fate, now that there is for the first time anything like a general demand for gas in the Armies, that the demand should be for projectors—which are less effective than Stokes Mortars or cylinders, and which actually require more labour for installation."[17] He continued to bristle at infantry resistance to the brigade's frequent requests for personnel for carrying parties. While expressing himself "in full sympathy" with infantry commanders, he stressed the point that if they could only realize the superior results capable of being achieved by gas, they would agree that "no more remunerative use could be found [for infantry] than in gas installation."[18]

Foulkes had hoped his reorganized unit might become an invaluable "Fifth Arm," as he called it (in addition to the infantry, cavalry, artillery, and engineers). But few commanders shared Foulkes's true-believer enthusiasm for gas warfare in any form. Later in the year a divisional commander mocked the projector efforts of A Company at Langemarck: "Does as much good, in this wind, as a horse farting in the desert."[19]

14
"G" Is for Gas

"G" is for the poisonous GAS that's emitted
By fighters behind the lines only half-witted,
But very pugnacious, and much to be pitied
By those who live in the trenches.[1]

The end of the fighting season of 1916 brought the usual period of reassessment, recrimination, and shuffling of leadership. Tired generals and marshals, exhausted by the destruction of frightening numbers of their men and arsenals, gave way to yet more eager players. In France the Western Front commander in chief, Papa Joffre, left the active playing field to be replaced by Gen. Robert Nivelle, and in March 1917, Premier Briand followed Joffre into unwanted retirement. From the French press Georges Clemenceau ordered victory and the dashing and enthusiastic Nivelle guaranteed that coordinated Allied strikes in the spring would lead to decisive breakthroughs. In Britain Lloyd George, an outspoken critic of the Western Front strategy, replaced an exhausted Asquith in December 1916. Only Haig stayed on, though he was intensely mistrusted by the new coalition prime minister and still wedded to an unwavering faith in victory through attrition.

The winter break in the fighting allowed time to formulate new plans for further impossibly ambitious offensives in 1917. After protracted Allied political maneuvering, Haig and Robertson (Chief of the Imperial General Staff) managed to salvage much of a British plan of attack for the BEF in Flanders, preferably in the fall. Nivelle set his sights on a spring attack at the Aisne culminating with a breakthrough within twenty-four to forty-eight hours through a policy of "violence, brutality and rapidity." The final compromise scheme committed the British to an April offensive at Arras and Vimy, in preparation for Nivelle's attack just to the south; a second offensive later in the summer at Messines Ridge; and then Haig's much-vaunted all-out independent British breakthrough in Flanders in late summer.

Foulkes envisioned a commensurately major role in Allied operations for the again restructured Special Brigade. Its various companies spent the winter months training with both cylinders and projectors, improving old techniques and experimenting with new ones. Morale was high. The gasmen were anxious to demonstrate their improved capabilities and ready to support all actions—from routine raids to full-scale offensives—with keen enthusiasm and new skills. In spite of indecisive results in 1916, they felt that gas, if used cleverly, might yet become a war-winner.

One of the first innovations introduced by the Special Brigade in 1917 was both ingenious and potentially spectacular. In late 1916 a captain of the South Staffordshires, A. Reid-Kellett, had suggested a boring machine that promised to deliver the highest concentration of gas to the enemy with the least difficulty. The plan involved boring an underground hole with a water-drill, then inserting and pushing a smaller gas pipe through the hole toward the enemy's trenches. The device was named the Reid-Kellett push-pipe. In late December 1916, the captain persuaded GHQ of the feasibility of his idea. On Christmas Day, the Third Army approved the scheme and agreed to host its trial.

In January 1917, Reid-Kellett was attached temporarily to the Special Brigade to provide instruction and, together with a section of B Company, carried out some preliminary experiments. Jesse Berridge, from Chelmsford, had transferred to the Special Companies in 1915 at the age of nineteen, had been wounded in October 1916, and rejoined the unit later the same year.[2] He was now in command of B Company. Reid-Kellett and Berridge selected a suitable dugout near Blangy just east of Arras from which to direct the actual installation of the push-pipe.[3] Under their supervision, Q Company personnel, in the line with the 15th Division at that point, enlarged the dugout in question, inserted the boring machine, and began drilling. With the aid of a constant water flush, Reid-Kellett's hydraulic drill bored deep holes beneath no man's land. Several holes had to be abandoned when they hit obstructions or enemy saps, but by 11 January the first completed hole reached 279 feet. Although J Company replaced Q Company in February, the work continued without interruption. By early March the gasmen had drilled seven $1^1/_2$-inch tunnels out an average of 200 yards, ending near the German wire. They then pushed seven one-inch gas pipes through the larger conduits and connected forty gas cylinders to each of the seven pipes. Extremely cold temperatures froze the water used in the drill and extensive leaking of gas forced all personnel working in the dugout to wear special breathing aids. Reid-Kellett himself examined the nozzles protruding from the ends of the pipes up into no man's land to make sure that the nozzles were clear and free of dirt or other obstacles. By 12

March all seemed ready and J Company stood by for discharge, but un-favorable weather forced postponements for six successive nights.

On 18 March, a steady southwest wind at three to four mph promised excellent conditions, and zero hour was set for 11 P.M. Accompanied by an intelligence officer of the 15th Division and Capt. C. Laycock, sec-ond in command of J Company, Reid-Kellett took his place at the obser-vation post at the foot of Ivory Street with the South Wales Borderers. J. A. Carpenter, in command of J Company, stood by with the 44th Bri-gade. At zero hour, Berridge gave the order to turn on the gas valves. The pressurized gas shot through the underground pipes beneath no man's land, and as the observers watched intently from their observa-tion posts, surfaced directly in front of the enemy trenches. "The cloud traveled well coming from the hostile wire and moving forward in a very low cloud about 15' high, 100 yards wide." Not until forty-five minutes had passed did the gas cloud appear to thin perceptibly, and not until 12:20 A.M. did it disappear altogether.[4]

Unfortunately for the Allies, the Germans opposite escaped the push-pipe surprise by less than forty-eight hours, having just executed a stage of their strategic retirement to the northern extension of the Siegfried Line, or, as the British called it, the Hindenberg Line. What-ever gas reached the ends of the seven pipes drenched abandoned trenches. Ironically, the British once again suffered far more irritation than their enemies, for trouble with leakage had prevented the dis-charge of more than 150 of the 280 cylinders, and four days later the British dugout still reeked with gas. Not until 29 March could the last of the push-pipe cylinders, called Berridge Babies, be carried out of the dugout along Impotent Avenue. Because Foulkes considered the experi-ment very much of a failure, quite apart from the bad luck of the Ger-man withdrawal, and because of the extraordinary additional labor in-volved, the "obviously unsuitable" push-pipe was never attempted again.[5]

The strategic German pullback ruined other gas operations as well. Hundreds of man-hours of arduous portering and installation were wasted up and down the line. P Company, for example, had carried in and installed some five hundred projectors on the 14th Division front (Third Army) just north of Beaurains on 18 March, only to see the Ger-man retreat take their targets out of range.

Far from demonstrating improved effectiveness, the gas companies suffered a wave of mishaps from the very beginning of the year. One of the keenest disappointments occurred in late February and early March during a routine cylinder operation in the Vimy sector. The success of the entire Arras undertaking depended on the Allied capture of this ridge. General Horne assigned this crucial task to the four divisions of the Canadian Corps under Sir Julian Byng. That assault on Vimy Ridge on 9 April was to pass into legend, the most well-known and one of the most costly Canadian engagements of the war.[6] The role of the gas companies is less known.

Operations by C, J, and M Companies in late February in the area of Vimy illustrate the kind of persistent difficulties typically encountered by the cylinder companies.[7] In support of an earlier preliminary reconnaissance raid by the 4th Canadian Division, M Company had planned a two-wave cylinder discharge along a gas frontage of about 2,600 yards in the vicinity of Berthonval. Unfavorable winds forced postponement of the raid for several nights, but the last day of February, though cold and drizzly, promised a favorable wind, and so M Company moved up the line again. In the early hours of 1 March, the men released the first wave of 1,308 cylinders of White Star (the usual 50 percent chlorine and 50 percent phosgene mixture) in an almost ideal west-southwest wind of eight to ten mph.[8] Enemy shellfire, however, punctured several pipes during the discharge, filling the trenches with gas. Casualties in M Company totaled nine killed and thirty gassed and wounded, the great majority of gas casualties caused either by shattered pipes or carelessness in removing helmets too soon. An unfortunate change of wind to north-northwest forced the cancellation of all but eighty cylinders of the planned 4:45 A.M. second wave of 680 cylinders. By zero hour, the German defenses had had ample time to recover from the effects of the first gas wave, so that when the Canadian raiding parties went over the top they encountered a lethal combination of withering machine-gun fire and lingering gas. They sustained forty-five casualties, including eight killed, an extraordinarily high casualty rate for a mere raid.

The Canadian officers were quick to blame the gas company for the failure of the raid and the loss of life. Criticism and accusation rained down upon the gasmen, denouncing every aspect of the gas operation. The infantry carrying parties complained of the labor and strain of portering the 2,000 gas cylinders: "Strong men fainted with exhaustion." The terrain had not been suitable in the first place. The weather had been too cold. The enemy trenches had been too distant. The gas company had been very inexperienced and "afraid of its own gas. . . . it was very much up in the air, and its work was not satisfactory." There had been a glaring insufficiency of both men and officers in the gas company. The Canadians attributed cancellation of most of the second wave of gas on "demoralization of the gas personnel" rather than on wind change. All gas ought to have been discharged in one wave. Of forty-four captured German prisoners, only one stated that he had seen a German killed by gas. None of the raiders had seen a German wearing a gas mask. The gas had merely alerted the enemy to the imminent raid. The Canadians concluded that the gas attack was counter-productive and that their losses were far heavier than they would have been without gas.

In the temporary absence of Garden and Foulkes, the former on leave and the latter again in bed with a cold, it fell to Lieutenants Bassett and Davies to defend the gas action. They responded that the overriding cause of the failure was the unfortunate but unpredictable wind change which prevented the second discharge and thus gave the Germans time to recover. Only a few pipes actually leaked. As for prisoners' statements about the innocuousness of the gas, Davies countered with reports of several of the infantry who saw Germans "coughing violently." Since forty-three tons of gas had been discharged, no doubt the enemy must have suffered heavy casualties. As for the alleged inexperience of the gas personnel, although 2d Lt. A. J. Dean (one of the section leaders) admitted that many of his men were raw pioneers, M Company had been actively employed in cloud gas attacks on the Second Army front since June 1916 and had achieved an average 92 percent discharge rate. "Because opposition was met it does not necessarily follow that the gas was ineffective. It will never be possible to cause the whole of the enemy subjected to Gas Attack to become casualties."

Several weeks later less vitriolic assessments surfaced. The commander of the Canadian 4th Division admitted that he had "overestimated" the effect of the gas and placed "too much reliance" on it. Lt. Gen. Byng concurred: "I consider I was wrong in thinking the gas would be more effective on the morale of the enemy than events proved. I was under the impression that this gas used in large quantities had the effect of placing men temporarily out of action." This mistaken impression was not an isolated one. Paradoxically, some commanders still expected near miracles from gas while others harbored the greatest skepticism of it. In his book, Foulkes mentions the Canadian incident only obliquely, as explaining a Canadian "prejudice" against cloud gas.[9]

Regardless of blame, the unfortunate Vimy incident eroded even further any remaining confidence in gas, and the Special Companies found themselves hindered by an even greater obstructiveness in carrying out routine gas operations, especially those by cylinder discharge. Shortly after the Vimy accident, General Horne's First Army summarily suspended all gas operations: "Under no circumstances . . . would they allow the cylinders to be discharged." On 9 March, the 1st Canadian Division and the 51st Division demanded that E Company immediately remove all its cylinders from their sectors. On 20 March the company received word that its operations were to be abandoned: "In view of uncertainty inseparable from action of cylinder gas, added to the immense labour involved in its installation, the Corps Commander did not wish any more cylinders to be installed on the Corps front. The use of projectors and gas shell was advocated." E Company thereupon began the task of removing the cylinders and pipes, intending to substitute projector apparatus. The next day, however, the 3d Canadian Division "would give no definitive assurance" it would permit even gas projectors. Nagging reminders about removal of all remaining front-line cylinders arrived at gas company headquarters almost daily. On 24 March the 2d Canadian Brigade issued an ultimatum that all 296 remaining cylinders be removed by the night of 27/28 March, followed by a "warning order" the next day. When, on the twenty-sixth, two gas sections proceeded up the line to do so, none of the lorries promised by the Canadians turned up, and the men had to hide the cylinders temporarily in two nearby tunnels. The beleaguered E Company was soon to move to Minx, but not before the Canadians peremptorily disconnected the phones they had lent.[10]

In spite of the Vimy debacle Foulkes hoped for impressive results from the massive combined projector and cylinder discharges which were planned to accompany the Arras Offensive, set for 9 April. Allenby's Third Army was to spearhead the attack in front of Arras while Horne's First Army struck just to the north and Gough's Fifth Army provided supporting attacks to the south. As at the Somme, the Special Companies discharged virtually all the cylinder gas during the preparatory stages, but the greatest part of the projector shoots were to be saved for the concentrated barrage just before zero hour. It would constitute the first large-scale projector attack of the war. Roughly half the gas companies participated, and although all had received some projector training during January and February, most had been practicing with dummy projectiles since the real ones did not arrive at Calais until the first days of April, shortly before the first scheduled projector shoots. Only Z Company had any experience "firing in anger."

As the inexperienced gas troops began hauling thousands of projectors "up the line" during the first days of April, the usual problems quickly surfaced, in addition to new ones unique to projector operations. Lorries transporting the heavy equipment to communication trench storage depots lost their way, frequently arriving only hours before zero hour. Infantry carrying parties found their routes barricaded by heavy shellfire. Many of the projectors' electrical connections broke in transit as the drums scraped the sides of the communication trenches, necessitating last minute rejoining and retesting. Frequently, lack of time prevented proper use of base-plates. Lack of clinometers rendered accurate angle alignment of the projectors impossible. Infantrymen tended to trample and sever the lengthy circuit leads. Enemy

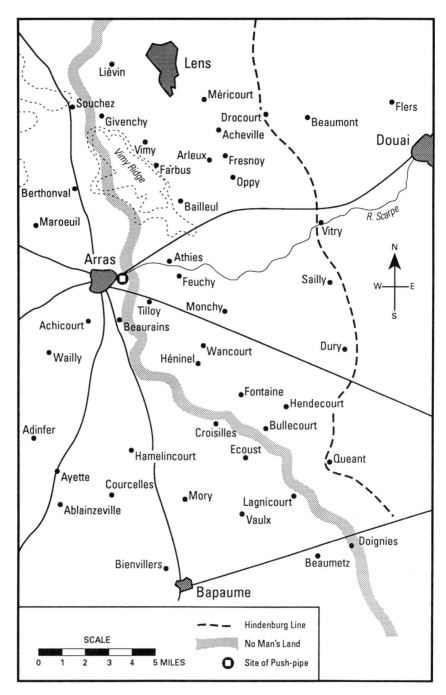

Map 14.1. Arras front: 1917

shellfire damaged crucial parts of equipment. The usual explosions of battle brought down avalanches of loose earth, breaking circuits and burying equipment in mud. When the projector firing began, the thudding impact of the machine's recoil on the trench system proved more damaging than had been anticipated. As the soft ground gave way, each subsequent firing became more and more difficult. Many projector guns had to be dug out of the ground and reset.

In dealing with these seemingly insuperable problems, the men of the Special Companies displayed extraordinary courage and ingenuity. In many cases they had to perform repairs and reset the projectors out on top of the parados in full view of the enemy. It was in this way that Lance Cpl. Robert Seaman, J Company, earned his Military Medal. Working at the front line near Iodine Street, Seaman noticed that some of the gas batteries had not fired because of circuit breakage. Repeatedly he carried exploders into the line, mounted the parados, and made the connections to get the batteries fired—all in daylight.[11] In spite of all difficulties, the Special Companies succeeded in firing 2,340 drums in one attack on 4 April alone.[12]

Meanwhile the Fifth Army had followed the retreating Germans to within projector range of the Hindenberg Line and the village of Bullecourt. On short notice, the Fifth Army requested the firing of up to 2,000 projectors against Bullecourt. Major Pollitt, formerly in command of the mortar battalion and now the commander of the Special Companies attached to the Fifth Army, could hardly refuse, for he had repeatedly asserted that the Special Companies were capable of carrying out small operations either with projectors or Stokes mortars at short notice, and that army failure to recognize this had led to many missed opportunities.[13]

Under severe time constraints, Pollitt sent for P and G Companies from their Third Army fronts where the retreating enemy had just deprived them of targets. P Company, following its gas discharge at Arras, had just been withdrawn from the line for much needed rest but, on 4 April, began a three-day route march southward to the area of Croisilles and Ecoust. Both companies spent most of three days slogging through snow and heavy rain. On the night of 6 April, wet and exhausted, they rushed up the line to support the short-notice Bullecourt operation of V Corps and I Anzac Corps.

Miserable weather contributed to greater-than-usual transport problems. According to Campbell-Smith, the track from Mory dump to Ecrolles was virtually impassable: "The state of this road almost defies description; a great part of it was built of sleepers and was only a single track. Being the only road on the V Corps front to Ecoust, it was full of traffic the whole night and blocks due to breakdown of horses or lorries

Flooded trenches at Laventie. (Courtesy of Imperial War Museum)

were frequent.'' In spite of these obstacles, the men succeeded in bring-ing 450 projectors, drums, and charges to the off-loading station at Ecourt crater.

Having thus overcome the first-stage transport problems, Pollitt learned during the evening of 8 April that the promised infantry carry-ing parties were a hundred men short. Under these circumstances both G and P Companies, after a night of unloading and storing the drums and charges, negotiated three successive round-trips up the line, wres-tling 320 of the 450 projectors into firing position. The next morning, the two companies, working under cover of the houses, carried the bombs from the crater to the center of the village, and later that night, the rest of the way to the front. The projector shoot of 9/10 April was mechanically flawless and the wind a perfect west-southwest at five to ten mph. When the infantry went over the top, however, they encoun-tered severe gunfire and were repulsed with heavy casualties. From the seventh to the fourteenth, both P and G Companies worked at the front, resetting and firing projectors and marching twelve miles to and from billets every night.

The concentrated projector barrages executed by the brigade at Arras were unmistakably impressive and played no small part in some local-ized initial advances. Foulkes was quick to claim great credit. J. Coch-rane, O Company, estimated that during these Arras projector shoots, ten companies fired about one thousand projector bombs each and that each two bombs resulted in one enemy casualty.[14] Except for the Canadian capture of Vimy Ridge on 9 April, however, significant British gains at Arras were virtually negligible, and the spring offensive subsided in bad weather about a week after its onset.

Gas operations in the Arras sector continued into May when a particularly tragic accident struck the Special Brigade. In preparation for another attack near Bullecourt, Z Company had assembled 250 projectors, high explosive bombs, propellants, and detonators to a forward position near Vaulx from Z Company headquarters at Bienvillers. From there the equipment had to be taken up to the front by 20 four-horse General Services wagons provided by 7th and 58th Division Ammunition Columns, led by guides from Z Company. The final off-loading point was a mere 250 yards from the crest of a ridge from which the projectors were to be fired, but hidden from direct view of enemy observation posts. It was at this forward point that the men of G and P Companies arrived the evening of 5/6 May to off-load and carry-in the remaining distance. Lieutenant Bansall, commanding Z Company, describes what happened next:

> The first ten wagons, containing projectors only, had arrived at their destination and been off-loaded with the exception of one, of which one horse was wounded and the wagon temporarily abandoned, but this was only a very short distance from the off-loading point. Carrying parties, each of strength 54 under an officer, were provided by G and P Special Companies, R.E. to assist in the work of moving the material from the off-loading point to the firing point. These parties were commencing their task when two other G.S. wagons containing charges arrived, one of which was offloaded, and the other rendered derelict by casualties to the horses, at the off-loading point. Four more wagons then appeared on the scene, containing bombs. (All these wagons were at intervals of 100 yards.) Unfortunately, the carrying parties were grouped thickly round the off-loading point, when a chance shell, probably from a minenwerfer, either struck the wagon containing propellant charges, or landed and exploded on the ground immediately beside it. All the propellants were exploded, and then it was that 90 percent of the casualties occurred.
>
> Immediately after the explosion, the enemy proceeded to search the ground behind the ridge with every piece of artillery that he could bring to bear against it. By this time, however, the survivors from the explosion had taken cover in the "cubby holes" in the sunken road nearby, but during the bombardment a shell, landing

on the top of the bank of the sunken road, buried more or less completely some seven or eight members of this unit. Of these, all were recovered except two. One, however, died immediately afterwards. The two others were buried beneath several tons of earth, and rescue was impossible.

Under harrowing circumstances, the stunned survivors struggled to bring the wounded and dying through the twisting communication trenches to dressing stations. Five men of the 58th Division were killed and one wounded from the 7th, but the three Special Companies sustained the greatest number of casualties. Z Company lost fourteen killed and seven wounded; P Company, which came to be known as the "suicide company," lost twenty-one killed and fourteen men wounded; G Company, eight men and one officer killed, seventeen men wounded. The dead were buried where they lay. The total number of casualties was eighty-eight. Nine horses were either killed outright or had to be put down.[15] It was the brigade's most costly single accident of the war. Strangely, Foulkes makes no mention of this tragedy in his book.

Continuing chemical research at home provided an increasing diversity of chemical compounds for use in cylinders, projectors, and mortars. None proved as consistently effective as White Star, but it was thought a variety of compounds might pose more problems for the enemy's defensive measures. A mixture of 30 percent chloropicrin and 70 percent chlorine, called Yellow Star, yielded additional lethal quality plus a strong lachrymatory effect. (Yellow Star should not be confused with Yellow Cross, the common symbol for mustard gas.) It was found that, for undetermined reasons, cylinders containing Yellow Star tended to leak and to become duds far more than others.[16] C Company, which Foulkes seems to have used as his primary unit for cylinder experimentation, also received cylinders containing 65 percent chloropicrin and 35 percent hydrogen sulfide, called Green Star, but the mixture proved so dangerous in field tests that it was never used.[17]

The mortar companies by mid-1917 were also using thermit, a mixture of powdered aluminum and iron oxide, which, when ignited with a special explosive called ophorite, produced a spectacular inflammatory effect, a metal-melting heat that doused enemy trenches with a rain of molten fragments. On occasion the brigade also used prussic acid, stannic tetrachloride, carbon disulfide, and, for smoke, various types of phosphorus. Dichlorodiethyl sulfide, commonly called mustard gas (also known as Yperite from the place of its initial German use and Yellow Cross from the German shell markings), was an extremely persistent blistering agent dispersed only from shells. Although British artillery employed it extensively during the last year of the war, usually mixed with other chemicals, the Special Brigade never included mustard gas in its repertoire.

In June 1917, the simmering policy disagreements between Foulkes and Thuillier ended when Thuillier left the gas directorship for promotion to a divisional command (15th). Foulkes replaced him, retaining also the command of the Special Brigade and obtaining promotion to the rank of brigadier-general. Harold Hartley, who had been serving as Gas Advisor to the Third Army, replaced S. L. Cummins as Assistant Director of Gas Services on the defensive side, and B. L. Eddis, formerly brigade major, became Assistant Director of Gas Services on the offensive side, continuing to work closely with Foulkes in the daily running of the brigade. In July the Special Brigade welcomed King George, Queen Mary, and the Prince of Wales.[18] For Queen Mary, the Helfaut contingent fired a *Flammenwerfer* shot, gas, and oil drums from Bilques Common, then thermit, gas, and smoke shells from Helfaut common, repeating much of the demonstration two days later for King George and the Prince of Wales.[19]

Despite some strong personal preferences in tactics, for the most part Foulkes allowed for a fair degree of improvisation among his chemists and engineers, providing each company with a workshop with facilities for carrying out experiments. Throughout the year not only did Foulkes constantly suggest new tactics and techniques, but both officers and men within and outside the brigade came up with variations and suggestions for improvements. In early June, K and O Companies hurled oil drums into the Wytshaete Woods north of Messines to burn off the underbrush—an early attempt at defoliation. In spite of the firing of 322 guns, the wood did not actually ignite, though "the moral effect [on the enemy] must have been considerable."[20] Many suggestions reflected a fairly sophisticated level of chemistry and mechanical and electrical engineering skills. Lt. William Gilliat, A Company, and Lt. Donald Wilson, M Company, hoping to reduce or eliminate chemical residues which collected on the ground after gas discharges, devised a jet attachment based on the principle of the Bunsen burner which vaporized heavy mixtures by drawing in a current of air behind the blast, but they found that even more unwanted liquid collected than with the old jets. Sgt. J. A. Miller, also A Company, produced an improvement in the tube helmet which kept the eyepiece in place and away from the eyes. Guy Crowden, B Company, noticing that the sound of the company's gas discharges was heard by men a mile away, wrote to Foulkes about a stovepipelike silencer attachment to a Vickers machine gun which disguises the fact that gas has been released.[21] Capt. Norman Campbell, N

Company, suggested an automatic trench gas alarm, based on the sensitivity of an electric cylinder to gas, which would be triggered automatically by the presence of gas in the trenches.[22] Some suggestions were workable, others not; but innovations and experiments continued at all levels.

The rivalry between advocates of cylinders and those of projectors intensified during 1917, especially during the summer and autumn. Cylinder detractors might quite handily have won a debate based solely on logic, because the problems and failings of cloud gas were manifold. The cylinder discharges involved a greater technical precision, greater inconvenience to infantry, a welter of pipes, connectors, spigots, and, once installed, greater vulnerability. Most exasperatingly, defects in cylinder equipment persisted. In March 1917, C Company had found 20 percent of a shipment of 457 newly filled cylinders to be defective.[23] Infantry carrying parties in 1917 echoed the same resentful complaints as those of 1915 and 1916. One infantryman, a private, cursed the cylinders claiming they weighed two hundred pounds![24] Occasionally mules were used for carrying, but they were prone to sudden panic and desertion.

Cylinder placement involved an extraordinary amount of work. Although the brigade experimented with a trench rope-way transit system called the Leeming ropeway, it was never made practical, and the perennial problems with carrying parties remained unsolved. Carrying out the empty and damaged cylinders might be as dangerous and arduous as the carry-in, though the empties weighed considerably less. Foulkes once told an amusing story about an infantry commander who doubled the carrying party for the carry-out on the mistaken supposition that the empty cylinders would be heavier without the gas.[25] One of the greatest unresolved drawbacks of the gas cylinders was their vulnerability to enemy shellfire and leakage during the many days and nights they sometimes had to remain in the front line awaiting favorable winds. "That's what the infantry feared," Edwards-Ker remembered, "that with the gas laid in there there might be a shell that would split open a cylinder."[26] Once installed, the gas cylinders had to be guarded twenty-four hours a day until discharged. C Company once "stood to" for twenty successive nights (21 June to 9 July 1917) nursing 1,064 cylinders in the front lines, during which time enemy fire buried over one hundred of them.[27] Not only did companies in charge of front-line cylinders have to mount twenty-four hour guards, but, anxious as they naturally were to fire them, several sections had to go up the line each evening on the chance of the favorable wind. Running the nightly gauntlet of shellfire was frequently the most dangerous part of a Special's work. Occasionally the men hitched rides on passing General Services wagons. Fox recalled one such adventure:

On one occasion, a moonlit night, some of us saw such a wagon coming, and raced to jump on it as it passed; clinging to the sides as we clambered in, we were horrified to find that it contained dead bodies jumping and jerking about as the vehicle swayed along the rough road; it was truly a "dead man's ride."[28]

If cylinders were not to be abandoned altogether, and Foulkes was firmly opposed to that, then radical improvements in the system had to be initiated. One such tactical innovation, which Foulkes had suggested as far back as May 1917, was what he called the "mobile cylinder" deployment.[29] The idea involved use of a smaller cylinder, advance storage in dugouts, and a postponement of the front-line carry-in until a favorable wind was most probable. The cylinders would then be carried the short additional distance from the dugouts, installed in boxed emplacements in the front lines, and discharged the same night. This system was intended to reduce the need for so much infantry portering, especially in advance, thus increasing the chances of surprise. The lighter cylinders (called "mice," as distinct from the larger "rats") weighed only fifty pounds and could be carried by one man by means of a shoulder sling.

Foulkes chose C Company, which many considered his favorite, for the first use of the new mobile cylinder method in mid-April. The gas reached the enemy lines in about forty-five seconds, no friendly infantry were gassed, and C Company sustained only slight gassing.[30] Trench emplacements were changed slightly so as to accommodate either rats or double that number of mice, and both were employed interchangeably from that point on. The new method, however, was actually not substantively different from traditional methods, and infantry complaints persisted. In July 1917, Capt. G. B. Riddell led a "working party" of fifty infantry from his B Company (Northumberland Fusiliers) to carry mice up the line for the Special Companies.

The party paraded at 8:30 P.M. and we marched the three miles to the line fairly well . . . and with few grouses. The cylinders were about sixty pounds each and we had only enough men for one to a cylinder. There were eight cylinders over. I impressed four R.E.s to their eternal disgust. It was very dark, the trenches un-duckboarded, and full of holes and covered with about two feet of mud and water. A man would fall into a hole and the next man came on top of him. Those behind halted and those in front kept on. A huge gap, and half the party lost. In half an hour the party had become a series of disconnected sections dragging, struggling on, not knowing whether they were going the right way or not, caring less. Anything to get those awful loads down. Men sank down from sheer exhaustion, but they had to be picked up, and had to carry on again. Men would fall over wires stretching under foot or get their rifles entangled in wires overhead. . . . The Bosch started to shell us. Men coming up got mixed up with men coming down. I cursed the returning party in many languages and put them on the right track. I hurried on over the top to where the cylinders were to be put. It would have taken too long to move along the trench, and would have blocked the traffic more than ever. Then the moon came up. The R.E.s refused to carry on till I used a little persuasion and a revolver. The cylinders came along one by one. The sight of the end of the task put fresh spirit into the exhausted lads, and the last cylinder was put into position.[31]

Since the mobile cylinder method often transferred the carrying duties from the infantry entirely to the Specials, it was by no means popular among the gas brotherhood. Several other companies occasionally used the mobile system, when sufficient mice were available, but the modification did not adequately address or solve the basic objections inherent in cloud gas operations.

The balance of evidence had clearly been tilting away from cylinders and in favor of projectors for some time. Had it not been for Foulkes's strong feelings on the matter, the Livens projector and the Stokes mortar might have replaced cloud gas altogether. Haig seemed to prefer the Stokes mortar and recommended early in April that several of the cylinder companies be converted to mortar companies.[32] Encouraged by the impressive results at Arras, most of the units except C Company were using projectors by the summer of 1917. The chief advantages of the projector were virtual independence from wind conditions, relatively easier installation, deployment in safer Reserve areas, and decreased vulnerability of trench personnel. The projector tube itself contained no gas, and when damaged or ruptured by shellfire, posed no gas hazard as did the gas-filled cylinders. It is easy to understand why most field commanders preferred the Livens projector to cylinders.

The projector, however, entailed disadvantages and dangers also. The guns tended to become more easily buried, both from repeated recoil and enemy shelling, as well as from natural sinking. They had constantly to be dug out of soft earth with picks and shovels and ropes.[33] Deeply buried projectors frequently had to be abandoned. A brigade veteran who returned to France after the war noticed that the French had salvaged many of these abandoned projectors and were using them as gateposts.[34] Installed on open ground behind the front lines, the projector, while not chemically dangerous if hit by shellfire, clearly posed a more visible and vulnerable target for enemy shelling than the cylinders sandbagged in the firestep. Moreover the projector operators had to work aboveground rather than in the relative safety of the trenches. When, in mid-May 1918, C Company was to carry out its first projector stunt, Fox wrote of feeling "naked" working out on top for the first time: "A deep protecting trench seemed Heaven compared to this."[35]

Nor was the projector an accurate weapon, thus adding the concern of projector shoots falling short and endangering friendly forces, as did those of H Company in late May.[36] In June, Foulkes distributed a warning memo:

> I wish to remind all officers as to their personal responsibility in regard to risky operations being undertaken. Unless the infantry can be temporarily withdrawn, for absolute safety, none of our troops in the line of fire should be at a less distance from the target than 40 percent of the range at which the projectors are set. Under special circumstances a Commander [infantry] might decide to take risks; but the latter must be pointed out to him.[37]

The installation and firing of projectors required as little professional expertise of chemists as did cylinders. New recruits voiced the same complaints as had those of 1915: "The need was for navvies who could dig fast and carry heavy weights, but nobody ever passed the news to England that a knowledge of chemistry was not of the slightest use, and chemists were being recruited until the end of the war."[38] The introduction of tanks during this period further complicated the deployment of projectors. The tank drivers tended to run right over them, completely flattening the lips of the protruding projectors.[39]

Z Company, usually in concert with other Special Companies, led the way in improving every aspect of the projector, both in the field as well as at its experimental camp at Toutencourt.[40] In an effort to simplify deployment and reduce manpower requirements, Z Company developed the open field system in which the projectors and base-plates were not dug deeply into the ground individually but were simply laid side by side, almost touching each other, in a shallow continuous trench with a forty-five-degree slope. Z Company practiced the open field routine until one officer and only three men could lay seventeen projectors, connect them, and fire, all in a time of fifty-five minutes. Unfortunately, as happened so often in experimental weaponry, improvements which solved one problem created others. In this case, some of the gun barrels suffered damage when fired so close together.[41] E Company buffered the drums to solve part of this problem by wrapping a tight-fitting coil of two-inch rope around the top and bottom of every other drum, but of course this procedure reduced the time saved.[42]

Though the projector method of gas discharge involved less heavy carrying than the cylinder method, the base-plates, detonators, cables, and projectors were clumsy and heavy enough. Each projector tube alone weighed about one hundred pounds. Where trench duckboards were either unsteady or damaged, as at Langemarck where the duckboards had been blasted to pieces by enemy shelling, it was simply impossible to transport heavy equipment. In an effort to reduce the carrying involved in projector shoots, Z Company tried firing the projectors without the base-plates. In soft ground, however, projectors without base-plates were too easily buried, sometimes to a depth of nine feet. Another way to reduce the recoil was to reduce the charge, but this also decreased the range.

In spite of difficulties inherent in both cylinder and projector discharges, by mid-1917 many of the gas companies were fast becoming professionally expert in both gas routines, as was the much smaller contingent of mortar companies. More and more operations passed off flawlessly, the result of hard work and conscientious leadership at the company level. The Special Brigade produced some excellent company commanders, among them Capt. A. J. Pelling, N Company, whose war diary shows a meticulous attention to detail. Pelling developed an exceptional proficiency in the coordinated use of both cylinders and projectors. His orders, in addition to specifying which side of the road the carrying parties should march on, the number of "spare" men carrying "spare" poles, and the number of guides and guards for the carrying parties, stated: "The utmost silence must be preserved throughout these operations, and no smoking will be permitted at any time, and stores are to be handled with care. In case of enemy shelling, no alarm is to be sounded and casualties must be handled only by 'spares.' "[43] For maximum effect, projectors were to be discharged three minutes after the onset of the cylinder discharge. Cylinder pipes were left hand-tight so that no spanners were needed for discharge. Pelling continued to fine-tune his operations. He provided empty sandbags for carrying crews to use as shoulder pads. Leaving as little to chance as possible, Pelling even arranged that the routes back from the trenches be taped out so that the crews would not lose the way. Based on his experience he came to the unorthodox conclusion that a strong wind was preferable, "even a gale of 40 mph or more."[44]

Pelling's secret codes were most ingenious. Numbers of "angle-irons" and "stakes," expressed in thousands, represented hours and minutes, respectively. To further confound enemy listeners, Pelling added 12,000 to the numbers, so that, for example, an order for 35,000 angle-irons and 42,000 stakes meant 11:30 P.M. As if additional coding were necessary, an accompanying message containing the word "full" meant that zero hour stood; a message with the word "empty" meant cancellation; and the inclusion of the word "buckets" meant that zero hour was postponed as many hours as the number of buckets (again in thousands). Thus an order for 35,000 angle-irons, 42,000 stakes, and 1,000 buckets meant zero hour 12:30. Less camouflaged codes Pelling used were FUN for favorable weather and GLOOM for unfavorable; FATHER for go, MOTHER for cancel, BROTHER for postpone. B Company used an alliterative series of code words—coffee, cocoa, chocolate, chicory, and candy—to designate various options. On one occasion JAM meant OK to discharge, and NO JAM not to; Lloyd George, yes, Asquith, no.[45] There must have been some cardplayers in C Company, whose codes on one occasion ran as follows: HOUSE, gas discharged as planned; BRIDGE, gas discharge canceled; POKER, gas discharge at zero hour plus one; WHIST, all clear.[46]

Early in the summer of 1917 Foulkes hired an intelligence officer for the brigade, Capt. T. H. Adams, a German literature scholar whose brother had been gassed in 1915 while serving with Company 186. Adams was largely responsible for a monthly publicity report that GHQ began publishing in July 1917.[47] Titled *Gas Warfare: Monthly Summary of Information*, the pamphlet consisted mostly of prisoner quotes and captured enemy documents substantiating the effectiveness of British gas attacks.

During the summer, several Special Companies operated along the Belgian coast between Dunkirk and Nieuport, on the far left of the Allied front. H and K Companies moved to St. Idesbalde in early July and fired projectors from the Nieuport front onto German positions at Lombartzyde.[48] But for the most part this sector was relatively quiet. Sid Fox, who joined H Company briefly at this time, recalled tenting on the sand dunes, relaxing and bathing in the North Sea, and listening to the unfamiliar sounds of waves breaking on the shore.[49] Cpl. T. Eden, K Company, thought the exercise a "seaside holiday" and employed his free time compiling a small herbarium of typical dune plants with the aid of a handbook, *Name This Flower*, sent from home. What he learned about the ecology of the sand dunes during his three-month stay in the area later became the basis of his first scientific published paper on the subject in the *Lancashire and Cheshire Naturalist*. For sports the men competed in running races through waterlogged tracks.[50]

From time to time, beginning in 1917, various Allied delegations visited Helfaut to study the gas tactics of the Special Brigade, among them Russians, Serbs, Portuguese, Italians, and Americans.[51] After comparing

French and British gas organizations, the Americans decided to model their own gas effort after that of the Special Brigade.[52] In October 1917, Maj. S. J. M. Auld, then Chemical Advisor to the Third Army, together with twenty-eight officers and twenty-eight men, sailed to the United States to give advice and training. Attached to the staff of the American Director of Gas Services, the delegation was called the British Gas Warfare Mission. To head the American gas effort, Auld advised a military rather than a civilian director, a post eventually filled by Maj. Gen. William L. Sibert, who remained at the head of the American gas effort and worked closely with Auld throughout the remainder of the war. About this same time, seven American officers of the 30th Engineers sailed to France and took up residence at Helfaut.

Seven Special Companies contributed to the great battle in Flanders, known as Third Ypres or Passchendaele, which began in late July. By this time, however, the work of the gas companies had became increasingly divorced from specific offensives and was more and more directed at a routine harassment of the enemy. In companies, sections, and even subsections, the gasmen played their part, not only in the major battles of Messines Ridge, Third Ypres, and Cambrai, but also in routine, almost nightly operations up and down the entire British line all year long.

Casualties in the brigade during 1917 were severe, certainly over 1,500, though Foulkes does not provide a breakdown of the 5,384 total wartime casualties. Only at the opening of the Somme battle in 1916 and at the beginning of the German spring offensive of 1918 did the casualties of the brigade exceed those attending the opening of Third Ypres. During the first three weeks of July, for example, N Company lost over 30 percent of its personnel—five killed and forty-three wounded. The company's war diary on 19 July showed only forty-five men fit for duty in the whole company. In what must be one of the most unusual sets of circumstances, Frank O'Kelly, No. 2 Mortar Company, was twice wounded on 24 May. In a thousand-to-one chance, at Ploegsteert Wood, a German machine-gun bullet struck the fuse of a shell O'Kelly was holding, blinding him in one eye. While at a dressing station, a direct hit from a German shell resulted in the loss of his other eye. He is perhaps the only soldier to lose the sight of both eyes on the same day—in separate accidents.[53]

The year 1917 saw the greatest gas activity of the war up to that time. From April to mid-December, the brigade carried out 348 separate operations, emptying nearly 12,000 cylinders and firing off 100,000 projectors. An additional 120,000 Stokes mortar bombs brought the total amount of discharged gas to about 2,050 tons.[54] By the end of 1917 Foulkes considered that gas had become, if not the decisive war-winner, at least a prime means of achieving substantial enemy casualties in a war of attrition and asserted that the Germans had "resigned themselves to these losses in despair."[55] He had not, however, given up on cloud gas as a primary, rather than secondary, weapon. During the winter lull, Foulkes worked out the major lines of a new mode of cylinder discharge called a "retired cylinder" attack and laid plans to employ this new method in a gas offensive early in 1918—one more massive and spectacular than any ever mounted before.

15
The Last Season: 1918

We went down to the Yankee front,
Oh, 'twas a lovely ride.
We had such gorgeous cattle-trucks,
With "forty hommes" inside.
But when we reached our journey's end
Just feeling slightly sore,
We found the Armistice was signed,
For the Yanks had won the war.[1]

In one of the more memorable scenes of the British antiwar film, *O, What a Lovely War*, Haig the attritionist prays for victory at Passchendaele "before the Americans arrive," but by the early months of 1918 such a prospect appeared quite improbable. The failure of the Brusilov Offensive in mid-1917 and the subsequent withdrawal of Bolshevik Russia from the war allowed Germany to focus virtually all its remaining resources on one last all-out attack on the Western Front. It remained for Germany to exploit the window of opportunity and win the war "before the Americans arrived." For the Allies the only question was the precise time and place of the German offensive.

In the classic battle in 490 B.C., Athenians faced Persians on the plains of Marathon, hoping to delay hostilities until the arrival of their seemingly dilatory Spartan allies. By much the same reckoning the Allied armies faced the Germans in the fourth spring of the war, waiting on the readiness of their new American ally. Pétain had successfully suppressed the French mutiny of 1917 largely on the promise that no further large-scale offensives would be mounted without America's help. Adopting a purely defensive posture for the first time in the trench war, the Allied infantry all along the Western Front entrenched even deeper and braced for the inevitable German onslaught.

Almost all of the Special Companies had been withdrawn to quiet villages in the Helfaut region by early December 1917. Only P Company remained in the front lines (with the Third Army) until mid-January, "and think ourselves hard done by," complained Robert Wilson. Three days later P Company trudged into Fruges, and Wilson enjoyed "a lovely warm shower bath" but "no change of undergarments, much needed after six weeks' wear."[2] This was to be the brigade's longest winter interlude, a period of relative safety from front-line dangers, but not entirely of rest and relaxation.

Strenuous training continued, both for initiating new tactics and for maintaining the usual rigors of military habit. Morning parades, route marches, practice attacks, and Saturday kit inspections all aimed at the preservation of discipline and readiness. Daily routine varied only slightly from company to company. The war diary of A Company indicates "cylinder training day and night," wind reading, map reading, camouflage, arms drill, and musketry, in addition to the routine physical drill.[3] Daily routine in N Company began with physical training from 7:15 to 8:15, followed by more specialized sessions involving wiring exercises, respirator drill, map reading, rifle exercises, wind vane construction, treatment of duds, and so on. The afternoon sessions usually ended at 3:30.[4] The evenings, however, remained quite pleasantly carefree, and Wilson recalled many "jolly evenings" spent at cards, talk, and sing-song.[5]

One of many urgent matters concerned the brigade's small arms. Most of the chemist soldiers still carried revolvers, which elicited constant curiosity and even suspicion from those unacquainted with the Special Brigade. On one occasion in 1917 a corporal in K Company, challenged to identify himself, had shown his Royal Engineers identification, whereupon the apprehending officer, noticing the anomaly of the revolver, arrested him as a spy. It was not until divisional headquarters verified that the identification number of his Colt revolver matched that shown in his pay-book that he was released.[6] During the German counterattack at Cambrai in late 1917, many of the gas personnel had found themselves at a distinct disadvantage manning the defensive line armed with revolvers. In view of these considerations and the enemy attacks expected in the spring, Foulkes ordered the call-in of all revolvers (and holsters) and their replacement with rifles, and an intense period of training in rifle handling and firing began.[7] In this new skill, the nonchemists drafted from infantry units, old hands at "sloping" and "fixing bayonets," showed the way. Only the commissioned officers retained revolvers.

Still privately cherishing his stubborn, outdated conviction that gas might yet break the deadlock and more than ever determined to overcome the bias against traditional methods of cylinder discharge, Foulkes passed the winter lull polishing various schemes for improving cylinder operations. In December 1917, he ordered all gas companies, including the mortar companies and even Z Company, to concentrate exclusively on cylinder practice during the winter months.[8]

In the search for improvements and simplification, the "mobile" deployment of "mice," added to the gas repertoire in 1917, had been one step in the right direction. Now, abandoning entirely the customary methods of digging in cylinders in the front-line trenches, Foulkes experimented with quite unorthodox techniques of pitching them into action at the last moment with as little front-line handling as possible. Several companies tried eliminating the pipes entirely, discharging the cylinders directly from the cylinder nozzles. A Company practiced laying the cylinders flat on the ground behind the front-line trenches, lashed together in bundles of three, erecting them just before zero.[9] Each of these methods eliminated some of the dangers associated with digging in the cylinders and then waiting for the wind. Since all of these new cylinder techniques, as well as the projector discharges, took place aboveground, Foulkes intensified training in camouflaging as well. To facilitate transport of gas equipment of all kinds, he obtained from the Ministry of Munitions a primitive model of a mechanical trench transport. The Leeming ropeway, as the contraption was called, was a motorized steel cable slung along the trench, suspended on trestles, and driven by means of a petrol engine. Foulkes set up a school for brigade training in its use, but the war ended before the mechanism could be perfected and delivered. Since the shortage of gas and cylinders that had hampered earlier gas offensives no longer existed, preparations proceeded for the most ambitious operations.

In mid-January 1918, D and K Companies moved to Fruges to make room at Helfaut for the first two of six American gas companies who were to train with the Special Brigade. Originally organized as the 30th Engineers, the unit was first renamed the Gas and Flame Companies, and finally the First Gas Regiment.[10] On 20 January, the regimental headquarters and most of the 1st Battalion arrived at Helfaut under the command of Maj. George Weinberg to begin training in all methods of gas warfare. There was some uncertainty as to what to call the new arrivals. Some of them protested against "Yankees," and although *Punch* suggested "Sammies," an unidentified American general was alleged to have said, "If there was anything the American soldier really dislikes it was to be called 'Sammies.'" Doughboys was preferred.[11] The American Gas Regiment requisitioned all supplies, gas masks, cylinders, mortars, and projectors from Foulkes's unit. Its own supplies did not arrive in France before the Armistice.

The winter intermission in GHQ Reserve areas terminated abruptly at the end of February when the Special Companies redeployed along the 120-mile-long British line. At a conference at Helfaut on 21 February 1918, Foulkes had announced a neat and orderly deployment of his forces, attaching three cylinder companies and one mortar company to each army; but even before the German offensive began, companies began to shift about as in earlier years. By the second week in March the Special Companies were once more in place all along the line. The purely defensive posture temporarily assumed by the British armies afforded the gasmen a brief opportunity for projector and cylinder discharges on the stabilized front before the German blow fell. They accomplished a number of releases along Third and Fifth Army fronts, between Arras in the north and St. Quentin to the south, where the German attack seemed most likely. At Queant, the Special Companies projected several thousand drums, while at St. Quentin, opposite Von Hutier's Eighteenth Army, they discharged nearly three thousand projectors the night of 19/20 March.[12] W. T. Stirling, a gas pioneer, left a vivid reminiscence of this attack, one of the last before the German offensive:

> We crept out without being observed, and when we got the order to fire the whole countryside was lit up with a sheet of flame and the peace of that quiet front shattered with a terrific blast. . . . Then we beat it across the open to find some cover from the hail of bullets that came over our way once the machine gunners got their gas-masks fastened.[13]

The American B (Gas) Company reached Bethune on 1 March 1918.[14] Its four platoons were distributed among B, M, O, and No. 3 Special Companies.[15] During the next several weeks various platoons of the American A Company left Helfaut to join L, Z, and F Companies for the most practical kind of field training. The pioneers and corporals worked side by side with the British Specials, sharing equally the onerous portering and the sergeants sharing dugouts and officers' mess. Wilson, M Company, regarded the arrival of the Americans at this time a "tonic" for weary Allies and remembers a warm and easy camaraderie.[16] Gen. William Sibert, chief of the American Chemical Warfare Service, and Gen. Amos Fries, commander of the 1st American Gas Regiment, both staunch advocates of all forms of gas warfare including cylinder clouds, got along well with Foulkes. The American gas companies scarcely had time to settle in, however, before confronting the great German spring offensive.

Simultaneously, Foulkes pressed forward with plans for the upcoming "retired cylinder" surprise. A huge and growing cache of cylinders collected in Mondicourt for this purpose required testing and guarding. In early March, P Company was sent to Mondicourt to be the Dump Company, and Wilson considered that P Company, seemingly always in the line, had drawn ''a snip job'' at last.[17] Then the storm broke.

In the morning fog of Thursday, 21 March, Ludendorff played Germany's last card. The long-anticipated and much-feared German attack began with a suddenness and a fury that soon threatened the breakthrough that neither side had been able to accomplish since the autumn of 1914. The German advance foiled all routine Allied gas operations on the fronts affected and forced indefinite postponement of Foulkes's ''retired'' operation as well.

The first German blow, code-named Michael, fell upon the British Fifth Army near Peronne. Its attached gas companies (A, E, H, and No. 1 Mortar), under the command of Campbell-Smith, converted hastily to infantry duty. Oakey was with No. 1 Mortar Company on 25 March:

> A strong attack on line held by the company was repulsed until noon when the left flank gave way and the company withdrew . . . to west of Maricourt after further attack on it at 2 P.M. A counterattack employing half the company among the troops engaged nearly re-established the line. At 11 P.M. the company withdrew to west of Bray to be held in reserve.[18]

The war diaries of each of the gas companies confirm in the starkest terms the desperation of the next several weeks as infantry and gasmen fought side by side in rearguard defensive operations. The retreat reached Ham, then Roye, then Quesnil. Such was the confusion that at times the gas companies found themselves mixed up with French troops. E Company, after a futile effort to help hold the line on the outskirts of Ham, had to withdraw, abandoning all its equipment stored at its Ham depot.[19] A Company destroyed all company orders on 31 March, and its war diary reported that ''men off strength and on strength from day to day could not be ascertained.''[20] The British Fifth Army checked the onslaught only forty miles from Amiens.

To the north with General Byng's Third Army, G, J, Q, and No. 3 Mortar Companies under Major Bunker stood and fought in similar manner. As the German advance rolled on, virtually all the gas units (except for a few in Flanders) became involved in bolstering the line wherever needed. C Company found itself attached in rapid succession to Third Army, First Army, Fifth Army, First Army, Third Army, to Fourth Army, and back to First Army, all within a period of less than six weeks.[21]

A member of Q Company remembered the most frantic days of the

German threat to Amiens as "the Nightmare of the Big Retreat."[22] Virtually the entire brigade worked on construction of defense breastworks; sixteen of the companies actually manned the defenses, and eight of these engaged in actual trench combat.[23] On 4 April, as an even more serious German breakthrough appeared imminent, Foulkes suggested that the gas companies be issued Lewis guns, add a machine-gun company, and convert temporarily to full infantry duty. Foulkes's plan was approved, and several companies began training with the Lewis guns; but before the plan could be fully implemented, the first German drive ground to a halt.[24]

The speed of the German advance meant for the Special Companies the loss of indispensable equipment—cylinders, mortars, and gas stores—near and in the front lines. On the first day No. 1 Company lost 17 mortars and 900 rounds. Where these could not be removed quickly small detachments of the Specials tried to get to them to destroy them, but many simply had to be abandoned. The German onslaught abruptly interrupted the "snip" duty of P Company, whose men sped off in lorries to retrieve as much as possible from the Courcelles dump, directly in the path of the enemy advance. They salvaged as much as time allowed and on 22 March blew up the remainder of the stores as the Germans closed in. Wilson's diary barely conceals the crisis atmosphere: "Heard that J Company has been sent in to help hold the line and very few had returned when we left. March 26: German advance continuing. Received order to pack kit and 'stand by' to protect dump. German cavalry said to be as near as Pas, four km. away."

In the ensuing few weeks, P Company was able to evacuate 80,000 cylinders by train. J. S. Heaton (L Company) recalled in 1976 a humorous aspect of one such otherwise perilous expedition:

> The C. O. sent for me and said "One of our companies has left some guns (projectors) in a dump on the Mont des Cats, and we don't want them to fall into the hands of the Germans. I want you to take a lorry and twenty men and see if you can recover them. You will have to be very cautious, for the Germans are very close to this point and may have over-run it by now. Choose your time very carefully. You will need enough light to find the guns and yet you must avoid observation." So I collected a lorry and twenty men, and we made our way to Boeschepe at the foot of the Mont des Cats. The place was absolutely deserted, the silence was uncanny. I told the fellows exactly what was required and when the time was right we crawled slowly up the hill. Nobody spoke. Just short of the top we stopped the lorry and turned it round ready for a quick get-a-way. No time was lost. We were quickly out of the lorry and

scouring the search area like a pack of dogs. We soon found ten guns but no more. We searched till it became quite dark. A flurry of light shells came over. Jerry was beginning to stir. We got back to the lorry and got away quickly.

The C. O. had not told me how many guns were involved, but, with twenty men, I expected about twenty guns and probably more. So, it was with some trepidation that I went to report my return with only ten guns.

He gazed sternly at me. "Dammit," said he. "There should only be eight."[25]

Along the relatively stationary fronts of the British First and Second Armies unaffected by "Michael," the interrupted projector gas attacks resumed, and planning continued for the long anticipated retired cylinder operation. C Company, while attached to First Army, managed a few cylinder operations in and around its old stomping grounds of the Loos area.

Ludendorff's second offensive, "Georgette," struck the British in the northern sector along the Lys River on the morning of 9 April. This time the initial blow fell upon Horne's First Army, crashing through the Portuguese 2d Division and scoring an advance of over three miles on the first day. (Gasmen had nicknamed the Portuguese the "Pork and Beans," but secret orders recommended public usage of the term "Our Oldest Allies."[26]) On the next day, 10 April, German divisions hit Plumer's Second Army on the left (north) of Horne's. A breakthrough on these fronts threatened potential disaster, menacing as it did not only Bethune and Hazebrouck, the important rail junction, but also a breakout right to the Channel ports, overrunning Helfaut and St. Omer along the way. It was on 10 April that Haig issued his famous "with our backs to the wall" order of the day.

The Germans advanced near La Bassée Canal with the benefit again of great quantities of mustard-gas shell, and the eight Special Companies operating with the First Army in this sector suffered severely, their war diaries indicating heavy casualties. Almost all officers of L Company were mustard gassed in early April, and replacements had to be sent from C Company.[27] On 13 April several bombs crashed into St. Omer, causing some civilian casualties.[28] Grantham noted in his diary that "civilians have wind up badly at Bosch advance," and summarized the situation in his characteristic vocabulary:

10 April: Inferno continues. Hun is nearing Bethune. Everyone clearing out. Everything in a muddle. Everyone flying. Refugees on road terrible. Have left behind in cellar pounds worth of kit.

13 April. All civilians ordered out this A.M. This place desolate. Never do I remember feeling so fed up as this afternoon. Took "Digne" the huge dog the Deldignes have left (and asked me to shoot) over to give him some dinner. . . . Bethune a mass of broken stones and glass everywhere. Hinges is worse—shelled to bits. . . . Bridges all mined.

14 April: Was told by Brigade Major (33th Bde) that all further carrying was washed out.

Fortunately Grantham found a new owner for Digne before French gendarmes physically ejected the Deldignes family members from their house. "One gendarme actually hit her [Mme. Deldigne] with a heavy stick."[29] The pages of Wilson's diary, too, convey the sense of emergency and war-weariness of these frantic days:

April 7: To Philosophe again, accompanied by a training squad of Americans, the first time they had been up the line. Great struggle through approach trench, half-filled with liquid mud, and party very slow. Most exhausting carry, 1 cylinder between 2, slung on a pole. One Yank, done up, swore he would carry the "go____-damned thing" to the top, for I had an idea that some had been dumped. On arrival at the trench he collapsed and had to be taken to the Medical Post.

April 8: Hun observation balloons up. Seen and shelled by Fritz for 3 1/2 hours with gas shell and shrapnel. Scattered, took shelter in dugout till 1 A.M., then no time to work, walked back over gas-ridden plain, stumbled along the Railway to billets. Many gassed in the several Companies.

April 9: Company a sight this morning on parade, eyes red and bleary from effect of gas.

April 11: The proportion of walk to work here is about 5–1.

April 12: Reported sick. Temperature 99.5, weak and feverish, eyes blood-shot, "gas" making itself felt. Throat sore too, and obstinate enough with big accumulation of phlegm. . . . all marquees crowded with cases, and many frightful sights. Forgot my own troubles in aiding the stretcher cases. . . .

April 14: Still no medical attention—but feeling no worse—certified for Light Duty. Aiding in Dispensary and stretcher-bearing to Operating Room and evacuating train for Base. Plenty of amputations going on and very bad gas cases in marquees.

Wilson spent over a month convalescing at the Casualty Clearing Station, simultaneously acting as orderly and attending wounded and doing light physical work around the camp. In mid-May he rejoined his company at Verquin.

For the remainder of April the military situation fluctuated between serious and desperate, reaching something of a crisis during the third week. Even military staff at the gas depot, both officers and men, except clerical, formed themselves into three emergency infantry companies to man the front line if necessary.[30] By the end of the month the most serious threats abated, and the Special Brigade returned to more normal activity. Enemy shelling in the Loos area continued, however, and on the afternoon of 17 May, Fox watched the final collapse of the Bethune cathedral.[31] During most of May, while the third and fourth German offensives targeted the French farther south, nineteen of the twenty-one gas companies worked with the First Army in Artois, where, though winds were generally unfavorable, the front had stabilized, and they carried out several small projector operations. As before, gas companies and sections were distributed among infantry units as needed and with scant regard to the brigade structure which existed on paper. On 13 June, for example, D section of No. 1 Mortar Company was lent to A Company to help with a smoke barrage while the rest of the company split between III Corps and the Anzac Corps.[32]

The American gas companies continued to operate in concert with the Special Brigade during the spring and with the French during the summer.[33] Subsequent to the arrival of Col. Amos Fries, Foulkes's American counterpart, the 1st Gas Regiment operated independently as part of the American Expeditionary Force. The numbers of the American gas soldiers were to reach a peak of 3,400 by the autumn of 1918.[34] Employing cylinder, projector, and Stokes mortar discharges, the American gas officers initially encountered resistance from their own infantry staffs almost identical to that met by the Special Brigade.[35] Neither Frederick March, chief of staff, nor Pershing were supporters of gas.[36]

In late May Foulkes finally was able to launch the first of his much-heralded retired cylinder operations. This ambitious technique, which he had outlined to his companies in the autumn of 1917, involved the discharge of a massive number of gas cylinders directly from light railway flatcars in "retired" rather than front-line areas. Gasmen loaded and secured hundreds of cylinders on railway flatcars in the safety of Reserve areas, usually in three to five tiers to facilitate wiring and handling. The simultaneous opening of the gas cylinders posed a problem, solved by Wilson of M Company, who suggested replacing the usual cylinder nozzles with breakaway spigots, to which were affixed detonators. With the cylinder valves closed, the Specials wired the detonators together. When optimal weather conditions obtained, petrol-electric tractors or light locomotives on either broad- or narrow-gauge lines propelled the entire train as close to the front as the main line extended.[37] On some occasions workmen separated the individual cars, then manually pushed each of them farther on separate rail-line extensions to broadside positions as close as a quarter of a mile to the front.

Just before zero hour, the gas personnel, in multicompany strength, opened the gas cylinder valves, the gas still contained by the spigots, and connected all the detonator wires together electrically to a remote plunger. At zero, with all infantry withdrawn from the front lines, the detonators exploded, the spigots blew off, and the gas hissed out of the hundreds of cylinders on each of the flatcars simultaneously. Following the discharge, the goal was to get away, in the words of one Special, "before all hell broke loose."[38] Within minutes the emissions from the various rail junctions converged and formed a cloud of more densely concentrated gas than obtained by any other method. The resulting spectacle resembled an arc or beam, and most gas soldiers referred to this method as the beam attack.[39]

The retired cylinder, or beam attack, offered distinct advantages over both projectors and earlier means of cylinder deployment. The method promised far greater safety, at least during most of the preparatory stages, since prior loading and wiring of the cylinders on the flatcars in safe Reserve areas avoided both the hazards of front-line installation as well as the arduous carry-in. Discharging the gas directly from the trains minimized the handling in the danger zones and kept the vulnerable cylinders protected until the last possible moment. The only apparent drawback was that the expected greater concentration of gas released all at once from behind the front lines would necessitate a temporary infantry evacuation from those affected areas. Foulkes entertained the greatest hopes, for the spectacular success of the retired cylinder method would conclusively corroborate his peculiarly unique faith in cloud gas. He originally proposed a huge, and he hoped devastating, attack involving the entire brigade in a simultaneous discharge greater than ever before, again envisioning a scenario in which the entire British Army awaited the Special Brigade gas to clear a path.

The opportunity to attempt such a discharge came the night of 24/25 May just southwest of Lens, along a part of the First Army sector unaffected by either of the first two German offensives. Three Special Companies, F, B, and O, prepared 4,725 cylinders and loaded them onto trains the evening of 24 May. B Company experienced severe difficulties as an early derailment smashed detonators, wires, and electrical equipment in several of the railcars. Then, as infantry parties pushed the railcars over banked track the last several hundred yards to the

Tram loaded for gas beam attack. (Courtesy of Imperial War Museum)

front, the track gave way under the weight, and three more cars tipped over, spilling the cylinders onto the ground. As some men repaired the track, others collected the scattered cylinders and stood them up in a shell hole from which they were fired simultaneously with the others.[40] Amid a burst of Lewis gunfire intended to muffle the explosions, the three companies successfully discharged 3,789 cylinders. B Company commander A. J. Sumner reported that "the cloud kept very low and did not appear to spread very much. It was possible to stand two yards to the side of it without being inconvenienced." Most of the 25 percent loss was due to the transport accidents, which smashed electrical circuits, and to faulty electrical detonators.[41] One of the officers of the 10th Canadian Railway Troops who had laid the narrow railway for this cylinder tram later claimed, "I even helped turn on the cylinders," a surprising revelation indeed, if true.[42] The technical execution of the new beam attack seemed successful, although once again there was no immediate indication of the effect on the German lines. B Company at once began preparations for another beam attack, but not before recommending that different railcars be supplied for the return journey because of the residual gas in the cylinder cars.

A month later P Company (Wilson's unit) staged the first of its several beam attacks in the Ypres area.

June 19: Warned about tea-time for line at 5 P.M.; just time for wash and tea. Work at same spot, restacking and testing cylinders in waggons. Got a good many "whiffs" of gas. Train ready by 8:30 P.M. Hands ached, and clothing reeked from testing (Phosgene Gas). This is quite a new type of stunt for Company.

June 21: Sent on to Dump at Piselhock at 9:30 A.M., to place detonators in cylinders and help in wiring the 2000 cylinders. Returned for dinner at 12:45 P.M. and on dump again at 2:15 P.M. Worked hard till 7 P.M. Back to camp at 8:10 P.M., had tea and walked into village to buy soap and a newspaper. Before "light out," Sergt. Botteril came in to warn the party for pooping off in stunt, 20 altogether, of whom I am one. The idea is to take waggons with cylinders up on Light Railway by petrol engine, then with aid of a party of infantry . . . to push and pull waggons to required point behind front line, about 1500 yards from Boche positions. Then run back with roll of wire about 50 yards, attach ends to exploders, push down handle and off go detonators and gas issues from broken nozzles. Slept well tonight as very tired; can sleep well now on boards when fatigued.

June 22: The longest day! Getting exploders and spanners ready for Poop tonight, if wind favourable. Looked to wiring and found it done wrongly. Made alterations and started the "turn-on" wheel. Train went off while still light, and moved slowly along the meandering line through fields of potatoes and ripening corn. . . . There were seven trains in all, our section having two trains, with a total of 49 trucks [railcars] and about 1000 cylinders in them. One engine left the line 4 times and caused delay. The moon was full, unfortunately from our point of view, but night beautiful, and our work ghastly; wind moderate. What a way of spending a pleasant Summer evening! Trains proceeded over road beyond Shrapnel Corner drawn by parties of infantry, 5 to a truck, and was carried out well. I was on third truck with Morris; carried out leads at once, and connected to exploders. Then on signal from left of train, put exploders down, and gas went over in a beautiful creeping cloud just above the surface. Continued delivery for about 5–10 minutes and then turned off. Found four cylinders had not gone off, in addition to four duds. Got a fair dose of gas. With Dan's arm for guide, stumbled down to asylum at Ypres. Last year a stunt of this nature would have been impossible during advance. In war of movement, gas stunts hardly possible, as far as I can see.

The largest of all beam attacks, involving four companies, B, C, F, and O, six separate railheads, and over 5,000 cylinders, took place near Hulluch the night of 12/13 July. A Company also participated in the preparatory work, but owing to an infantry relief (Canadian Corps) taking place on 12 July, A Company had to postpone its beam discharge for a week.[43] Fox rode C Company's pilot engine and officer Grantham the train of sixty flatcars stacked with 1,260 phosgene cylinders.

> On each truck one man was posted as guard. It did not require a very vivid imagination to imagine what would happen if our completely unprotected train came under fire. Out on the void of the plain the heavily-laden trucks produced more noise than was desirable as they continued nearer and nearer to the trenches. The main body of the Company walked up to the rendezvous in small parties where they waited for the train's arrival. At last it drew slowly into position and stopped. The driver removed his engine some distance back for safety. Sections took charge of the trucks as appointed and made the final adjustments and checks. After that, there was nothing to do but wait. For the greater part of two hours we waited orders and a favourable wind.
>
> Gradually, to our relief, the wind freshened and swung to the direction we needed. As Zero approached, conditions became eminently suitable. Thus at 1:40 A.M. Grantham "pooped" the whole train successfully. Everybody stood well back as the detonators showered in the explosion. Immediately there ensued a terrific hissing noise as a huge release of gas commenced. The dense, grey cloud made an awe-inspiring sight as it rolled steadily forward, widening as it went. We watched it as it poured over our own Front Lines and continued across No Man's Land. Such a threatening cloud as this we had never before witnessed. Over the enemy Lines the gas belt spread wider and wider, engulfing them from sight.

Fox found himself in charge of one of the return trains. Just as the driver reconnected the railcars to the engine, some enemy shells exploded nearby.

> Our engine-driver, who had been waiting for the order to go, at once took it upon himself to make the move. I was near the rear of the train at the time, when a sudden lurching and jerking of the trucks told me that it was off. I raced toward the front, but it was of no avail. Some of the guards scrambled onto the trucks as the train gathered speed. It rattled homewards across the plain at a frightening rate, with the men clinging on for dear life; they were enveloped in the gas which still issued from the dripping cylinders. Their respirators saved them, though it was a ghastly ride.[44]

The tone of Grantham's diary was more calm and succinct: "I fired train by switch near engine. Magnificent cloud."[45] B Company also experienced the usual derailment difficulties, this time losing thirty railcars down an embankment, but nevertheless achieving a 65 percent discharge.[46] Nor had things gone smoothly in O Company. On one rail line, six cars derailed because railway points had been wrongly set, and several others derailed due to spreading rails. Leaking spigot bursters forced premature discharge of many cylinders. The company found that 163 detonators malfunctioned and 353 spigots did not break off on detonation.[47] As with other gas stunts, the beam attack was not as easy to accomplish on the battlefield as on paper, but Foulkes sanguinely reported a huge success and noted reports of two hundred German casualties from one regiment alone.

A week later on 21 July, A Company, led by Adrian Hodgkin, was able to carry out its part of the beam attack originally planned to be in concert with that of 12/13 July. John Thomas in section 5 was in charge of the train from the dump to the discharge point:

The train went at a walking pace starting at 9 P.M. Passing through cuttings to the east of Arras I saw thousands of swallows, every little broken tree and shrub was covered with them. I thought they were resting perhaps on their journey south. I was glad they were on the right side of the gas beam. A few shells were falling here and there but we arrived at the firing position without mishap around 12 midnight. The wired circuits were tested and found O.K. The men turned on the spindles quickly and all was ready by 1:05. Capt. Hodgkin was responsible for the actual discharge, and my heart sank when he hesitated and wondered whether the wind was in the right position. Fortunately parts of the sky were clear and the Polar star could be plainly seen. I drew Hodgkin's attention to this and turning to face a westerly wind said that we would never get a better chance to release the gas. All the infantry had been withdrawn behind the firing position. Moving towards the little Petrol-Electric engine that had brought the train up, Hodgkin connected the ends of the cable to fire the train and pressed the firing button.

A dense cloud rose quickly from the train and was wafted forward by a light wind over the enemy lines. This occurred at 1:07 A.M. By 1:40 the discharge had finished and about 60,000 lbs. of gas had been released. The men then proceeded to turn off the spindles to avoid traces of gas being left to cause any trouble on the return journey. When the engine approached to take the train back (the engine was to the rear of the train and had pushed the train on the forward journey), a coupling broke and two trucks went careening towards the German line, where they were derailed at a broken part of the tramway. . . . It was found impossible to replace the trucks on the line, so the cylinders (empty) were removed and hidden in a dugout nearby. The empty trucks were left to be shattered by shell-fire when the enemy saw them at dawn. I took the remaining trucks back to Artillery Dump and we reached billets about 4:30 A.M.[48]

Hodgkin does not mention the moment of indecision alluded to by Thomas, but does admit to some anxious moments afterward: "There was a full moon and one could see the cloud well: it spread rather wide at first and frightened me awfully for fear it would go outside the danger limits. However it didn't, nor did the subsequent SE which sprang up about 4 A.M. seem to have any effect."[49] But the gas attack killed three Canadians who had somehow not been evacuated from the danger zone. Later "Chitty," Thomas's fellow section officer, worried that "we should be court-martialed if we [again] gassed our own men," but the fault really lay with the Canadian infantry officer in charge.[50]

The greater concentration of gas generated by the beam attack, unfortunately, greatly increased the dangers of blow-back. In late August, O and P Companies, after waiting on a favorable wind for several hours, pushed the plungers in an uneven wind with fatal consequences.

For the first time the wind did a complete turn-around and gas falling over side of trucks like a waterfall, came back on us. We retreated about 100 yards, leaving weapons near train. At this moment machine-gun played round us for a while. The pulling party of Yanks had settled down in shell-holes mostly waiting till stunt was over, and no doubt were dozing. A good many were caught and gassed; a couple unfortunately succumbed.[51]

This proved to be the last beam attack of the war, as the accelerating German retreat increasingly deprived the gasmen of the necessary range. All told, the Special Companies carried out ten beam attacks, one in May, one in June, five in July, and three in August, discharging slightly over 27,000 cylinders.[52] The effectiveness of the beam attack, however, remains questionable. In spite of Foulkes's usual sanguine appraisal, Fritz Haber told Hartley after the war that the Germans knew nothing about this kind of delivery system, so that either the brigade had been completely successful in its efforts at disguise or the results were indistinguishable from other methods of gas delivery.[53] Hartley considered the elaborate operation a waste of time.[54]

Meanwhile the last of Ludendorff's five spring offensives had sputtered out. Reinforced at Château Thierry and a few other crucial places by a modest injection of fresh Yanks, the Allied line had held. Germany had played out its last bid for victory. Foch launched the French counterattack on 18 July. It was everywhere successful. Three weeks later, in the predawn hours of 8 August, in front of Amiens, Rawlinson's Fourth Army joined in. With the benefit of over five hundred tanks, Australian and Canadian troops broke out of the trenches and scored gains measured in miles the first day, spreading panic and demoralization through German lines. On this, Ludendorff's "black day," sixteen thousand German prisoners surrendered. Three days later, 11 August, Byng's Third Army thrust forward toward Bapaume, and later in the month Horne's First Army moved forward in the Arras sector. By the end of August, Allied armies had recovered most of the territory lost in the five German spring offensives. The final Allied push was under way.

As the balance of battle tilted from defense to counterattack, the Special Companies continued to operate but were forced to accommodate to mobile warfare by means of more frequent but smaller extemporized strikes, usually without much infantry coordination. Fast retreating targets meant repeated cancellations and forced the abandonment of traditional gas tactics. The absence of a stabilized front precluded the orthodox installation of either cylinders or Livens projectors, for even a shallow retreat might take the enemy lines beyond the reach of gas. By early September A Company found that the mobility of the front made even projector attacks "almost impossible."[55] On 7 September C Company found itself preparing a projector attack against abandoned German trenches.

Innovations continued to the very last. One of the new transport methods introduced about this time was the tank projector sledge. The sledges could be loaded in safe Reserve areas in similar fashion to the trains and pulled into position by Mark IV tanks, which could be fitted with towing gear in about three hours. The sledge itself was constructed so that in folded position it served as a transport sledge, and when unfolded in the field by its eight-man team, functioned as the firing foundation base for the projectors. One tank pulled two such sledges, each of which might bear a weight of up to two tons. Four slotted wooden beams which held the projectors on the sledge during transport also served as foundation supports for six projectors in the field. The Third Army constructed sixteen of these sledges for use by the Special Brigade.

In early September sections of No. 1 Special Company laid plans for small-scale blitzkrieg tactics, with lorries permanently assigned, loaded, and "ready to move forward rapidly at short notice."[56] A Company sank projectors in shallower trenches, supported instead by sandbags, saving

Tank sledge loaded with sixteen projectors ready for transport. (Courtesy of Liddle Collection, Leeds)

time both in installing and removing.[57] Eventually even such extemporizing tactics became patently futile. The sudden German retreat from Amiens spoiled one of the most well-prepared Special Brigade operations. With the First Army, Hodgkin (commanding A Company) echoed a widely felt frustration at the loss of targets: "The Bosch will probably

Tank sledge deployed and extended, with sixteen projectors resting on slots in the extended sledge ready for firing. (Courtesy of Liddle Collection, Leeds)

withdraw after the fall of Cambrai and thus escape the 6 2/3 tons of gas that I have got waiting for him. . . . Very disappointing for us personally, but very good from all other points of view." More and more with each day's passing the prospect of the enemy's retreat threatened carefully planned operations. "Two sections making up the line tonight; I fear their work is wasted unless I can get Corps to order the discharge for tomorrow."[58]

Disagreements that had been going on between Foulkes and the Porton personnel continued. In early August rumors circulated that Foulkes was to lose his job because, in Hodgkin's words, "he makes himself so objectionable to Lt. Col. Crossley who runs our hopelessly inefficient Experimental Station at Porton. I hope the rumour is untrue."[59] Foulkes contended that observations of the effects of gases in true combat situations were invariably superior to laboratory simulations conducted at Porton and characterized these differences of opinion as a "friendly dispute."[60]

After about the first week of October, the Allied advance now in full swing, the battle zone intruded more and more into areas hitherto behind German lines, and the presence of great numbers of French civilians remaining in these areas retarded even localized gas activity on the British front.[61] As their specialized work gradually became more infeasible, the chemist-soldiers gained time for reflection and relaxation, for tennis and football. Tagging along with advancing infantry across the countryside that had been so desperately contested for over four years, they observed scenes of destruction which awed even these battle-hardened veterans. On the last day of September, Wilson's first unhindered look at no man's land along the Belgian front revealed

a vast devastated area of four years of trench warfare. As far as the eye can see truly a piteous spectacle. Trees standing dead, stark and bare, the remains of woods, shell-holes innumerable, pill-boxes rent by shell-fire, . . . debris of all sorts, munitions, rifles, equipment, bodies alas of Germans horribly battered, and of our Belgian allies.

October 15: The destruction over Passchendaele . . . is absolutely appalling. . . . Not a tree alive by road or in woods, each of them just branchless, topless, and withered, and torn by shell.[62]

The German retreat from Flanders accelerated to the point that Thomas considered "there seemed no chance of our being able to catch him in one position long enough to mount a gas attack."[63] Platnauer, with O Company, manned the Arras front: "There was not a live Hun in sight for miles facing that part of the 1st Army front, consequently no targets for our projector attacks or even the longer range Beam Attacks. We were, temporarily, out of a job." In lieu of its normal work, the company was ordered to search for and salvage projectors abandoned earlier in the war. "It was something of a picnic. We took a Company Cook and haversack rations and I remember that it was a bright, warm, autumn day with the promise of some interesting new terrain to explore in the sunshine. We had the whole day for a cushy job. . . . Everyone was in high spirits."[64]

During most of the last month of the war the companies engaged in railway repairs, crater-filling, de-gassing operations, and routine field labor. During one of these decontamination fatigues Platnauer encountered unexpected danger while on what he thought was a cushy job.

The Bosch were on the run at last and static warfare was over. . . . Soon we were found some work clearing out underground "barracks" which the Germans had constructed with such thoroughness as part of their Front Trench system.

I set off with half the Company on the first of these ventures. . . . It was something of a holiday, though I was worried about this new and unknown job. Our destination was Henin Lietard, a ruined small town some miles behind the old German Front Line on the road to Douai. Intelligence had reported that many of these large dug-outs were mined, booby-trapped and some filled with gas. The latter was our main objective. We carried an assortment of tools—wire-cutters, axes, electrical equipment for testing and detonating, cylinders of chlorine (it was said that chlorine neutralized mustard gas!) and drums of paraffin and petrol.

On arriving at our objective, I realized that it was useless and dangerous to take 150 men down dug-out steps into the unknown; though my rough plan, made from vague Intelligence reports showed at least four entrances and sleeping quarters underground for about 1000 men. Leaving the Company in the open, I took two senior sergeants and began to reconnoitre.

We trod warily on the way down; cutting anything that looked like trip wires—and there were quite a number. Then the three of us worked our way slowly to the lower level, and by torch light made our way gingerly along the corridors, noting with astonishment the strength and thickness of the concrete, and the tiers of well-constructed bunks—a veritable palace compared with our familiar infantry "hovels." One of the sergeants called back from a bend: "Some exploded shells in this corner! Maybe gas shells!" They were; 6" and 8" howitzer projectiles, split open with some

small explosive charge, the whitish-yellow powder of freshly exposed mustard gas in heaps beside them!!! Previously, I had been
working in my gas mask with mouthpiece and nose-clip in position but with eyes exposed at times because of the difficulty of seeing in unfamiliar surroundings. The smell of pungent "garlic"
made it essential to don the whole face-piece before going further.
Rounding the bend, to my consternation, I saw the two sergeants,
Jo Cross and Don Britton, bending over the big shells and examining the stuff *without their gas-masks on.* I yelled to them in no uncertain terms to put their gas-masks on immediately. Both were
old regulars; both wore Mons Stars; they should have known better. . . . I realized afterwards that, having worked so much with
our own gas, they had a contempt for gas in general. Though we
had all been through German mustard gas bombardments and
knew the smell of it and that, normally, it was not particularly lethal, this was their first experience of it in high concentration and
at close quarters; Alas, it was their last.

A small party brought down drums of paraffin and petrol, satu-
rated the wooden props and other combustible material and set the
place alight. I understand that the damn place underground burned
by slow combustion for days. I was not there to witness it; neither
were the two sergeants; Cross died in his billet the next morning
and Britton was taken to hospital in extremis. And I, having in-
haled comparatively little of the foul stuff, woke up the same
morning, temporarily blinded, sores on the forehead and under the
arms and with no voice.[65]

Platnauer, following a brief stay at Douai Hospital, was to spend Armistice Day in a Manchester Hospital, but eventually made a full recovery. Britton died in the hospital.

The brigade operated in 1918 far below normal strength. It began the
active season 700 men short, and by September, was under strength by
1,355, fully 25 percent of normal. Much of the shortage was attributable
to casualties during the year—11 officers and 124 men killed, 60 officers
and 1,326 men wounded.[66] In April, E Company reported two-thirds of
its men sick, and only 30 fully fit for work.[67] In July, C Company was
down to an average strength of only 170.[68] During the late summer a particularly virulent disease, possibly the Spanish flu, ravaged the brigade.
War diaries commonly referred to it as the "3-day fever," or, by this
time thoroughly addicted to alphabet abbreviation, P.U.D. (plague, unknown disease) or P.U.O. (plague of unknown origin). By mid-July it

was already decimating all ranks, and men from A Company had to be sent off to bolster B Company, which was especially hard hit.

As the Allied advance gained momentum the men of the Special Companies shared in the adulation and joy of the throngs of liberated French people. "I haven't been kissed yet," wrote Hodgkin in late October, "but I have been waved at several times. Nearly all the men take off their hats to us."[69] As rumors of the end of the war multiplied during the second week of November, a spirit of relief and excitement permeated the ranks of the gas companies. News of Kaiser Wilhelm's abdication circulated on 9 November, and the next day A Company beat G Company five to two in a football match.

Meanwhile the Americans were in the midst of their toughest fighting of the war. They had launched their offensive against St. Mihiel Salient on 12 September. In October General Fries asked Foulkes for some relief for his overworked gas companies, and as the rapid advance in the British sector prevented the Special Companies from operating normally in any event, Foulkes dispatched nine companies (C, D, E, F, J, O, P, Z, and No. 3 Mortar, under the commands of Bunker and Campbell-Smith) to the American sector during the first week of November. The Americans were by that time in the thick of the Argonne fighting and their own gas regiment was extremely active. From the following account, at least one American company had learned the game well.

> Just after midnight, 160 projector bombs went over, loaded with T.N.T. About 15 or 20 seconds later, another 160 bombs went over, loaded with phosgene/chlorine mixture. Zero was at 6 A.M. and we preceded this with several Stokes mortars sending over with rapid fire with bombs of Thermit and phosphorus. The first wave of Marines walked through our forward positions with their rifles slung over their shoulders and made several miles that day.[70]

None of the nine Special Companies arrived in time to commence actual gas operations with the Americans, but their too-late transfer meant that the men of these companies ended their war in the unfamiliar areas of Verdun and Metz. Wilson arrived at Verdun in time to hear of the Armistice: "November 11: God has indeed been good to have spared so many of us to see this day and enable us to return home to Blighty once again. And the enemy will one day thank us for bringing a murderous autocrat from his throne."[71] With these earnest words Wilson brought his wartime dairy to an end.

The men of the Special Brigade greeted news of the Armistice with mixed emotions. As is always the case at the end of wars, return to civilian life was a welcome relief to some, a difficult adjustment for others. Hodgkin did not learn of the Armistice until the day following its signing: "I feel most awfully at a loose end now and so does everyone else. Now that there is to be in all probability no more fighting one has no aim before one for which to work. . . . the thought of going back to regular office hours rather appalls me at times!"[72] On arrival home, however, one reaction was universal: "The people at home didn't want to hear anything about the war."[73]

As the Special Brigade did not participate in the occupation forces, its companies were gradually withdrawn to home bases around Helfaut. While awaiting demobilization, the army, true to form, kept everyone busy. Instructors offered a variety of useful courses, including shorthand, math, French, bookkeeping, mechanics, chemistry, botany, algebra, German, and chemical engineering.[74] Several of the Special Companies were occupied briefly in decontaminating cellars, filling in trenches, cleaning up villages, repairing roads and bridges, "dull and cold work."[75] In early November, N Company had begun the construction of a Leeming ropeway across the Sambre River at Berlaimont. The company completed it on 13 November and began disassembling it on 15 November.[76] One of the major long-term chores involved continued salvage operations. During the first three weeks of January 1919, No. 1 Special Company salvaged 704 projectors, 635 base-plates, and 7 1/2 tons of scrap iron.[77]

The end of the war stranded thousands of gas cylinders, all of which had to be carefully gathered in for emptying at decontamination dumps. Over forty tons of phosgene accumulated at the main gas dump at Les Attaques. The cylinder tops had been welded, but winter rusting created some leakage. Although the leaking cylinders were buried, an increasing number of complaints from barge workers on the nearby canal indicated the need for a more permanent solution. In July 1919, GHQ decided to send some of the gas cylinders to a factory in the village of Morecombe in England where the phosgene could be used to make dyes. The soldiers loaded 1,500 of the cylinders onto eight railway cars. D. C. Murphy, O Company, accompanied the strange train as guard. During the Channel crossing, gas seeped into the ship's engine room, and although the guards disposed of the leaking cylinder overboard, volunteers had to lend gas masks to the engine crew. On the English side, at Richborough, more leaks developed as the open cars paused at a siding all afternoon in the hot sun and Murphy and crew buried two more leaking cylinders. During the night the train slowly made its way through London, Murphy sleeping in the brake van with the guard at the rear of the train. In the countryside to the west of London he awoke to the unmistakable smell of gas, the guard already red and coughing:

The white cloud was traveling back down the train and streaming into the van. The train slowed and stopped at a signal. A cross wind took the gas over open fields until the cylinder was empty. A chorus of mooing and bleating arose and we learnt later that the War Office had to meet a heavy claim for animals killed by gas.

Following delivery of the gas to Morecombe, Murphy returned to Richborough where the remaining cylinders were guarded twenty-four hours a day. No further train transport was attempted, and after six weeks the guards buried the leaking cylinders ''on a deserted stretch of foreshore,'' amid rumors that the officer who ordered the shipment was facing court martial.[78]

Another group of Specials volunteered to accompany a mission to Russia to assist General Denikin's White Army, among them Davies, W. E. Saunders, J. Laycock, and Grantham. The small band left France in July 1919, sailing to Archangel via Murmansk. After a brief pause in Archangel for language study, they continued by boat to Obersaskaya. There the chemist adventurers demonstrated smoke clouds and released some arsenical smokes, Grantham and Laycock took advantage of the situation to study the geology of the area, and Saunders set up a profitable trade in furs. But nothing further of a military nature came of the expedition, and the British gas entourage shortly withdrew.[79]

Most of the Special Companies remained in skeletal existence until the summer of 1919 when demobilization was completed. Foulkes himself stayed in France until the last, departing for England on 22 May 1919, and at noon on that day the Directorate of Gas Services ceased. The experimental center at Porton in Salisbury, Wiltshire, continued after the war, its name changed to Chemical Defense Experimental Establishment, and again in 1991 to Chemical and Biological Defence Establishment. The memory of its Special Brigade origins was perpetuated by its adoption of the green, white, and red colors of the brassards worn by members of the Special Brigade in the early days.[80] During the Second World War the village of Helfaut became a German V-I site, and St. Omer, the headquarters of the brigade for much of the Great War, became a German air base.

16
No Humanitarian Scruples

"Chemical warfare has been branded as inhumane. Humanity is not a word to mention when discussing War."[1]

Since antiquity, states at war have utilized with few qualms whatever weapons contemporary science could suggest and technology could deliver.[2] Herodotus reported quite complacently the strategic placement of Bactrian baggage camels in the forefront of the Median battle line where their distinctive odor caused the horses of their Lydian enemy to bolt. Thucydides wrote with detachment of the primitive but inventive use of sulfur and pitch in the Peloponnesian War. Tacitus described occasional Roman use of another chemical blend, invented, like so much else that Rome appropriated, by the Greeks. Later called "Greek fire," it was the closest classical equivalent to chemical weapons until the invention of shellfire. The Chinese invented and used "stink-pots" with some success. Da Vinci, a military as well as artistic genius, suggested the bombardment of enemy warships with shells containing a mixture of sulfur and arsenic dust. Through the ages military science has welcomed the development of improved weaponry as ingenious and clever, a thoroughly natural employment of chemistry, physics, and engineering technology in the interests of battlefield success, and not in any way diabolical or unfair.

However that may be, it remains difficult to regard 20th century chemical weaponry dispassionately.[3] The post–World War II development of horrific nerve gases has but added to the stigma. No weapons are ever pleasant, but some are less pleasant than others, and "poison gas" would seem to fall into the latter category. One feels intuitively something unfair and inhumane, something inherently different, something sinister about poison gas that makes it an outlaw weapon. To this day news of the use of chemical warfare by any nation evokes a greater emotional recoil than the use of conventional weapons and conjures images of villainous atrocity.

Citizens and pundits ignorant of the modern battlefield almost universally stigmatized poison gas as uniquely diabolical and assumed that the soldiers widely shared similar sentiments. In this assumption, as with so much else, they were quite mistaken. It is true that virtually everyone in the Allied armies condemned the German first use of gas: Sid Fox thought it "diabolical,"[4] Lefebure, "monstrous."[5] But their initial outrage was based less on the weapon itself than on the callous violation of the spirit if not the letter of international accords that its introduction represented. James Pratt was a lieutenant commanding an infantry platoon in April 1915 when the first German gas attack took place. In the 1970s oral historians at the Imperial War Museum interviewed Pratt:

Q. Do you remember whether there was any particular reactions amongst the troops to the German first use of gas?
A. Not among the troops themselves. We took it all as part of the war. . . . In war, you can expect anything, you see.
Q. But it was a particularly novel and insidious weapon; I'm surprised you didn't have a slightly different reaction to it.
A. It was only later on when we heard the views expressed by the politicians and so on that this was a breach of the Hague Convention and so on that we began to think about it in that strain.[6]

Soldiers tended to direct any moral outrage at war itself rather than at the use of a particular weapon such as poison gas. In a surreal world of random danger and discomfort, where rats and lice brought constant misery, the unexpected whizz-bang or underground mine explosion might bring unspeakable mutilation, or a sniper's bullet instant death, there seemed little reason to differentiate weapons in any rational fashion: "If you are a combat soldier, there is not a great deal of difference between being gassed, having a bayonet through the chest, an incendiary bullet through the lungs, a belly ripping hunk of shell casing or a squirt of napalm. The quickest way to get it over with is the most humane."[7]

But what of the chemist-turned-soldier asked to orchestrate the discharge of poison gas on his fellow man? Did he ever ponder the ethics of his mission? Surprisingly the gasmen's diaries reveal no hint of guilt or self-recrimination associated with the kind of warfare the Specials were waging. They, like Tommies in general, tended to regard gas as just another weapon. For Ashley, gas was no more objectionable "on moral or any other grounds" than high explosives.[8] Capt. Norman Campbell, deeply religious, conscientious, and sensitive to his fam-

Line of gassed soldiers. (Courtesy of Imperial War Museum)

ily's sentiments, wrote candidly to his wife of these concerns about a year before his death in 1917:

> In case you have any doubts . . . as to whether my particular job is an honourable one or not, I should just like to say this, that except for a few days at the very beginning out here, I have never had any doubts about it being right. The old knightly rule of warfare was to give every man a fair chance individually, but I cannot see that is based on any essential principle, or it has been washed out by such things as shells and mines, if nothing else.[9]

Many others in the brigade were men of conscience who wrote of morality in their letters and diaries and likewise seemed undisturbed by gas retaliation. Pioneer Percy Dixon, C Company, was a candidate for holy orders. Berrisford, one of the battalion commanders, became a Hampshire rector and joked with his parishioners about his gas experiences. The sensitive and conscientious Parkes nowhere in his diary suggests any scruples about the gas mission. Even Garfield Powell, a vitriolic critic of war and its cruelty, never once attached any special onus to poison gas.

Another popular myth of the Great War was that gas was an unnecessarily cruel weapon. For those unfortunate initial victims who ingested large amounts of chlorine or phosgene without adequate protection the answer would seem to be undoubtedly in the affirmative. All statistical studies indicate, however, that after the introduction of appropriate protective measures, the overall ratio of deaths to casualties was dramatically lower for gas casualties (3–4 percent) than for other types of injuries (over 25 percent).[10] In the majority of cases of minor gassing, the invariable result was temporary incapacitation rather than permanent injury. Even some severe cases of phosgene poisoning recovered completely over time. Dr. Claude Douglas, Royal Army Medical Corps, who certainly ought to have known better than anyone, considered that in comparison with permanent injuries associated with shell and bullet wounds, gas poisoning was "more humane."[11] J. B. S. Haldane, professor of biochemistry at Cambridge and a well-known and ardent supporter of gas warfare, castigated the double standard by which death by poison gas was condemned while death by high explosive was condoned. In the 1920s Haldane only half-jokingly urged the greater use of mustard gas in any future war as a humanitarian act.[12]

One of the most sensationalizing and evocative images of gas warfare is John Singer Sargent's picture of eleven pitiful and blindfolded gas victims hobbling along the road to Amiens, each soldier's hand resting on the shoulder of the one next in line. The huge painting, measuring over seven-and-a-half-feet high and over twenty-feet long and displayed prominently in the Sargent gallery of the National Army Museum in Chelsea, in no way suggests the reality that 75 percent of these victims suffered only temporary eye irritation and were fit for duty again within three months or less.[13] A. L. Robins, gassed at Cambrai, experienced a bad cold and sore throat and took to bed for a week. "This was just the treatment needed. . . . I was fit and back with my unit." Robins's case was not in the least unusual.[14] The following letter, "to Mother," written in uneven lines weaving diagonally across the page by a soldier with bandaged eyes, is typical:

> I am afraid the War Office may have alarmed you with a lot more of their insensate telegraphing. The truth is that I have had a touch of gas and the trouble about gas is that it is apt to get at your eyes a bit. Mine are kept at the moment under bandages, so that accounts for this scrawly letter. In every other way I am perfectly cheerful and well. . . . In about three days I expect to go back to the battery.[15]

Scratched across a copy of Sargent's picture among the Foulkes Papers at King's College London is the notation in his son Tom's hand: "CHF hated this picture and considered such things demoralizing."[16] Thuillier, too, regarded the painting as "maudlin sentiment."[17] The stark truth, surprising as it sounds, is that for the most part, soldiers wounded by gas rather than shrapnel or bullets were the lucky ones.

Gen. William Sibert, who headed the American Chemical Warfare Service, was asked in a congressional hearing whether he considered gas to be a cruel method of warfare: "Not a cruel method. I look upon it as the most humane element in War. It should be said that of our [gas] casualties only 3 or 4 percent died and of those that lived nearly all of them are getting well.[18] This is all the more compelling since the American soldiers, brashly heedless of safety, suffered more from gas per day in action than any other national combatants: 75,000 gas casualties out of a total of 275,000.[19] Liddell Hart, a veteran who served in three different British divisions in the Great War and later became one of the most prominent military historians in Britain, characterized gas as an "ideal weapon" and, as employed in that war, the "least inhumane" of all weapons.[20] This may seem to be going too far, but it was the virtually unanimous verdict of those who were most familiar with gas on the Great War battlefield. More recently, the head of the United States Army's weapons modernization program, Col. Robert Orton, stated the modern case simply and dispassionately: "People say that coughing your lungs out in three minutes because of nerve agent is an immoral way of dying, while bleeding to death in twelve because your leg has been shot off is better. Those arguments leave me cold."[21]

Furthermore, defensive gas capability far outpaced the offensive. Improvised gas masks appeared in the trenches within days of the first German gas attack and continuous improvement of defensive equipment followed. Gas advisors, gas schools, gas training, and a system of gas alerts all lessened the threat. Correct wearing of the mask minimized or prevented most serious gas injuries. With the exception of the steel helmet, the Great War soldier had virtually no equivalent protection against the myriad other hazards of front-line duty. A prudent soldier was better protected from severe gassing than from rifle- or shellfire, shrapnel, or any other weapon.

Foulkes had little patience with sentimentality or moral hand-wringing concerning the ethics of particular weapons. In a speech in late 1916 the commander of the Special Brigade brushed aside the view that gas warfare was a new type of warfare which was subject to moral debate. "We are not concerned with the ethics of the use of gas in civilized warfare."[22] Neither Foulkes nor most of his Specials, it seems, harbored any moral qualms about their gas mission. Gas warfare was admittedly atrocious, but most felt, like Lefebure, that it was nonetheless "less atrocious" than other forms.[23] It fell to Gale to answer the question at hand most directly and succinctly: "We feel no humanitarian scruples on the subject."[24] A reasonably thoughtful person may well believe war to be morally indefensible, but a term such as "inhumane weapon" seems indeed an oxymoron par excellence.

Aside from the moral questions, a second set of more practical issues concerns the strategy and tactics of gas warfare as waged by the Special Brigade. The effectiveness of any military arm depends to a large extent on integration and close cooperation with the other branches. Both were lacking in this case, and in fact, the Special Brigade's mission suffered to a considerable degree from a pervasive spirit of ignorance and obstructiveness on the part of the high command as well as from widespread infantry resentment. George Pollitt, member of the Special Companies from 1915 to 1917, when he took over an infantry battalion, commented that "the staff were determined not to make use of it [gas] and queered it always."[25] Walter Campbell-Smith, citing an unnamed corps commander who "scornfully condemned the use of gas as a most unsporting form of warfare," concluded that the notion of gas was "profoundly distasteful" to the army.[26] Also working against acceptance was the fact that the army command could not document substantial enemy casualties directly attributable to gas. Furthermore, Maj. J. C. Hill, Chemical Advisor to the Third Army, claimed that the Army regarded chemists as "faddists" whom it had to tolerate. "The Army machine doesn't understand what Research means. *Immediate* results are wanted."[27] Many of those most knowledgeable about the Gas Services in all its forms complained about a generalized scientific ineptitude in higher ranks. "Hopelessly unscientific" staffers, inadequate preparation, and general disinterest regarding the gas potential constantly irritated Hodgkin: "My own view is that the paid expert (myself) should either be sacked or else his views should be acted on."[28] Sir William Pope, Cambridge chemist, president of the British Chemical Society, and member of the Chemical Advisory Committee, who favored more intensive but knowledgeable use of gas, wrote in 1917 that "the whole conduct of chemical warfare on our side is a disgraceful scandal. . . . the whole thing is being run in the spirit of the little village publican doing his two barrels a week."[29] Arthur Smithells, a professor of chemistry at the University of Leeds, who volunteered his civilian services as a Chemical Advisor in France and also wrote some of the antigas pamphlets for the War Department, soon became disenchanted with the scientific and chemical "illiteracy" he found in military circles at every level. For his outspoken criticism of the military reliance on unthinking gas discipline rather than on an understanding of the scientific principles of gas, he was sent back to England where he became chief Chemical Advisor to the home front, advising on all forms of civilian antigas policy.[30] The vast majority of army commanders regarded gas at best as a nuisance. According to Foulkes, even Thuillier, for a time the Director of Gas Services, was "not a gas enthusiast."[31]

The attitude of the PBI (poor bloody infantry) was even more antagonistic, as illustrated in a verse of the improvised song "Corporals All":

> We went up to the trenches, and we filled 'em full of fear,
> We gassed a Major-General, and we gassed a Brigadier.
> The infantry detest us, and make remarks at us,
> As we ride up to the Line in a posh motor-bus.[32]

Early in the war Foulkes became acutely aware that both the front-line troops and their commanders "disliked gas and did not believe in its success."[33] Although he mounted a strong public relations campaign in early 1917 to counter this attitude, he candidly admitted it to be an "apparently hopeless task."[34] After the war Fritz Haber told Hartley that German troops similarly disliked the discharge of gas from their own trenches.[35]

There were many understandable reasons for this infantry hostility. Gas in the trenches inevitably meant leaks, which made life miserable and necessitated the wearing of uncomfortable masks. The use of gas represented quite a jarring intrusion into infantry routine, and the presence of gas in the front lines made divisional work harder. Men at rest quite naturally resented the extra work required for the carrying parties, which tended to be far more exhausting than they were accustomed to. This debilitating portering imposed on troops, especially those destined shortly to go over the top, also rankled infantry commanders. Brig. Gen. C. D. Bruce, 27th Infantry Brigade, 9th Division, wrote to Edmonds several years after the war:

> The battalions in my brigade, *all ranks*, disliked very strongly the use of poison gas, the wind and weather being what they were. The Jocks particularly hated the very severe fatigues entailed by carrying up hundreds of the gas cylinders when they felt, and rightly, that they ought to have been given every chance of being fresh and fit for the kick-off.[36]

Much the same, or course, might be said of extra labor imposed by other units of the Royal Engineers. Machine-gunner Victor Fagence explained that because the infantry was frequently called upon to provide the hard labor for the Royal Engineers, their attitude toward them was "sort of a mild hate, really, a dislike. They didn't like them, and they used to swear about them. And they would refer to them as the bloody R.E.s and that sort of thing."[37] Infantryman George Grossmith considered the foot soldiers the "dogsbodies" of the Royal Engineers.[38]

Another reason for the aversion to gas was not often or openly articulated. The introduction of gas shattered the "live and let live" system which frequently developed either in relatively quiet sectors or between major offensives.[39] The too candid excuse that "the Division wanted a quiet front" goes to the heart of the matter.[40] Release of gas invariably elicited heavy retaliatory bombardment from the enemy. Since the gasmen quickly retreated to less forward zones following release, the poor bloody infantry remaining in the front lines had to absorb the retaliatory shelling. It was they who had to pay for the success of the retreating gasmen.

Much the same was true of snipers. They, too, like the gas personnel, brought enemy retaliation in their wake and incurred infantry hostility. Bill Howell was a sniper at Loos:

> Nobody liked us snipers. The men loathed us, and the officers hated us. They could not order us out of their sector. The trouble was, we would watch through a loophole for hours, and when we were absolutely sure of a target, we would fire. No other firing went on without an order, and Jerry knew it was a sniper, and he would let everything he had loose on that section. Of course we hightailed it out, as fast as our legs would carry us, and poor old Tommy had to take it.[41]

The gas companies resembled the snipers (and trench mortarmen) in that the effect of their actions in the front lines was to elicit enemy retaliation though on an even larger scale.

Whatever the causes, this widespread resistance to gas at most levels was particularly unfortunate for it contributed to a more significant failure, the failure to effectively integrate gas strategy into those of the other arms, in particular, the infantry and artillery. As Bidwell and Graham have shown, the lack of coordination which already marred prewar inter-force tactical links made it less likely that new weapons could be advantageously entered into the combined military equation. Administrative inertia militated against the efficient orchestration of additional new weapons systems such as the machine gun, the tank, and gas.[42] In few cases, however, was this inertia compounded by such outright hostility, as with gas.

Unlike the other service branches, no prewar gas doctrine on either strategy or tactics existed. Foulkes was forced to blaze new trails. Under these circumstances mistakes were inevitable, but these were exacerbated by his singular reluctance to accept their consequences. Foulkes from the first harbored the false hope that a massive cloud gas attack might be the centerpoint of a British strategy ending the Western Front stalemate, a hope reminiscent of that of Fritz Haber earlier in the war. The Battle of Loos should have clearly demonstrated the futility of such a gas scheme, both in terms of strategic soundness as well as tactical implementation. The effectiveness of cloud gas attacks depended on too many unpredictable and uncontrollable variables. The requirements of a stabilized front, appropriate terrain, sufficient preparation, protective cover for cylinder emplacement, and the most exacting wind conditions meant that any precise synchronization of gas emission with any sizable infantry assault, whether a night raid or a major offensive, was extremely improbable. All other aspects of battle timing had to be subordinated to that single variable, and in the case of major infantry advances, such as at Loos or the Somme, this was impossible. The only solution to this problem was to reverse the priorities and, instead of timing the gas to coincide with an established infantry offensive, to time the offensive to a favorable wind. But no large-scale infantry offensive preceded by extensive bombardment could be maintained indefinitely at "zero minus an hour or so and holding" while waiting for a favorable wind.

Even where favorable winds prevailed at the moment of discharge, without a steady velocity of at least 3 to 4 mph in the right direction, there was no guarantee that a sudden calm would not eddy the gas into the path of advancing infantry, or, even worse, a change in wind direction would not blow the gas back into the British trenches. Even with the most ideal wind conditions, the chances of an attacking force running into its own gas were very great. This was exacerbated by the natural tendency of most heavier-than-air gas to sink into holes, craters, and trenches, and there to form deadly concentrated pools of gas, thus depriving the attacking force of cover in the face of opposing fire. Perhaps the most fatal flaw of gas warfare was, after all the expense and trouble, the very real risk of doing as much damage to one's own troops as to the enemy's.

The beam attack sought to ameliorate the hazards associated with carrying parties and front-line installation. But it added others: It avoided the arduous human carry-in, but required light railway manpower; it necessitated the temporary but complete evacuation of front-line troops; and the loaded railway trains, unless elaborately camouflaged, posed an even greater concentration of gas as a target for enemy artillery than the isolated projectors or cylinders. As an offensive weapon however dispersed, gas by cloud had far too many inherent and fatal flaws and handicaps. Hartcup concludes that chemical warfare "failed in its original purpose."[43]

For these and other reasons both the French and the Germans gave up on cloud gas early in the war. The French, sensitive to the danger of their own nationals behind German lines, rejected all large cloud gas operations.[44] Because of contrary prevailing winds and indecisive results, the Germans soon became disenchanted with cylinders, and their last cloud gas attack took place on 8 August 1916.[45] Only the British persisted in cloud gas dispersion, and that was entirely due to the influence and persuasion of Foulkes.

If gas proved ineffective as an accompaniment to assault, it was nevertheless manifestly effective as an agent of harassment. Haber alleges that even Foulkes changed his mind on this point after Loos and acquiesced, however grudgingly, to this less glamorous use of gas.[46] On one occasion long after the war Foulkes finally did admit that gas had come to be used most of the time "for inflicting casualties in a war of attrition," though this was not the role he would have chosen for it.[47] In any event, whether Foulkes approved or not, in 1916 and afterward gas increasingly became a weapon of opportunity, merely an "accessory" (ironically, an early code word for gas itself) rather than a "fifth arm." For such a role, gas by artillery shell and by projector was far more appropriate than cloud gas. Released from the constraints of synchronized timetables, gas by projector could be discharged whenever and wherever minimal wind conditions obtained.

An important but easily overlooked aspect of this harassing gas and smoke campaign was the anxiety and uncertainty such attacks engendered in the enemy forces. Since harmless smoke and lethal gas were virtually indistinguishable, use of either forced the enemy to don awkward and inconvenient protective masks. The infantry called these harmless discharges "pseudo-gas" and used such discharges frequently as cover for raiding parties, following the release of toxic gases.[48] Edwards-Ker explained the clever "cat and mouse" game:

> We used to mix with our phosgene, smoke, and we used to mix with the whole thing SK [tear gas] and then of course . . . one could cut out the gas altogether and simply send over smoke as a result of which the Germans, of course, were sitting in their trenches with their gas masks on because they didn't know whether there was gas in with the smoke or not. So we teased the Germans very considerably in that way by mixing in with phosgene sometimes smoke, sometime sending over smoke only, and our troops going over with the smoke.[49]

For example, in June 1918 No. 3 Mortar Company discharged both gas and smoke the night before an infantry raid and then exclusively smoke on the night of the raid.[50] It is all but impossible to calculate the degree of effectiveness of such tactics beyond recognizing that they constituted a clear though indirect contribution to infantry operations.

The concept of cost-effectiveness was not used at the time, but Great War commonplace had it that it took roughly a ton of lead to kill a man. In the context of such imprecise standards of measurement, the answer to the question "Was gas cost-effective?" is probably no. But analysis of cost-effectiveness is dependent on figures of enemy gas casualties—figures forever unrecoverable because the Germans kept no separate gas casualty tallies. In lieu of hard evidence Foulkes relied on circumstantial and anecdotal evidence collected by any means possible, and in 1917 he was estimating that on average the Germans suffered one casualty for every gas cylinder discharged.[51] In a report on operations during 1918 Foulkes repeated the cylinder claim and additionally reckoned one enemy casualty for every five projector drums discharged.[52] After the war he urged that the Allies "try to extract or purchase" from the Germans official evidence of the results of our gas attacks.[53] Their rejection of this suggestion did not deter Foulkes from further estimating the enemy's total gas casualties at between one and two hundred thousand.[54] George Pollitt, originally in intelligence before serving with the Special Brigade, considered these estimates as highly exaggerated—"Foulkes's and Adams's fairy stories."[55]

Another aspect of cost-effectiveness was the waste of trained scientists in digging trenches and portering cylinders. The virtually unanimous consensus both inside and outside the brigade was that the offensive gas organization did not require such a large number of chemists. "The War Office asked for chemists when they wanted gas fitters and plumbers," grumbled Livens.[56] No more consistent pattern of complaint emerges from the gasmen's diaries than this disillusionment that their authors' chemical expertise and training was not being tapped in any useful or significant way. The recruitment of chemists produced not a few square pegs to be fitted unnecessarily into round holes. While the experimental work had of necessity to be carried out by the scientific community, there was little need for qualified chemists in the Special Brigade. They went about their work of digging, portering, and plumbing with an air of some cynicism: "We are the blokes who will turn on the bloody gas taps. Some bloke at the War Office decided that to turn on the taps properly one must have an honours degree in chemistry, so here we are, a bunch of chemistry teachers."[57] Pratt, a chemist, decided not to join the brigade because he felt it did not need chemists at all:

Their main job was really to carry gas cylinders into and out of the trenches and to operate them when the attack took place. In fact, any ordinary individual could have done that. . . . The whole thing was absolutely misconceived and a tremendous number of very valuable chemists served and served well in that Brigade when they could have been employed much more usefully back in this country in our explosive and chemical factories. There was work for a few chemists in the way of advisors in connection with gas masks and so on. But there was no real need for a Special Brigade of the sort they had.[58]

Before World War II, J. B. S. Haldane again argued that scientists, rather than being wasted in the trenches, should be assigned to laboratories. He cited the egregious case of Henry Moseley, the brilliant English physicist, who was killed at Gallipoli at age twenty-eight.[59] Hindsight does seem to corroborate the need only for laborers, plumbers, and engineers, but it was not so obvious at the beginning of this pioneering endeavor that chemical retaliation would not require trench-chemists. And to the original collection of chemist-corporals Foulkes did add a growing number of ordinary infantry. It is the nature of an army at war to waste individual talents. Rarely is there time to allocate men with specialized training to best advantage. Doubtless countless others in all World War I armies considered their peculiar talents and intellect misspent or untapped. Assuming that chemists would not all be assigned to laboratories, where else in the army would their chemical expertise be put to any more appropriate use? Was Pratt, for example, applying his knowledge and training in chemistry any better while riding about repairing telephones for the Gordon Highlanders than he would have been portering cylinders in the Special Brigade?

Perhaps the greatest limitation of gas was that given the state of the art that existed at the time, gas was too easily defended against, a fact recognized by the Germans early on. Fritz Haber told Hartley in 1958 that "as soon as you had a Box Respirator, I knew it was a waste of time."[60] Edmonds, himself a Royal Engineer, concluded in the official history, much to Foulkes's consternation, that gas achieved sporadic and local success, but nothing decisive. "It made war uncomfortable, to no purpose."[61]

In 1960 Hartley, the greatest British authority on gas and highly critical of the inflexible way Foulkes conducted the gas mission, contemplated writing an exposé, to be titled *Chemical Man, 1915-1918*, but was reluctant to do so while Foulkes was alive since, he wrote to Pollitt, it would mean "torpedoing" what Foulkes had said in *Gas!*[62] Six years later Hartley still did not want to "upset the old man."[63] The book in fact was never written, but Hartley's association with Ludwig Haber, Fritz Haber's son, inspired the latter's own book, *The Poisonous Cloud* (1986), which reflected Hartley's views. A full discussion of both sides of the question of gas effectiveness, as well as a synopsis of opinion from professionals in and outside the Special Brigade, may be found in Ludwig Haber's penultimate chapter, "Was Gas a Failure?" where he asserts unequivocally that the answer to the question is yes.[64]

Was Foulkes, then, the right man for the job? A hands-on, self-confident leader, he seemed utterly undaunted by either physical dangers or policy difficulties. He was extremely self-demanding and hard-working, at times to the detriment of his own physical health, but was careful to allow for a moderate amount of relaxation and pleasure to maintain emotional stability. He was personally outspoken, even abrasive and brusque, and could be difficult at times. It was common knowledge that he and Thuillier did not get along.[65] Peter Liddle, keeper of the Personal Experience Archives at Leeds University, during the course of taped interviews in the 1970s and 1980s with two officers of the brigade in a position to know Foulkes well, asked them directly about Foulkes the man. Both responses sound enigmatically evasive. Douglas Edwards-Ker was a gas company commander, Army Chemical Advisor, and, in 1918, Assistant Director of Gas Services:

Q. What sort of man was Foulkes?
A. Charming man.
Q. What were his particular merits?
A. (hesitantly) His merit was involving a new Arm. Gas was a new Arm. It had never been used before and no one knew what the difficulties were and Foulkes was very clever indeed at starting this new form of warfare which had never been used before.

Dr. Walter Campbell-Smith was one of Foulkes's company and battalion commanders, rising to the rank of lieutenant colonel in the brigade:

Q. What sort of man was Foulkes?
A. Ooooo, that's very hard—difficult—to answer. (long pause) He inspired confidence and was very cheerful.[66]

Strong-minded, opinionated, and assertive, Foulkes frequently got his way through bluster rather than diplomacy. But the successful introduction of a weapon as unusual and unpopular as gas demanded initiative, and it was perhaps for this reason that Ludwig Haber concluded that Foulkes was "just the man for the job."[67] If the British gas mission did not live up to expectations it was hardly Foulkes's fault.

Throughout the war years Foulkes had spent a great deal of effort seeking to vindicate gas. To the extent he became aware of the prevailing sense that gas had been a disappointment, especially cloud gas, he was very much distressed, but he never admitted failure. In his book he alleges that some of the gas offensives "were shown subsequently to have been the most successful in the whole war. . . . Unfortunately, this was not realized by the majority of our commanders."[68] Foulkes remained sanguine to the end, proclaiming in 1922 that each man in the Special Brigade was worth ten of those in any other branch of the army.[69]

Regardless of the controversies surrounding chemical warfare, the men of the brigade deserve recognition for a job well done. They performed their uniquely difficult tasks with a dedication and professionalism that was exemplary. They were innovative, hard-working, and, under the most trying circumstances, maintained for the most part an excellent esprit de corps. Eden considered his friends in K Company "a band of brothers."[70] Fox characterized his company commander as a "fond father of a happy family."[71] A keen sense of humor ameliorated many of the miseries of everyday life even in the front lines. Outrageous extemporized songs radiate a healthy badinage during grueling marches, and the personal diaries evoke images of equally outrageous but rollicking good times, camaraderie, and shared danger. Along with the frequently expressed wishes for the minor wounds that ensured return to Blighty, the memoirs of the gasmen betray as well a certain unwillingness to leave comrades. Stricken with trench fever, Corporal Dalton strongly resisted orders to report to the hospital, not wishing to be separated from chums.[72] At the section level in particular, the gas units developed a special kind of group bonding that frequently developed into life-long friendships—a phenomenon analyzed by Tony Ashworth in his sociological study *Trench Warfare, 1914–1918: The Live and Let Live System.*[73]

At its greatest strength the Special Brigade numbered 258 officers and 5,832 men. The brigade conducted 768 gas operations involving 88,000 gas cylinders, 197,000 projectors, 178,000 Stokes mortar bombs. It discharged 5,700 tons of various gases. Foulkes estimated that from Loos to the Armistice the gas companies discharged gas two nights our of every three. Total brigade casualties were 5,384, close to 100 percent of its total strength. The brigade won 557 decorations, including Dawson's Victoria Cross.[74]

After the war, the question of gas warfare once again became a diplomatic and ethical issue rather than an active military one. Germany's use of gas was of course one of the thirty-two listed war crimes in the Versailles documents, and the League of Nations considered a renewal of the Hague prohibitions on chemical warfare. Meanwhile, Foulkes served briefly in India, where he and Churchill vainly urged British use of gas against the Afghan rebels.[75] "If the wind conditions were found to

Photo of the trenches at Festubert taken by Foulkes just after the war ended. (Courtesy of Liddell Hart Centre for Military Archives).

be favourable the whole of the occupants of the Tochi valley, for example, from Darpa Khel to Datta Khel, a distance of about 15 miles, would be either killed or severely incapacitated.[76] As before, Foulkes disposed of the morality issue off-handedly. Gas was now "openly accepted" and recognized as a fair weapon. The tribesmen are not bound by Hague anyway and "our commanders consider the tribesmen as vermin only fit for extermination, and the troops regard them as blood-thirsty, treacherous savages."[77]

Between the wars a healthy debate raged in the military journals concerning assessments of Great War gases, the future likelihood of chemical warfare, predictions as to what form it might take, and the value of international agreements. The majority opinion contended that improved chemical weapons posed a great threat in any future war but that attempts to forestall their use, either by industrial restriction or international agreements, were likely to prove futile. Victor Lefebure not only served with the Special Brigade during part of the war, but participated in the post-Armistice monitoring of the German gas facilities. In his book, *Riddle of the Rhine* (1921), Lefebure contends that it would be impossible to suppress chemical warfare by edict and that no treaty safeguard would ever deter resort to chemical warfare on the part of a state which saw winning advantage in first use. Nevertheless in 1925 the Geneva Protocol banned first use of all chemical and biological weapons, though not their development and stockpiling. Nor did the final wording include provisions for verification, enforcement, or penalties. Britain agreed, with qualifications; the United States signed but did not ratify until 1974. The Machiavellian Foulkes, of course, deprecated all international pledges on the subject as patently worthless.

That Germany did not resort to chemical weapons in World War II was in no way due to the Geneva Convention. Hitler simply did not choose to do so, convention or no—his crass disregard for other international agreements surely suggests that it was not the Geneva Convention that tied his hands. Other explanations seem far more plausible. Hitler, having personally suffered from mustard gas in 1918 (from British artillery shells, not Special Brigade gas), possessed a twisted and contorted notion of honor and considered the use of poison gas dishonorable. More likely, Germany calculated that its western enemies were this time fully prepared for retaliation and that, based on dubious results from the use of gas in the earlier war, the advantages of first use were not sufficiently compelling. And so gas was to be the only weapon introduced in World War I that was not used in the second. Chemical warfare was to be reserved for surprise use against states or ethnic groups without the industrial capacity for effective retaliation in kind—against Ethiopia by Italy in the 1930s, by the Japanese against China in the same decade, and, more recently, by Iraq against its own people.

Epilogue

After the war, surviving members of the Special Brigade began or continued the usual variety of mostly professional careers—as leaders of industry, rectors, schoolmasters, physicians, university professors, research scientists, company presidents, Members of Parliament, museum curators, artists, society presidents, barristers, authors, and businessmen.

Harold Hartley rejoined the faculty of Balliol College, Oxford, in 1921. After a distinguished academic career, he died in 1972 at the age of 94. His funeral took place in Westminster Abbey. Dr. Gordon Monier-Williams worked for the Ministry of Health in charge of the food-research laboratory, published articles in chemistry, and was very active in the Society for Analytical Chemistry, serving as president in 1945/46. An accomplished watercolor artist as well, his landscape paintings were exhibited in the Royal Academy and elsewhere. He died in 1964 at age 83. George Pollitt, commander of the mortar battalion and wounded three times in the war, went on to become a managing director of the Imperial Chemical Institute. E. A. Berrisford, commander of the 3d Battalion, who once told Foulkes he was struggling with theology ("What the devil for?" asked Foulkes), went on to become a rector in an obscure Hampshire country parish where his wartime activity was not generally known. "There is, I believe, a vague impression that the Rector had something to do with gas in the war and that . . . gives the village wits a chance for an obvious jest or two. I can of course reply that I also learnt a little about flames and can threaten the jesters with what is waiting for them."[1] Berrisford, who conducted Foulkes's memorial service in 1969, himself died in 1980. Dr. Walter Campbell-Smith worked as an assistant curator at the Natural History Museum in London. Sidney Bunker, commander of the 4th Battalion, died in June 1968.

James L. Dawson, winner of the Victoria Cross, spent much of the rest of the war in a number of antigas instructional capacities in London, France, and America and after the war served in the Indian Army until 1946. He died in 1967, willing his Victoria Cross to Glasgow University. William Livens became assistant editor of *Country Life*. Livens died in 1964 and his friend Harry Strange the year following. Ernest Gold, chief meteorologist of the brigade, lived until 1976, age 94.

As for the other gas veterans whose diaries have constituted a major part of this book, Martin Sidney Fox resumed his schoolteaching career at Leeds, became science master, and privately published two recollections, "With the Special Brigade" in 1957 and "Corporals All" in 1965. Fox died of a coronary attack while working in his garden at Eastbourne in 1966 at age 78. Donald Grantham and Ronald Purves died in 1969. Charles Ashley became professor at Trinity College in Toronto, living until 1974. Alex Uvary—who had enlisted at the age of sixteen by falsifying his age, was wounded at Loos, and subsequently gassed three times while with B Company—after the war opened his own heating and ventilating business. He also survived active service in World War II and died in 1974. Guy Crowden became professor of Applied Physiology at the University of London. Richard C. Gale, Fellow of the Royal Institute of Chemistry and professor of Chemistry and Metallurgy at Ordinance College, Woolwich, died in 1975 at age 87. Dr. D. A. Clibbens, "the professor of the broom," became a lecturer at King's College London. He died 1975. T. H. Adams, the brigade's intelligence officer and a fluent German scholar, became a headmaster and a barrister. Thomas Davies, C Company, returned to his native Tasmania and served as a prominent member of the Tasmanian Parliament. John Oakey became a barrister in Eastbourne, Sussex.

Frank O'Kelly was one of three brigade soldiers permanently blinded in the war. After long residence at St. Dunstans, a hospice-school for the blind, he trained as a telephonist. O'Kelly died in 1980. John A. Oriel, chlorine gassed at Loos in 1915 and mustard gassed at Passchendaele in 1917, became chief chemist with Shell Petroleum Company (1935–1950). Despite his eventually total blindness, he was elected to the presidency of the Institution of Chemical Engineers and in 1960 earned an "Extraordinary Fellowship" at Churchill College, Cambridge. He died at the age of 71 in 1968. Thomas Ap Rhys, No. 4 Mortar Company, who was totally blinded by mustard gas at Vimy Ridge on 9 April 1917, returned to Bangor University and received an Arts degree with three first class distinctions in 1921, became a Justice of the Peace, ran for a Commons Carnarvon seat on the Labour ticket (losing to Lloyd George), and practiced physiotherapy until close to his death in 1978 at the age of 82.

The camaraderie of the Special Companies remained very strong— many brigade gas veterans had spent the better part of three years together. One of the most frequent demobilization parting promises involved "getting together again" sometime. As early as the 1920s several of the gas companies began to discuss the possibility of company reunions. Initiated by Donald Grantham and others, the first C Company reunion was held 3 December 1920 at the Imperial Hotel in Russell Square in London's Bloomsbury district. Q Company organized in December 1922 as Scottish Pals, then Pals of Q, and finally, simply Q Club.

In World War II several members of the brigade joined the new 1st Chemical Training Battalion, Royal Engineers, described by R. H. Thomas as "a sorry imitation of the Special Brigade. It is a really good show really, and it is hardly fair to expect it to equal the old Special Brigade."[2] After the war, the company reunions resumed, but by the late 1950s the number of members able to attend was dwindling. At the annual reunion in 1958 only thirty C Company veterans attended and at that time decided to publish a periodical newsletter to keep in better touch. Filled with survivors' recollections of wartime experiences, these newsletters contain a wealth of information and human interest. In 1960 the Royal Engineers Museum in Chatham placed on exhibit a small collection of items illustrating the experiences of the Special Brigade. These postcards, gas masks, trench maps, slides, and other souvenirs, together with several sets of personal diaries and letters, became the foundation for the permanent archive of the brigade.

In commemoration of the fiftieth anniversary of the Loos gas attack, 135 members of the brigade attended a gala Special Brigade reunion at Eastbourne in 1965. In attendance were Foulkes, Ernest Gold, J. Oriel, James Lennox Dawson (the Victoria Cross winner), and, though he was never a brigade member, Harold Hartley. Foulkes made a brief speech in which he described the brigade as "a small semi-civilian kind of secret society."[3] The fiftieth reunion, however, was to be his last. He suffered from severe arthritis during the 1960s but still drove his car until the eve of his ninetieth birthday. He was deaf by the last part of the decade, and failing sight prevented his reading or writing. Foulkes's wife, Dorothy, died in 1967, age 87, having lived with Foulkes for 63 years. He then went to live for a time with his son Tom and transferred to a nursing home shortly before his death in 1969.

In the 1960s the few remaining reunions merged to offset the dwindling membership. In 1968 at the forty-second reunion of Q Club, its president Louis Fletcher collapsed on the podium and died in the hospital the next morning. Q Club held its fifty-first and last reunion in 1977 when there were only three members left.[4] Combined newsletters and brigade reunions held on for a few more years. On 25 September 1981, in the familiar surroundings of the Imperial Hotel in Russell Square, a final Special Brigade reunion convened. Only ten members were able to attend, the youngest well into his eighties. One month later the last newsletter went out, describing to those absent the last moments of the last Special Brigade reunion: "From this point onwards, members began to drift away. There were no fireworks, no singing of Auld Lang Syne, no histrionics. The Special Brigade's reunions simply faded away in the old tradition of the British Army." The last entry on the last page of the last newsletter reproduced the most memorable lines of perhaps that most memorable of all Great War poems, written by Robert Laurence Binyon in 1914:

> They shall not grow old as we that are left grow old.
> Age shall not weary them, nor the years condemn.
> At the going down of the sun and in the morning
> We shall remember them.

Appendix A: Structural Chart

COMPANY STRUCTURE 1915

Companies			
186	187	188	189
Sections			
1	11	21	31
2	12	22	32
3	13	23	33
4	14	24	34
5	15	25	35
6	16	26	36
7	17	27	37
8	18	28	38
9	19	29	39
10	20	30	40

BRIGADE STRUCTURE 1916

Battalions				
1st	2d	3d	4th	5th Mortar
Companies				
A B C D	E F G H	J K L M	N O P Q	1 2 3 4 Z
Sections				
1 7 13 19	25 31 37 43	49 55 61 67	73 79 85 91	A E J N 1
2 8 14 20	26 32 38 44	50 56 62 68	74 80 86 92	B F K O 2
3 9 15 21	27 33 39 45	51 57 63 69	75 81 87 93	C G L P 3
4 10 16 22	28 34 40 46	52 58 64 70	76 82 88 94	D H M Q 4
5 11 17 23	29 35 41 47	53 59 65 71	77 83 89 95	
6 12 18 24	30 36 42 48	54 60 66 72	78 84 90 96	

BRIGADE STRUCTURE 1917

Battalions

1st	2d	3d	4th	5th Mortar

Companies

A B C D	E F G H	J K L M	N O P Q	1 2 3 4	Z

Sections

1 6 11 16	21 26 31 36	41 46 51 56	61 66 71 76	A E J N	1
2 7 12 17	22 27 32 37	42 47 52 57	62 67 72 77	B F K O	2
3 8 13 18	23 28 33 38	43 48 53 58	63 68 73 78	C G L P	3
4 9 14 19	24 29 34 39	44 49 54 59	64 69 74 79	D H M Q	4
5 10 15 20	25 30 35 40	45 50 55 60	65 70 75 80		

Appendix B: The Royals Keep a Distance

Already disappointed that in his view the Special Brigade was not fully credited for its contributions to the war, Foulkes especially resented what he considered the official history's short shrift of the brigade's activities. He therefore published his own account in 1934. Though somewhat amended by a War Office reticent to acknowledge Britain's full role in chemical warfare, the book served its author's purpose in justifying the actions of the brigade and its commander. In researching the book Foulkes found that the British war documents were in a "chaotic" state—scattered and "unclassified and haphazard"—but his own admitted failure to keep an official war diary before 1916 surely did not help.[1]

Foulkes asked one of the keenest advocates of gas warfare, Winston Churchill, to contribute an introduction, but he refused somewhat brusquely in one sentence: "I have enough troubles to bear without associating myself with what I am sure will be your deeply interesting book."[2] Eventually, Lord Cavan, Frederic Rudolph Lambart (tenth earl), Foulkes's first superior officer in the Engineers, wrote a brief but discursive piece which Foulkes thought "pretty feeble," but he included it anyway in the hope that the author's status might ease War Office approval.[3] The completed manuscript, titled "Frightfulness: The Story of the Special Brigade," was sent to the War Office in October 1933. War Office censors returned it five months later with "trivial alterations," deletion of the word frightfulness in the title—which in their opinion might have created a wrong impression in the minds of a generation "un-versed in war humour"—and elimination of all references to exact numbers of gas cylinders used in various places. Foulkes thought this last objection "ludicrous," but acquiesced.

Buckingham Palace also refused permission to publish photographs of the royal family associated in any way with gas warfare. Sir Clive Wigram, aide to the royal family, wanted to know whether the Special Brigade referred to "Gas Bombers."[4] That cleared up, a letter from Clarence House still wished to learn "the exact connection in which you wish to use" the photographs.[5] In a protracted correspondence involving Wigram, Cavan, and Foulkes, it was tentatively agreed that there would be no objection to photos captioned "visiting the front," but that any photos that associated any royal with "frightfulness" would not be acceptable.[6] Lord Cavan also urged deletion of all references to the attendance of any royalty at gas demonstrations. Wigram wrote to Cavan that the title was "abhorrent."[7] Foulkes agreed to omit the offending passages and proposed the captions "H.M. Visiting a Gas School" and "H.M. the King and Queen Watching a Smoke Demonstration."[8] That was still not acceptable. Cavan responded: "I foresee hostile criticism if their Majesties are associated with gas development whether defensive, retaliatory or protective."[9] In the end Foulkes had to exclude all pictures of the royal family except one of King George crossing a trench bridge with the innocuous caption "His Majesty at the Front (attended by the Author)."[10]

Foulkes first suggested changing the offending title to "Gas!!" But the publishers thought one exclamation point enough, and the book finally came out as *Gas! The Story of the Special Brigade*.[11] Though Foulkes explored the possibility of publishing *Gas!* also in Germany, Blackwood, the publisher, sensibly suggested that this was improbable.[12] Response to the book was unfailingly positive: "absorbing" (*Times Literary Supplement*); "extraordinarily interesting, sober, authoritative" (*Daily Mail*); "quite unlike any other war book" (*Birmingham Post*); "one of the most valuable war histories and one of the most fascinating" (*Army, Navy, and Air Force Gazette*); "the fullest account." (*Telegraph*); "the best book that has been published on gas warfare" (*Nature*); "the gap in history has now been filled" (*Times*). The National Institute for the Blind requested permission to transcribe it into Braille. The U.S. Chemical Warfare Service distributed copies to its officers.[13] Foulkes no doubt felt satisfied that he had finally set the record straight.

Abbreviations

CAC   Churchill Archive Center, Churchill College, Cambridge
IWM   Imperial War Museum, Lambeth
LC   Liddle Collection, Leeds University
LHCMA Liddell Hart Centre for Military Archives, King's College London
NAM   National Army Museum, Department of Documents, Chelsea
PRO   Public Record Office, Kew
REL   Royal Engineers Library, Chatham
REM   Royal Engineers Museum, Chatham

OTHER

ADGS Assistant Director of Gas Services
AEF   American Expeditionary Force
BEF   British Expeditionary Force
CCS   Casualty Clearing Station
CIGS Chief of the Imperial General Staff
CT   Communication trench
DGS   Director of Gas Services
HE   High explosive
JSAHR *Journal of the Society for Army Historical Research*
MoM   Ministry of Munitions
RA   Royal Artillery
RAMC Royal Army Medical Corps
RE   Royal Engineers
REJ   *Royal Engineers Journal*
RFA   Royal Field Artillery

RUSIJ   *Royal United Services Institution Journal*
SBNL   *Special Brigade Newsletter*
SBR   Small box respirator
SK   Tear gas (first developed at South Kensington)

Notes

INTRODUCTION

1. Henry Williamson, *A Fox under My Cloak* (London, 1955), p. 272.

2. IWM, Department of Manuscripts, Adrian Hodgkin Diary, 30 January 1916.

3. *SBNL* 46 (November 1979): 7.

4. Sir Basil Liddell Hart makes a strong case for soldiers being poor historians in *Through the Fog of War* (London, 1938), pp. 39-40.

5. The best German work of this interwar period was undoubtedly Rudolf Hanslian, ed., *Der chemische Krieg* (Berlin, 1925). A. M. Prentiss, *Chemicals in War* (New York and London, 1937) heads the list of many general accounts in English.

6. An example is Robert Harris and Jeremy Paxman, *A Higher Form of Killing: The Secret Story of Gas and Germ Warfare* (London, 1982). The one brief chapter dealing with the Great War is inadequately researched, contains nothing new, and is suspect in many respects. For a scathing review see *Stand To!* 6 (Winter 1982): 20.

7. PRO/WO33/1072, Harold Hartley, "Report on German Chemical Warfare Organization and Policy, 1914-1918." Every one of the thousands of official war diaries at the PRO was closed until 1965. Others are gradually becoming public. A card index record of every Special Brigade officer was opened in 1991 (WO 142/338).

8. John Keegan, *The Face of Battle* (Sandhurst, 1974).

CHAPTER 1. THE GERMANS DO IT FIRST

1. IWM, DS/MISC/35, microfilm account of Lt. Col. G. W. G. Hughes. A series of three photos taken 2 May 1915 of thirteen British gas victims swathed in blankets is reproduced in *Stand To!* 13 (Spring 1985): 38-39.

2. CAC, Hartley Papers, Box 39, unpublished article, "Fritz Haber," written about 1960, p. 3.

3. See Edward M. Spiers, *Chemical Warfare* (Urbana and Chicago, 1986), p. 14; Guy Hartcup, *The War of Invention* (London, 1988), pp. 94-95; J. E. Edmonds, *Military Operations: France and Belgium* (London, 1922-1949), III: 193-194.

4. PRO/WO33/1072, Harold Hartley, "Report on German Chemical Warfare Organization and Policy, 1914-1918."

5. CAC, Hartley Papers, Box 39, "Fritz Haber," pp. 2–3.

6. Hartcup, *War of Invention*, p. 114.

7. Ibid., p. 96. After the war Haber told Hartley that the Germans refrained from use of gas from the air in 1917–1918 because "they were afraid of the effect of retaliation against civilians in the Rhineland" (CAC, Hartley Papers, Box 35, Letter from Hartley to R. H. Peck, assistant chief of Air Staff, 19 August 1941).

8. Spiers, *Chemical Warfare*, p.15; Ludwig F. Haber, *The Poisonous Cloud* (Oxford, 1986), pp. 24–25.

9. Hartcup, *War of Invention*, p. 96.

10. "Es war nur ein Versuch," Herman Nernst, a noted German physical chemist, explained (CAC, Hartley Papers, Box 39, "Fritz Haber," p. 5).

11. Charles Howard Foulkes, *Gas! The Story of the Special Brigade* (Edinburgh and London, 1934), pp. 31–34.

12. IWM, Dept. of Sound Recordings, 000495/06 RO3, Tape of James Davidson Pratt. Pratt was serving with the 4th Battalion of Gordon Highlanders, near Hill 60.

13. James L. McWilliams and R. James Steel, *Gas! The Battle for Ypres, 1915* (St. Catharines, Ontario, 1985).

14. Hugh Popham, *The Dorset Regiment* (London, 1970), p. 74.

15. PRO/PRO30/57/50.

16. McWilliams and Steel, *Gas!* p. 86.

17. PRO/WO142/90/DGS3, Memo dated 5 May 1915. Simon Jones has provided a most informative study of early British respirators and defensive actions in "Gas Warfare: The British Defensive Measures. Part I: The Second Battle of Ypres"[*Stand To!* 14 (September 1985): 15–23].

18. IWM, Dept. of Sound Recordings, 000554/18 R12, Tape of Charles Robert Quinnell.

19. IWM, Dept. of Sound Recordings, 000495/06 Ro3, Tape of James Davidson Pratt.

20. IWM, MISC/82/35/1, Letter from Capt. H. V. Parker to "Tommy," 12 May 1915.

21. IWM/PP/MCR/86, Memoirs of H. G. R. Williams, pp. 166–167.

22. IWM, Dept. of Documents, F6, Memoirs of A. E. Coleman.

23. NAM, 5010/29, Regimental Orders, 1 May 1915 (Royal Irish Regiment).

24. PRO/WO32/5169.

25. IWM, Richard Gale Diary, 13 and 14 May 1915. In Gale's diary is a photocopy of the list of the Original Special Service Party.

26. At that time, rumors circulated that the Germans had poisoned streams with arsenic, rumors shortly found to be unsubstantiated.

27. IWM, Gale Diary, 17 May 1915.

28. One joined the First Army at Aire and the other the Second Army at Hazebrouck.

29. "How the Special Brigade Began" (extracts from the Diary of Donald Grantham), *SBNL* 6 (February 1962): 11.

30. IWM, Gale Diary, 24 May 1915.

31. "How the Special Brigade Began," p. 12.

32. Taped interview by Peter Liddle, Leeds.

33. "How the Special Brigade Began," p. 11.

CHAPTER 2. THE DECISION TO RETALIATE

1. LHCMA, Oakey Papers, poem of unknown authorship, found on a New Year's card among Oakey's papers.
2. Sir George Douglas and Sir George Dalhousie Ramsey, eds., *The Panmure Papers*, vol. 1 (London, 1908), pp. 308, 340. The details of Dundonald's scheme were summarized clearly in J. B. Poole, "A Sword Undrawn: Chemical Warfare and the Victorian Age," Pt. 1, *Army Quarterly* 106 (October 1976): 463-465. See also C. Lloyd, *Lord Cochrane* (London, 1947), pp. 105ff.
3. See files in PRO/MUN5/385/1650/9; and Ludwig F. Haber, *The Poisonous Cloud* (Oxford, 1986), pp. 20-21.
4. Charles Howard Foulkes, "Fire, Smoke and Gas," *JSAHR*, 19 (1940): 148.
5. The Cabinet files are in PRO/CAB21/83.
6. PRO/CAB21/83, File 27/E/24, Maurice Hankey to Col. Ernest Swinton at GHQ, 15 May 1915.
7. See H. C. Peterson, *Propaganda for War*, (Norman, Okla., 1968), p. 63. Editors noticeably muted gas commentary following British retaliation.
8. *Times* (London), 29 April 1915.
9. Basil Collier, *Brasshat: A Biography of Field Marshall Sir Henry Wilson* (London, 1961), p. 224. At the time Edward Grey was secretary of state for foreign affairs.
10. PRO/WO32/5171, Memo by Col. Lucius Jackson, "Gas in Trench Warfare—Summary of what has been done to date, June 30, 1915."
11. PRO/CAB45/120, Lucius Jackson to Edmonds, 10 December 1925.
12. LHCMA, Foulkes Papers, J-1, Lucius Jackson to Charles Foulkes, 8 August, 1921. Another officer in Jackson's new department, J. C. Matheson, made some of the initial appointments and interviewed many of the officer candidates in London. He also exploited a contact at Cambridge who fed him suitable recommendations. LHCMA, Foulkes Papers, J-1, Matheson to Foulkes, 22 March 1922. See also Charles Howard Foulkes, *Gas! The Story of the Special Brigade* (Edinburgh and London, 1934), p. 47.
13. PRO/WO32/5173, War Office circular letter, 11 May 1915.
14. PRO/WO32/5171, Jackson, "Gas in Trench Warfare."
15. IWM, Richard Gale Diary, 18 May, 1915.
16. PRO/MUN5/385/1650/9.
17. LHCMA, Foulkes Papers, K-1(b), manuscript of unpublished book "Savage Africa," p. 21b.
18. "My best performance was with one [dumbbell] weighing 140 pounds, lifted with one hand from the floor to the shoulder and then pressed slowly to arm's length above the head" (LHCMA, Foulkes Papers, D-14). While at Chatham, Foulkes would lift a fellow cadet weighing eight stone "by the belt, with one hand, from the floor to the shoulder, and then press him slowly to arm's length above his head" [*REJ* 83 (March–December 1969): 236]. Among the Foulkes Papers at King's College London (D14), is a list, written for his son Tom, of all his sports accomplishments, his medals, cups, trophies, candlesticks, "many solid silver." After a three month course in muscle-building at Sandow's School, he boasted of fifteen-inch biceps and posed for photos advertising the school. LHCMA, Foulkes Papers, K-1(b), manuscript of "Savage Africa," pt. 3, "Boer War."
19. Charles Howard Foulkes, "The Anglo-French Boundary Commission, Niger to Lake Chad," *REJ*, 73 (March–December 1959): 429-437.
20. LHCMA, Foulkes Papers, D14.

21. Foulkes, *GAS!* p. 11.
22. Ibid., pp. 13, 15.
23. Charles Howard Foulkes, "Chemical Warfare Now and in 1915," *REJ* 76 (March–December 1962): 177.
24. LHCMA, Foulkes Papers, K-1(c). Quoted in *Times* (London), 15 June 1958.
25. Foulkes, *Gas!* pp. 13-15.

CHAPTER 3. CORPORALS ALL

1. Martin Sidney Fox, "Corporals All" (typescript, 1965), p. 38.
2. PRO/WO32/5171, Memo by Col. Lucius Jackson, "Gas in Trench Warfare—Summary of what has been done to date, June 30, 1915."
3. LHCMA, Foulkes Papers, Diary, 31 May 1915.
4. PRO/MUN5/197/1650/8.
5. PRO/WO32/5171, Jackson, "Gas in Trench Warfare." See also Charles Howard Foulkes, *Gas! The Story of the Special Brigade* (Edinburgh and London, 1934), p. 40.
6. Throughout the war, cylinders of a variety of sizes saw service as it proved impossible to supply the necessary number of uniform cylinders. This accounts for infantry carrying parties' widely divergent estimates of the weight of cylinders.
7. PRO/WO32/5173, Sir John French to War Office, 16 June 1915. Foulkes omitted the provisional nature of the establishment in his own account of French's recommendation in *Gas!* p. 46.
8. PRO/WO32/5173, Secret Memo, War Office to Sir John French, 30 July 1915. The War Office reserved ten company numbers (186-196) for the future expansion of Foulkes's unit, but used only four. When the unit expanded to brigade strength in 1916, letters replaced the numbers.
9. PRO/WO32/5173, Sir John French to War Office, 25 June 1915.
10. PRO/WO32/5173, Memos, Adjutant General to Sir John French, 19 June 1915; War Office to French, 25 June 1915.
11. IWM, Richard Gale Papers, War Office flier, 28 May 1915.
12. The soldier was F. S. Shadbolt [*SBNL* 23 (January 1970)].
13. Fox, *Corporals All*, p. 2. Foulkes does not seem to have been involved in the actual selection of any of the men except the senior officers.
14. Martin Sidney Fox, "With the Special Brigade" (typescript, 1957), p. 3.
15. *SBNL* 32 (November 1973): 11.
16. The soldier was B. R. Heaseman [*SBNL* 17 (March 1967): 8].
17. *SBNL* 42 (November 1977): 10.
18. IWM, Dept. of Sound Recordings, 000495/06 ROI, Tape of James Davidson Pratt.
19. *SBNL* 7 (April 1962): 10.
20. The soldier was M. Stevenson [*SBNL* 17 (March 1967): 14].
21. LC, Recollection of Cpl. T. Eden. Fred Karno was a popular comic entertainer of the era.
22. *SBNL* 40 (February 1977): 2.
23. REM, 6106-06, S.4(h), "Q Special Company, R.E., 1916-1918," by "Anguish" (Angove), p. 1.
24. The story is told by R. F. Dalton [*SBNL* 44 (November 1978): 9].
25. IWM, Charles Allen Ashley Diary, 19 July 1915.
26. Jack Sewell Diary, *SBNL* 7 (April 1962): 10.
27. IWM, Luther Gordon Mitchell Diary, 16-17 August 1915.

28. Typescript account of L. W. White, in author's possession.
29. Foulkes, *Gas!* p. 57.
30. Martin Sidney Fox, "With the Special Brigade" (typescript, 1957), p. 14.

CHAPTER 4. PUTTING THE HELL INTO HELFAUT

1. This parody of a popular Irish poem, "The Mountains of Mourne," portions of which also appear at the beginning of chapters 5 and 9, caricatures the experiences of C Company [CAC, Hartley Papers, Box 31, Harmon Gas Warfare Papers, Songs of Company C].
2. LHCMA, Charles Howard Foulkes Diary, 24 July 1915.
3. Gale refers to the initial unit as the 250th R.E. [IWM, Richard Gale Diary, 5 July 1915].
4. IWM, G. O. Mitchell Diary, 18 July 1915.
5. R. H. Atkinson, "Recollections of the Gas C'oys," *SBNL* 40 (February 1977): 1; IWM, Charles Allen Ashley Diary, 19 July 1915.
6. REM, 8403-15/1, "An Account from the Diaries Made during the Great War by John Miles Thomas," 11 August 1915. See also Charles Howard Foulkes, *Gas! The Story of the Special Brigade* (Edinburgh and London, 1934), p. 57.
7. IWM, Gale Diary, 15 July 1915.
8. Ernest Gold Diary, *SBNL* 41 (May 1977): 1.
9. IWM, Gale Diary, 10 July 1915.
10. *SBNL* 7 (April 1962): 11.
11. PRO/WO32/5170, Army Council to Sir John French, 24 June 1915.
12. REM, Ronald B. Purves Diary, 5 September 1915.
13. Martin Sidney Fox, "With the Special Brigade" (typescript, 1957), p. 16.
14. IWM, Ashley Diary, 19 July 1915.
15. IWM, Gale Diary, 17 July 1915.
16. PRO/T173/702, p. 34.
17. IWM, Gale Diary, 4 September 1915.
18. CAC, Hartley Papers, Box 43, Letter from J. A. O. to Hartley, undated, but after the war. J. A. O., otherwise unidentified, served in section 7 of Company 186 and is probably John A. Oriel.
19. REM, 8103-02.
20. IWM, Gale Diary, 12 August 1915.
21. IWM, G. O. Mitchell Diary, 18 July 1915.
22. IWM, Gale Diary, 6 July 1915.
23. IWM, 76/211/1T, Frank G. Cousins Papers, manuscript of "Billets."
24. IWM, Gale Diary, 14 July 1915.
25. F. A. R. Hopkins, "Memories of Helfaut and Chickory," *SBNL* 10 (February 1964): 14.
26. Ibid.
27. IWM, Luther G. Mitchell Diary, 13 September 1915.
28. LC, Meiron Thomas Papers, October 1915.
29. IWM, 76/211/1T, Cousins Papers, "Billets."
30. *SBNL* 20 (July 1968): 9–12.
31. *SBNL* 40 (February 1977): 2.
32. IWM, Gale Diary, 26 August 1915; Sir Basil Liddell Hart, *History of the First World War* (London, 1972), p. 198.
33. In his diary Foulkes wrote 1 September, but in his book *Gas!* he gives 9 September.

34. REL, Donald Grantham Papers, Circular Letter, October 1915.
35. These sections came from Companies 186, 187, and 188.
36. IWM, Gale Diary, 4 September 1915.

CHAPTER 5. UP THE LINE TO LOOS

1. NAM, Henry Rawlinson Papers, 5201-33-25, Diary (shortened), 20 August 1915.
2. PRO/CAB44/22, draft chapter 6 of official history by J. E. Edmonds, p. 22. In the manuscript margin Haig penned, "This is quite true." Gen. J. E. Edmonds was designated after the war to write the official history of the war. The series as a whole is popularly called the official history, but the Western Front volumes commonly appear in bibliographies as *Military Operations: France and Belgium*. Before publishing, Edmonds sent copies of the draft manuscript of pertinent parts to various appropriate persons for comment and verification of fact.
3. PRO/CAB45/121, R. D. Whigham to J. E. Edmonds, 1925. According to Gen. Hubert Gough, the demonstration under favorable wind conditions had "raised great hopes in our minds" [*The Fifth Army* (London, 1931), p. 101].
4. Gas, however, was not the only factor in Haig's decision. On 23 August 1915, Sir John French ordered Haig to support the French attack "to the full extent of your available resources" rather than the scaled-down alternative [J. E. Edmonds, *Military Operations: France and Belgium* (London, 1922–1949), 4: 153].
5. NAM, Rawlinson Papers, 5201-33-18, Rawlinson to Wigram, September 1915.
6. Robert Blake, ed., *The Private Papers of Douglas Haig, 1914–1919* (London, 1952), 16 September 1915.
7. NAM, Rawlinson Papers, 5201-33-18, Rawlinson to Fitzgerald, 29 August 1915.
8. CAC, Rawlinson Diary, 26 June 1915. Rawlinson's biographer quotes the phrase "as 'flat' as the palm of my hand" [Sir Frederick Maurice, *The Life of General Lord Rawlinson of Trent from His Journals and Letters* (London, 1928), p. 137].
9. After the battle of Loos, headquarters ordered that this cherry tree be cut down and made into souvenirs. Philip Warner, *The Battle of Loos* (London, 1976), p. 148.
10. LHCMA, Foulkes Papers, J-1, manuscript draft for "A History of the Royal Engineers," vol. 5, chap. 20, p. 6.
11. PRO/WO32/5170, Sir Alexander Keogh to Jackson, 5 July 1915.
12. REM, John Thomas Diary, 2d version, p. 1.
13. IWM, G. O. Mitchell Diary, 4 September 1915.
14. Atkinson Diary, *SBNL* 40 (February 1977): 6. Atkinson served in section 14.
15. R. F. Dalton, *SBNL* 36 (July 1975): 5.
16. IWM, 86/57/1, reminiscences of Richard Foot, p. 38.
17. IWM, Richard Gale Diary, September 1915.
18. *SBNL* 7 (April 1962): 11.
19. *SBNL* 17 (March 1967): 7.
20. *SBNL* 42 (November 1977): 11.
21. CAC, Hartley Papers, Box 31, Harmon Gas Warfare Papers, Songs of Company C.

22. *SBNL* 10 (February 1964): 14.

23. REM, Grantham Papers, Letter, October 1915.

24. IWM, Charles Ashley Diary, September 1915.

25. IWM, Gale Diary, 17 September 1915.

26. LHCMA, Charles Howard Foulkes Diary, 25 September 1915.

27. Warner, *Battle of Loos*, p. 10. Sid Kemp, signaller with 6/Royal West Kent Regiment, wrote that during the summer of 1915 the Germans displayed a six- to eight-foot banner indicating the number of Russian ships the German Navy had sunk in the Baltic (PRO/85/28/1).

28. REM, Grantham Papers, 6911-03, Circular Letter, October 1916.

29. REM, Grantham Papers, 6911-03, Ciruclar Letter, July 1916.

30. LHCMA, Kerrich Papers, Diary, 5 June 1915.

31. IWM, Gale Diary, 6 September 1915.

32. IWM, Cousins Diary, 10 September 1915.

33. PRO/WO95/1911, War Diary, 15th Division, "Instructions as to IV Corps as to gas," 31 August 1915.

34. IWM, Gale Diary, 6 September 1915.

35. NAM, Rawlinson Papers, 5201-33-18, Rawlinson to Wigram, September 1915.

36. LHCMA, Foulkes Papers, J-32, J. B. K. Crawford to Tom Foulkes, 7 October 1969.

37. *SBNL* 40 (February 1977): 5-6.

38. Robert Graves, *Good-bye to All That* (London, 1929), p. 125. German circulars would seem to corroborate this point [Ludwig F. Haber, *The Poisonous Cloud: Chemical Warfare in the First World War* (Oxford, 1986), p. 53 n. 25].

39. Sir Frederick Maurice, *The History of the London Rifle Brigade, 1859-1919* (London, 1921), Appendix A, "Details of Work Leading up to and the Attack with Asphyxiating Gas at Loos, September 25, 1915."

40. PRO/T173/702, pp. 34-36.

41. PRO/WO95/120, War Diary, Special Brigade Depot, 13 September 1915.

42. CAC, Rawlinson Papers, Diary, 17 September 1915.

43. IWM, G. O. Mitchell Diary, 17 September 1915.

44. Blake, ed., *Private Papers of Douglas Haig*, 16 September 1915.

45. Charles Howard Foulkes, *Gas! The Story of the Special Brigade* (Edinburgh and London, 1934), p. 64.

46. Blake, ed.,*Private Papers of Douglas Haig*, 16 September 1915.

47. NAM, Rawlinson Papers, 5201-33-18, Rawlinson to Fitzgerald, 29 August 1915.

48. NAM, Rawlinson Papers, 5201-33-25, Diary (shortened), 16 September 1915.

49. PRO/WO158/184, Haig to GHQ, 18 September 1915.

50. Blake, ed., *Private Papers of Douglas Haig*, 20 September 1915.

51. CAC, Rawlinson Papers, Diary 1/3, 17 September 1915.

52. This happened at Gorre rail siding according to A. B. White (London Rifle Brigade) and is recounted in Henry Williamson's story, *A Fox under My Cloak* (London, 1955), p. 276.

53. REM, John Thomas Diary, p. 6.

54. Maurice, *Rifle Brigade*, p. 352; Williamson, *Fox under My Cloak*, p. 277.

55. From the recollection of Capt. W. M. Escombe, 1/20 London Irish Rifles, in Warner, *Battle of Loos*, pp. 85-86.

56. Obituary of Charlie Chance by C. S. Harmon in *SBNL* 20 (July 1968): 16.

57. Alan H. Maude, *The 47th (London) Division, 1914–1919* (London, 1922), p. 26.

58. PRO/WO95/1361, War Diary, 2d Division, 18 September 1915.

59. Graves, *Good-bye to All That*, pp. 143, 129.

60. *SBNL* 7 (April 1962): 11; *SBNL* 48 (November 1980): 9.

61. Martin Sidney Fox, "Corporals All" (typescript, 1965), p. 12.

62. PRO/CAB45/121.

63. Lt. Jack Sewell was in command of section 1, Company 186.

64. *SBNL* 7 (April 1962): 11.

65. REM, Grantham Papers, Circular Letter, November 1915.

66. IWM, L. G. Mitchell Diary, 24 September 1915.

67. PRO/WO95/120, War Diary, Special Brigade Depot, 24 September 1915.

68. Foulkes indicated 800 (*Gas!* map facing p. 84), but Campbell-Smith stated clearly in a brief account of Loos that only 160 arrived [LC, Campbell-Smith Papers].

69. PRO/WO95/1911.

70. IWM, Sir John French Diaries, 23 September 1915.

71. IWM, Ashley Diary, September 1915.

72. IWM, Gale Diary, 18 September 1915.

73. IWM, L. G. Mitchell Diary, 24 September 1915.

74. LC, Campbell-Smith Papers.

75. CAC, Hartley Papers, Box 43, J. A. O. to Hartley.

76. REM, John Thomas Diary, 24 September 1915, 2d version, p. 6.

77. IWM, G. O. Mitchell Diary, 24 September 1915.

78. Maurice, *Rifle Brigade*, p. 352.

79. LC, Meiron Thomas Papers, Letter to his mother, 24 September 1915.

80. REM, Ronald Purves Diary, 24 September 1915.

81. LHCMA, Foulkes Papers, J-1, manuscript for vol. 5, chap. 20, of "History of the Royal Engineers" (unpublished).

82. "The Meteorological Service in France," *SBNL* 34 (November 1974): 8.

83. Rawlinson wrote that Gold "seemed to know his job" (CAC, Rawlinson Papers, Diary 1/3, 24 September 1915). In his newest book, however, Denis Winter unfairly characterizes him as a temporizer at best and an incompetent at worst: "His reports were often little better than hunches" [*Haig's Command: A Reassessment* (London, 1991), pp. 39–40, 278].

84. REM, John Thomas Diary, 24 September 1915.

85. Percy and Geoffrey Higson were brothers from Birkdale.

86. IWM, Frank Cousins Diary, 24 September 1915.

87. Foulkes, *Gas!* p. 70.

88. *SBNL* 34 (November 1974): 8.

89. PRO/CAB45/120, Charteris to Edmonds, 24 February 1927.

90. CAC, Rawlinson Papers, Diary 1/3, 24 September 1915.

91. Henry Williamson fought at Loos as an infantryman. In his novel based on personal experience, his chief character, Philip Maddison, was a gas officer positioned near the Vermelles-Hulluch Road with the 1st Division [Williamson, *Fox under My Cloak*, p. 303].

92. IWM, Gale Diary, 25 September 1915.

93. REM, John Thomas Diary, 2d version, p. 7.

94. Typescript account of L. W. White, in author's possession, p. 1.

95. See William Robertson, *Soldiers and Statesmen, 1914–1918* (London, 1926), vol. 1, p. 112; Sir Basil Liddell Hart, *A History of the First World War, 1914–1918* (London, 1972), pp. 198–199.

96. Charteris confirms that except for being awakened to receive weather reports at 2 and 3 A.M., Haig slept soundly thorough the night [John Charteris, *At GHQ* (London, 1931), pp. 112–113].

97. LHCMA, Foulkes Papers, Diary, 25 September 1915. Foulkes adds the words "but the battle could not be postponed."

98. Gough, *Fifth Army*, p. 107; Foulkes, *Gas!*, p. 68. Charteris later wrote that Haig "was very upset" upon hearing this [*At GHQ*, p. 114]. Anthony Farrar-Hockley states that the reason Gough believed it was too late was that the telephone lines between corps headquarters and the field commanders were not sufficiently reliable to guarantee transmission of messages in so short a time as thirty minutes. But he incorrectly fixes this incident at 6A.M. rather than 5 A.M. [*Goughie, The Life of Gen. Sir Hubert Gough* (London, 1975), p. 168].

99. LHCMA, Foulkes Papers, J-31, Ernest Gold, "Draft of an unpublished letter to the editor of *The Times*," written about 1964.

100. Blake, ed., *Private Papers of Douglas Haig*, 25 September 1915.

101. IWM, 87/33/1, Maj. E. S. B. Hamilton Diary, 25 September 1915.

102. Martin Sidney Fox, "With the Special Brigade" (typescript, 1957), p. 24.

CHAPTER 6. LOOS—THE FIRST BRITISH GAS ATTACK

1. Walter Campbell-Smith's recollections, L. W. White's diary, and Charles Howard Foulkes's own account [*Gas! The Story of the Special Brigade* (Edinburgh and London, 1934), pp. 70–71] all contradict Warner's statement that gas was not employed at Aubers Ridge on this occasion, although it is true that contrary winds and the factors to which White alludes prevented the opening of most of the canisters. [Philip Warner, *The Battle of Loos* (London, 1976)]. This unsubstantial book is marred by other mistakes as well. For instance, on page 8, I Corps contains six divisions and on page 9, only four; I Corps sector at Loos ran from the Vermelles-Hulluch Road northwards to La Bassée, not from Grenay northward (p. 8); at the time the Special Companies were not a brigade (p. 54), and so on.

2. LC, taped interview by Peter Liddle.

3. Terry Cave, "The Indian Army Corps," Pt. 2, *Stand To!* 14 (September 1985): 28.

4. LC, typescript recollections of Walter Campbell-Smith.

5. PRO/T173/702, pp. 36–37.

6. LHCMA, Foulkes Papers, J-31, R. Ridgeway to Foulkes, 15 February 1920. Ridgeway was commander of 33d Punjabis, Bareilly Brigade (Meerut Division) at Loos.

7. Typescript account of L. W. White, in author's possession, p. 1.

8. Both the Meerut and Lahore Divisions of the Indian Corps contained battalions of non-Indian regiments.

9. LC, George W. Grossmith, Letter written from hospital, 27 September 1915.

10. Foulkes, *Gas!* pp. 70–71.

11. E. Wyrall, *The History of the 19th Division, 1914–1918* (London, 1932), pp. 12ff.

12. I Corps, commanded by Gen. Hubert Gough, consisted of three divisions, 2, 9, and 7. Horne's 2d Division sector was the most northern and astride

La Bassée Canal. Horne deployed the 5th Brigade on its left (north) side and the 6th and 19th Brigades on its right.

13. *SBNL* 7 (April 1962): 11. Jack Sewell was in command of section 1.

14. LHCMA, Foulkes Papers, J-31, Foulkes to Gold, 22 September 1964, and J. K. B. Crawford to Tom Foulkes, 25 September 1975.

15. Robert Graves, *Good-bye to All That* (London, 1929), p. 134. The RE captain was, of course, Percy-Smith.

16. Sir Frederick Maurice, *The History of the London Rifle Brigade, 1859–1919* (London, 1921), Appendix A, "Details of Work Leading up to and the Attack with Asphyxiating Gas at Loos, September 25, 1915," p. 357.

17. REM, 8403-15/1 and 2, "An Account from the Diaries Made during the Great War by John Miles Thomas," 25 September 1915. This file contains two parallel versions of the Thomas Diary. In this chapter I have merged both where sensible.

18. REM, Thomas Diary, 25 September 1915.

19. IWM, Ashley Diary, 25 September 1915.

20. R. H. Atkinson, "Recollections of the Gas C'oys," *SBNL* 40 (February 1977): 3.

21. LHCMA, Foulkes Papers, J-2, Memo regarding J. A. Oriel, by D. M. Wilson, 12 February 1969. Oriel and Wilson were both in section 7 of Company 186 during the Loos battle. Wilson's reference to a favorable wind in this sector is contradicted by nearly everyone else at the time. Since he wrote this statement in 1969, it may reflect either forgetfulness or the fact that a wind so variable may well have impressed different observers differently.

22. REM, R. B. Purves Diary, 25 September 1915.

23. Jack Sewell Diary, *SBNL* 7 (April 1962): 12.

24. PRO/WO95/1347, War Diary, 1/9 Glasgow Highlanders (5th Infantry Brigade), 25 September 1915.

25. Maurice, *Rifle Brigade*, Appendix A, p. 357.

26. L. W. White typescript, p. 1.

27. REM, Donald Grantham Papers, Circular Letter, November, 1915.

28. Martin Sidney Fox, "With the Special Brigade" (typescript, 1957), p. 27.

29. Graves, *Good-bye to All That*, p. 134.

30. IWM, L. G. Mitchell Diary, 25 September 1915.

31. IWM, Richard Gale Diary, 25 September 1915.

32. This was the 22d Brigade in Capper's 7th Division in I Corps.

33. IWM, Dept. of Sound Recordings, 000322/06, R04, Tape of J. P. O. Reid. Reid served with the 6th Gordons, 7th Division.

34. Maurice, *Rifle Brigade*, p. 355.

35. PRO/WO95/1911, War Diary, 15th Division, 25 September 1915.

36. IWM, Frank Cousins Diary, 25 September 1915.

37. Gas officer Lieutenant Charles, quoted in Maurice, *Rifle Brigade*, pp. 353–354.

38. IWM, Cousins Diary, 25 September 1915. While discharging his cylinders, a whizz bang hit the parados just in front of Cousins and "showered me over."

39. Account by a Captain Wyllie, quoted in Warner, *Battle of Loos*, p. 163.

40. IWM, G. O. Mitchell Diary, 25 September 1915.

41. Sir Frederick Maurice, *The Life of General Lord Rawlinson of Trent from His Journals and Letters* (London, 1928), pp. 138–139.

42. CAC, Henry Rawlinson Papers, Diary 1/3, 26 September 1915.

43. PRO/WO95/1229, 1st Division War Diary.

44. NAM, Rawlinson Papers, 5201-33-67, "Minutes of G.O.C. (General Officer Commanding) Telephone Conversations during Battle of Loos."

45. PRO/WO95/1911, War Diary, 15th Division, 25 September 1915.

46. John Stewart and John Buchan, *The Fifteenth (Scottish) Division, 1914–1919* (London, 1926), p. 32.

47. IWM, Cousins Diary, 25 September 1915.

48. Lieutenant Lovell, quoted in Warner, *Battle of Loos*, p. 119.

49. Recollection of C. Arthus, a soldier with the London Irish Rifles (1/18 London Regiment), quoted in Warner, *Battle of Loos*, p. 80.

50. IWM, Ashley Papers, 25 September 1915.

51. Graves, *Good-bye to All That*, p. 140.

52. Warner, *Battle of Loos*, p. 163. The officer was Captain Wyllie.

53. REM, Grantham Diary, 25 September 1915.

54. REM, Purves Diary, 25 September 1915.

55. Maurice, *Rifle Brigade*, p. 354.

56. IWM, G. O. Mitchell Diary, 25 September 1915.

57. Sewell Diary, *SBNL* 7 (April 1962): 12.

58. REM, Thomas Diary, 25 September 1915; IWM, L. G. Mitchell Diary, 25 September 1915.

59. IWM 87/33/1, Maj. E. S. B. Hamilton Diary, 25 September 1915.

60. IWM, Gale Diary, 25 September 1915; L. W. White typescript, p. 2.

61. *Sapper* 21:250 (May 1916): 243.

62. LC, Meiron Thomas Papers, Letter to his mother, 26 September 1915.

63. Maurice, *Rifle Brigade*, pp. 354–355.

64. For a personal account of the forlorn attack of the 21st Division and some excellent maps, see Harry Fellows, "The Battle of Loos: An Eye-witness Account of the Attack on Hill 70," *Stand To!* 4 (April 1982): 8–14.

65. REM, John Thomas Diary, 27 September 1915.

66. Maurice, *Rifle Brigade*, pp. 358–359.

67. LHCMA, Foulkes Papers, Diary, 27 September 1915; Foulkes, *Gas!* p. 86.

68. The corporal was J. B. Ventham, later of Z Company [*SBNL* 36 (July 1975): 12].

69. REM, Purves Diary, 27 September, 1915.

70. PRO/WO142/100, file DGS/M/12; Ludwig F. Haber, *The Poisonous Cloud: Chemical Warfare in the First World War* (Oxford, 1986), p. 57. Foulkes disputed these figures, contending that a larger proportion of this number was attributable to German gas (Foulkes, *Gas!* pp. 93–94).

71. Haber, *Poisonous Cloud*, p. 245; PRO/WO95/120, War Diary, Special Brigade Depot, 25 September 1915.

72. LC, "Recollections of Professor Leonard E. S. Eastham of his service as a corporal with J Company, Special Brigade."

CHAPTER 7. BOOMERANG ALLY

1. Sir Hubert Gough, *The Fifth Army* (London, 1931), p. 101.

2. LHCMA, Charles Howard Foulkes Diary, 25 September 1915.

3. LHCMA, Foulkes Diary, 22 and 25 August and 20 September 1915.

4. Account of George W. Grossmith, 2d Leicestershire Regiment, Meerut Division, quoted in Philip Warner, *The Battle of Loos* (London, 1976), p. 194.

5. Charles Howard Foulkes, *Gas! The Story of the Special Brigade* (Edinburgh and London, 1934), p. 77.

6. LHCMA, Foulkes Diary, 25 September 1915.

7. H. Cotton, "Memoirs of an Army Meteorologist," Pt. 1, *Meteorological Magazine* 108 (August 1979): 241. Cotton's full memoirs may be found in IWM, 79/17/1T.

8. IWM, MISC 26, Item 469. Captured Germans claimed that the hammering on metal gave away the gas surprise on other occasions as well.

9. PRO/CAB45/120, Braine to Edmonds, 18 September 1926.

10. IWM, L. G. Mitchell Diary, 28 September 1915.

11. V. E. Inglefield, *The History of the Twentieth (Light) Division*, (London, 1921), p. 58.

12. IWM, Richard Gale Diary, 28 September, 1915. An anonymous gasman waited until 1960 to publicly criticize many technical aspects of the gas operation, mentioning prominently the awkward pipes as well as the lack of foresight ["The First British Gas Attack," *Chemistry and Industry* 46 (November 1960): 1395].

13. Foulkes, *Gas!*, p. 87.

14. LHCMA, Foulkes Papers, J-2, Memo regarding J. A. Oriel by D. M. Wilson, 12 February 1969.

15. Maurice, *The History of the London Rifle Brigade, 1859–1919* (London, 1921), p. 358.

16. PRO/T173/702, p. 37.

17. Charles Howard Foulkes, "Chemical Warfare Now and in 1915," *REJ* 76 (March–December 1962): 179.

18. Martin Sidney Fox, "With the Special Brigade" (typescript, 1957), pp. 29–30.

19. A. B. Swaine, Kent Cyclist Battalion, quoted in Philip Warner, *The Battle of Loos* (London, 1976), p. 148.

20. PRO/CAB45/121.

21. Warner, *Battle of Loos*, p. 196.

22. LHCMA, Foulkes Papers, J-32, Crawford to Tom Foulkes, 7 October 1969.

23. The phrase comes from the account of a Loos survivor, C. J. T. Johnson, quoted in Warner, *Battle of Loos*, p. 43.

24. PRO/CAB45/121, Col. H. C. Potter to Edmonds, 1927. Potter was C.O., 1/King's (Liverpool), 6th Brigade.

25. Warner, *Battle of Loos*, p. 124.

26. Henry Williamson, *A Fox under My Cloak* (London, 1955), p. 269.

27. NAM, Henry Rawlinson Papers, 5201-33-67.

28. PRO/T173/702, Pt. 2, p. 52.

29. PRO/T173/702, Pt. 2, pp. 46–47.

30. PRO/WO95/1911, War Diary, 15th Division, "Report on Operations 21–30 September, 1915."

31. PRO/CAB45/121, Lt. Gen. Robert Whigham to Edmonds, 1927. Whigham was a general staff officer in 1915.

32. CAC, Hartley Papers, Box 43, Letter from George Pollitt to Harold Hartley, 30 October 1960. Pollitt was among the earliest group of officers to join the unit. He commanded several sections of the "composite" companies at Loos and replaced the gassed Percy-Smith after the battle as commander of Company 186.

33. LHCMA, Foulkes Papers, J-1, manuscript of "Responsibility versus Privilege."

34. Foulkes, "Chemical Warfare Now and in 1915," p. 179.

35. Ludwig F. Haber, *The Poisonous Cloud: Chemical Warfare in the First World War* (Oxford, 1986), p. 57.

36. Trevor Wilson, *The Myriad Faces of War* (Oxford, 1986), p. 257 n15.

37. LHCMA, Foulkes Papers, J-1, Speech to Reunion Dinner, 2 April 1933.

38. IWM, Gale Papers, Foulkes to Hitchins, 8 October 1915. Yet, Foulkes alleges that he received "detailed reports" from every one of the forty section officers, as well as from company and other commanders, in the few days following the attack (Foulkes, *Gas!* p. 79).

39. "It was undoubtedly the neglect to collect information from prisoners on the effects of the gas which produced the impression . . . that the gas had produced unimportant results" (PRO/CAB45/120, Foulkes to Edmonds, 20 December 1925).

40. LHCMA, Foulkes Diary, 5 October 1915; Foulkes, *Gas!* p. 175.

41. IWM, L. G. Mitchell Diary, 30 September 1915.

CHAPTER 8. THE SPECIALS' FIRST WINTER

1. LC, Meiron Thomas Papers, Letter to his mother, dated Monday (probably 4 October), 1915.

2. The soldier was A. G. Lipscomb, Company 186 [*SBNL* 17 (March 1967): 13].

3. IWM, Richard Gale Diary, 13 December, 1915.

4. Charles Howard Foulkes, *Gas! The Story of the Special Brigade* (Edinburgh and London, 1934), pp. 66–67; Martin Sidney Fox, "Corporals All" (typescript, 1965), p. 28.

5. IWM, Richard Gale Diary, 10 October 1915.

6. Jack Sewell Diary, *SBNL* 7 (April 1962): 11.

7. Typescript account of L. W. White, in author's possession, p. 2. The Cambrin gas sector was merely a diversionary feint, and no infantry attack was planned there in any case.

8. IWM, 85/28/1, Memoirs of Sid T. Kemp, p. 31. The 6/Royal West Kents were in the 12th Division, which had replaced the 21st Division in the interval between 25 September and 13 October 1915.

9. LC, Higson Papers, Diary, 13 October 1915. "Got badly dosed, and was out in trench bottom. Crawled round to dugout and after three hours or so felt better."

10. IWM, Frederick Hunt Papers, p. 17.

11. IWM, 78/57/1T, James Dawson Papers.

12. Charles Howard Foulkes, "Chemical Warfare Now and in 1915," *REJ* 76 (March–December 1962): 178.

13. IWM, Gale Diary, 20 November 1915.

14. Fox, "Corporals All," p. 30.

15. Foulkes, *Gas!* pp. 88–89.

16. NAM, Henry Rawlinson Papers, 5201-33-67.

17. PRO/WO95/120, War Diary, Special Brigade Depot, 13 October 1915.

18. Foulkes, *Gas!* pp. 88–89.

19. IWM, L. G. Mitchell Diary, 2 December 1915.

20. REM, Donald Grantham Papers, Circular Letter, October 1915.

21. PRO/T173/702, p. 26.

22. *SBNL* 19 (March 1968): 5.

23. Corporal Nye recollection in *SBNL* 17 (March 1967): 10.

24. IWM, L. G. Mitchell Diary, 21–23 December 1915.
25. Fox, "Corporals All," p. 32.
26. IWM, Gale Diary, 13 December 1915.
27. REM, John Thomas Diary, 13 November 1915.
28. Fox, "Corporals All," pp. 27–28.
29. IWM, Gale Diary, 13 November 1915.
30. REM, Thomas Diary, 15 December 1915.
31. REM, Thomas Diary, 21 December 1915.
32. IWM, Gale Diary, 13 December 1915.
33. Fox, "Corporals All," p. 31.
34. IWM, L. G. Mitchell Diary, 20–23 December 1915.
35. IWM, Gale Diary, 20 December 1915.
36. *SBNL* 17 (March 1967): 15.
37. IWM, L. G. Mitchell Diary, 25 December 1915.
38. Martin Sidney Fox, "With the Special Brigade" (typescript, 1957), pp. 37–38.
39. IWM, L. G. Mitchell Diary, 1 January 1916.
40. IWM, L. G. Mitchell Diary, 31 December 1915.
41. Sewell Diary, *SBNL* 8, (February 1963): 15.
42. Fox, "Corporals All," p. 32.
43. All of the account of this gas operation is taken from REM, Thomas Papers, 8403-15/2, "The Gas Attack at Armentières, January, 1916."
44. Foulkes, *Gas!* p. 90.
45. The respective strengths of the four companies were: Company 186, 7 officers and 373 men; Company 187, 8 officers and 369 men; Company 188, 9 officers and 442 men; and Company 189, 9 officers and 335 men [PRO/WO95/120, War Diary, Special Brigade Depot, 12 January 1916].

CHAPTER 9. EXPANSION INTO THE SPECIAL BRIGADE

1. Charles Howard Foulkes, *Gas! The Story of the Special Brigade* (Edinburgh and London, 1934), pp. 109–111.
2. See Edwin M. Spiers, *Chemical Warfare* (Urbana and Chicago, 1986), p. 24.
3. Guy Hartcup, *The War of Invention* (London, 1988), p. 101.
4. Foulkes, *Gas!* p. 57.
5. R. H. Atkinson, *SBNL* 40 (February 1977): 8.
6. Foulkes, *Gas!* p. 96.
7. Detailed reports on the effects of the 19 December phosgene attack both from the field commanders and the various medical staffs are found in PRO/WO142/99/DGS/M/2.
8. PRO/MUN5/385/1650/9.
9. *SBNL* 33 (July 1974): 7. See also Foulkes, *Gas!* p. 112; Ludwig F. Haber, *The Poisonous Cloud: Chemical Warfare in the First World War* (Oxford, 1986), p. 85. On Sundays they scheduled two shifts of twelve hours each.
10. LHCMA, Foulkes Diary, 1–27, March 1916.
11. PRO/WO95/61; Foulkes, *Gas!* p. 97.
12. PRO/MUN4/1281. Report of interview between Mr. G. H. West, Professor Gardener, Lieutenant Alesandroff, Captain Stomm, and Captain Starforth, 8 March 1916.
13. LHCMA, Thomas Parkes Diary, 20 March 1916.
14. LC, T. Eden Papers.

15. The soldier was T. Evans, J Company [*SBNL* 33 (July 1974): 11].

16. PRO/WO95/121, 2d Battalion Programme of Training, Week ending 26 March 1916.

17. LHCMA, Thomas Parkes Diary, 27 and 29 March 1916.

18. IWM, L. G. Mitchell Diary, 11 February 1916.

19. *SBNL* 34 (November 1974): 5.

20. LHCMA, John Oakey Diary, 1 May 1916.

21. Ibid.

22. PRO/WO95/120, War Diary, Special Brigade Depot, 2 March 1916, 28 March 1916, 12 April 1916, 16 April 1916, 24 May 1916, 7 July 1916.

23. IWM, L. G. Mitchell Diary, 23–26 February 1916.

24. REM, Donald Grantham Papers, Circular Letters, January and June 1916.

25. IWM, Frank Cousins Diary, April and May 1916.

26. LHCMA, Foulkes Diary, April and May 1916.

27. REM, Thomas Diary, 22 May 1916.

28. REM, Grantham Papers, Circular Letter, June 1916; Foulkes, *Gas!* pp. 96–97.

29. LC, Meiron Thomas Papers, Letters to his mother, 2 and 4 June 1916.

30. LHCMA, Foulkes Papers, J-56, Thuillier to Foulkes, 26 June 1934.

31. REM, R. B. Purves Diary, 14 June 1916.

CHAPTER 10. WHITE STAR OVER THE SOMME

1. Dr. H. Cotton, of the Meteorological Service, after describing a particularly successful attack in which heavy phosgene poured almost like a liquid into the German trenches [H. Cotton, "Memoirs of an Army Meteorologist," Pt. 5, *Meterological Magazine* 109 (February 1980): 59].

2. IWM, Frank Cousins Diary, 31 May and 11 June 1916.

3. REM, John Thomas Diary, 30 June 1916.

4. Martin Sidney Fox, "With the Special Brigade" (typescript, 1957), p. 59.

5. Paul Fussel, chap. 7 "Arcadian Resources," in *The Great War and Modern Memory* (Oxford, 1975), pp. 231–269.

6. REM, Donald Grantham Diary, 25 June 1916.

7. IWM, Cousins Diary, 18 June 1916.

8. Charles Howard Foulkes, *Gas! The Story of the Special Brigade* (Edinburgh and London, 1934) p. 121. For continuing deficiencies in equipment delivery, see also PRO/WO95/120, War Diary, HQ, Special Companies, June 1916.

9. REM, Grantham Diary, 8 June 1916.

10. R. B. Carver and J. M. Fenwick, *A History of the 10th (Service) Battalion, the East Yorkshire Regiment (Hull Commercials), 1914–1919* (London, 1937), p. 83.

11. LHCMA, Thomas Parkes Diary, 17 June 1916.

12. REM, Grantham Diary, 17 June 1916.

13. J. B. Platnauer Diary, *SBNL* 32 (November 1973): 11. Platnauer was in O Company.

14. IWM, Cousins Papers, a brief essay titled "A Night Fatigue," p. 1.

15. LC, Henry Venables Papers, Letter to his mother, 26 June 1916.

16. Malins's colleague was J. B. McDowell.

17. Ludwig F. Haber, *The Poisonous Cloud: Chemical Warfare in the First World War* (Oxford, 1986), p. 91.

18. LC, taped interview by Peter Liddle.

19. PRO/WO95/121, War Diary, 2d Battalion, Special Brigade, 16–18 June 1916.

20. Foulkes, *Gas!* p. 139.

21. Foulkes had long urged instead the withholding of gas until the moments before the actual attack, the soldiers following in the path of the neutralizing gas cloud. The overriding objection to Foulkes's plan of action, however, was the impracticality of timing the assault in advance, for although the season of the year afforded a fair probability of generally favorable wind conditions, there could be no certainty of predicting this in advance.

22. Foulkes, *Gas!* p. 123.

23. IWM 73/222/1, Maj. William Gilliat Papers, corps commander Sir Aylmer Hunter-Weston to 4th Division commander William Lambton, 25 June 1916. Hunter-Weston, who was not liked by either Haig or Rawlinson, was shortly to come under heavy criticism from Haig for not raiding during the pre-Somme as well as for ordering premature lifting of artillery the morning of 1 July. That Hunter-Weston was especially attentive to gas matters is shown by an incident that occurred some weeks later, when, while inspecting one of the battalions in his VIII Corps, without any warning he shouted "Gas!" and then watched the scramble for masks [Capt. G. K. Rose, *The Story of the 2/4 Oxfordshire and Buckinghamshire Light Infantry* (London, 1920), p. 114].

24. IWM, Cousins Diary, 25-29 June 1916.

25. NAM, Henry Rawlinson Papers, 5201-33-26, Diary (shortened), 24 June 1916.

26. PRO/WO95/122, War Diary, 4th Battalion, Special Brigade, 27 June 1915.

27. Foulkes, *Gas!* p. 123.

28. PRO/PRO30/57/51, Rawlinson to Kitchener, 24 April 1915.

29. NAM, Rawlinson Papers, 5201-33-17 Letter Box, vol. 1, Rawlinson to Lt. Col. O. A. G. Fitzgerald, 29 April 1915.

30. NAM, Rawlinson Papers, 5201-33-17 Letter Box, vol. 1, Rawlinson to Wigram, 8 May 1915.

31. PRO/PRO30/57/51, Rawlinson to Fitzgerald, 24 May 1915.

32. NAM, Rawlinson Papers, 5201-33-18-94, Rawlinson to Fitzgerald, 21 June 1915 (microfilm copy). The original of this letter is in the Kitchener Papers at the Public Record Office (PRO30/57/51).

33. The main diary, averaging one page or more of text per day, is at Churchill College, Cambridge; a much abbreviated version is in the Rawlinson Papers at the National Army Museum.

34. NAM, Rawlinson Papers, 5201-33-18, Rawlinson to War Office (Sclater), letter undated, but sometime during the last weeks before Loos.

35. CAC, Rawlinson Diary, September 1915.

36. PRO/WO158/233, Rawlinson to GHQ, 19 April 1916, p. 9. See also Tim Travers, *The Killing Ground: The British Army, the Western Front, and the Emergence of Modern Warfare, 1900–1918* (London, 1987), p. 141.

37. CAC, Rawlinson Diary, 19 June 1916.

38. CAC, Rawlinson Diary, 26 June 1916.

39. PRO/WO95/121, War Diary, 1st Battalion, Special Brigade, Appendix 2, "Report on Gas Attack from III Corps Front," 26/27 June 1916.

40. REM, Parkes Diary, 28 June 1916.

41. PRO/WO142/90/DGS4, Notice, 30 June 1916. Care in the tight fitting of the nose-clip was considered so important that GHQ ordered urgent "all night" printing of the notice to expedite distribution.

42. PRO/WO142/300, "Operations Orders by Captain A. E. Kent, O. C. #4 Co'y, 5th Battl., Spe. Bde.," 25 June 1916.

43. REM, R. B. Purves Diary, 1 July 1916.

44. LC, Geoffrey Higson Diary, 1 and 2 July 1916.

45. Foulkes, *Gas!* p. 131.

46. REM, Parkes Diary, June 28 1916.

47. *SBNL* 32 (November 1973): 11.

48. *SBNL* 20 (July 1968): 13.

49. See Lyn Macdonald, *Somme* (New York, 1983), pp. 161–166.

50. PRO/WO95/122, War Diary of Battalion 4A, another composite battalion, commanded by Captain Garden. J Company was commanded by Captain Carpenter.

51. IWM, 69/25/1, Geoffrey Boles Donaldson Papers, Letter to his mother, 16 July 1916.

52. PRO/WO95/121, War Diary, 3d Battalion, Special Brigade, 30 June 1916. The sergeant was W. Harrower.

53. *SBNL* 17 (March 1967): 7.

54. PRO/WO95/122, War Diary, 4th Battalion, July 1916; Foulkes, *Gas!* p. 90.

55. REL, Crowden Papers, Memorandum by Foulkes, 17 July 1916.

56. IWM, Cousins Diary, 18 July 1916.

57. LHCMA, John Oakey Diary, 1–3 July 1916.

58. IWM/85/28/1, Sid T. Kemp Memoirs, signaller with the 6th Royal West Kent Regiment, p. 57.

59. IWM/PP/MCR/289, Lt. Col. Sir Robert Tolerton to his fiancée, 10 July 1916.

60. IWM, 69/25/1, Donaldson Papers, Letter to his mother, 16 July 1916.

61. PRO/WO95/121, War Diary, 2d Battalion, Special Brigade, 18 February 1916.

62. Martin Sidney Fox, "Corporals All" (typescript, 1965), p. 95.

63. LHCMA, Foulkes Papers, J-50.

64. IWM, Dept. of Sound Recordings, 000490/06, Tape of Maurice Edward Seymour Laws.

65. IWM, 84/11/2, Maj. H. J. C. Marshall Memoirs, vol. 3, p. 4.

66. Sir Basil Liddell Hart, *A History of the First World War, 1914–1918* (London, 1972), p. 319.

67. LC, R. E. Wilson Papers, Letter to his mother, 13 August 1916.

68. REM, Parkes Diary, 21 August 1916.

69. REM, Purves Diary, 4 August 1916.

70. R. F. Dalton Memoir, *SBNL* 48 (November 1980): 9–11.

71. Mrs. Norman P. Campbell, *N. P. Campbell: Scientist, Missionary, Soldier* (Cambridge, 1921), p. 35.

72. IWM, Adrian Hodgkin Diary, 26 October, 1916.

73. Foulkes, *Gas!* p. 77.

74. IWM, Dept. of Manuscripts, PP/MCR/11, First World War Letters of Lt. Col. Vivian M. Fergusson, DEF/2 (Correspondence from the Western Front), Fergusson to D'Ewes, 16 October, 1915.

75. *SBNL* 18 (July 1967): 4. The soldier was Frank White, C Company.

76. PRO/WO142/99 DGS/M/10, "Report on German gas casualties," Memo by Capt. Claude Douglas, RAMC, 23 November 1916.

77. PRO/WO95/121, War Diary, 3d Battalion, Special Brigade, 10–11 July 1916.

78. PRO/WO95/121, War Diary, 3d Battalion, Special Brigade, 21 August 1916, "Interrogation of Prisoners."

79. PRO/WO158/270, Report No. 916, 13 August 1916, signed by Lt. Gen. C. M.

Kavanagh, C.O., I Corps. The attacks in question took place 27/28 June and 5/6 July. See also PRO/WO95/122, War Diary, Garden's 4A Gas Battalion.

80. Foulkes, *Gas!* p. 168.

81. LC, R. Dawson Papers, Diary, 14 September 1916.

82. Typescript account of L. W. White, in author's possession, p. 3.

83. See voluminous files and reports on the operation in PRO/WO158/270.

84. Fox, "Corporals All," p. 58.

85. Foulkes, *Gas!* pp. 136–138.

86. LHCMA, Foulkes Papers, J-56, Edgar A. Cross to Foulkes, 21 February 1937.

87. Fox, "With the Special Brigade," pp. 61–62; *SBNL* 46 (November 1979): 6.

88. Foulkes, *Gas!* p. 138.

89. PRO/WO158/270, Report on 5-6 October 1916 Operation, by Lt. Gen. C. A. Anderson, C.O. I Corps, 21 October 1916.

90. Foulkes, *Gas!* p. 138.

91. Ibid., pp. 138–158. See also voluminous official reports on this and related gas attacks in PRO/WO158/270.

92. *SBNL* 10 (February 1964): 12. Armstrong further embellished this same story in 1972, placing the incident in July instead of October 1916 [*SBNL* 28 (June 1972): 8–9].

93. PRO/WO158/294, "German Attack Made by the British on the French Front near Nieuport on the 5th October, 1916."

94. Foulkes, *Gas!* p. 144–152.

95. *SBNL* 33 (July 1974): 10–13.

96. *SBNL* 20 (July 1968): 9–12. Fox claimed it was in 1917, but Clibbens remembered 1916.

97. PRO/WO95/120, War Diary, Special Brigade Depot, 18 January 1917.

98. LHCMA, Foulkes Diary, 27 July 1916.

99. LHCMA, Foulkes Papers, Diary for 1916.

100. Fox, "Corporals All," p. 60.

101. Ibid., p. 61.

102. REM, Parkes Diary, 9 January 1917.

103. Severe food shortages during this winter reduced German civilians to the consumption of turnips, hitherto considered suitable only for animal fodder.

104. Fox, "Corporals All," p. 64.

105. IWM, 84/11/2, H. J. C. Marshall Memoirs, vol. 3, p. 4.

106. LC, Eden Papers.

107. PRO/WO158/270, Memo to First Army, 2 July 1916.

CHAPTER 11. LIVENS AND THE *FLAMMENWERFER*

1. PRO/T173/702, Pt. 2, pp. 24–25. Foulkes recollected that Livens saw him at Chatham and asked that he be taken in, but Livens did not remember this.

2. LHCMA, Charles Howard Foulkes Diary, 16 October 1915.

3. LHCMA, Foulkes Papers, J-4, Foulkes to War Office, 7 October 1921; Charles Howard Foulkes, *Gas! The Story of the Special Brigade* (Edinburgh and London, 1934), p. 87.

4. Foulkes, *Gas!* p. 105.

5. LHCMA, Foulkes Papers, J-4, memo, 5 February 1964.

6. PRO/WO142/250, "A Brief Record of Flame Projector Work at Wembley Experimental Station."

7. Foulkes, *Gas!* p. III n3.

8. PRO/T173/702, Pt. 2, p. 67.

9. For a further discussion of the flame-throwers, see Guy Hartcup, *The War of Invention* (London, 1988), p. 68.

10. PRO/T173/702, Pt. 2, p. 48.

11. J. B. Ventham, "Z Special Company R.E.," *SBNL* 36 (July 1975): 11–15.

12. LHCMA, Foulkes Papers, J-32, Col. J. K. B. Crawford to Tom Foulkes, 25 December 1975. Crawford was a cousin to Bansall, who later commanded Z Company.

13. Ventham, "Z Special Company R.E.," pp. 11–15.

14. LHCMA, Foulkes Papers, Box 1, J-4, J. W. Bansall to Ken Crawford, 12 October 1969.

15. Z Company at this time consisted of 15 officers, 18 sergeants, 168 men, 38 attached infantry, and 14 drivers.

16. Foulkes mistakenly wrote that Z Company only brought two machines to the Somme in *Gas!* p. 112.

17. PRO/WO95/122, War Diary, Special Sections (Z Company), 1 July 1916.

18. LHCMA, Foulkes Papers, Box 1, J-4, J. W. Bansall to Ken Crawford, 12 October 1969.

19. PRO/T173/702, Pt. 2, p. 11, Livens to Mackintosh (director of the Trench Warfare Department), 21 July 1916.

20. Ibid.

21. Ibid.

22. PRO/WO95/122, War Diary, Special Sections, 3 September 1916. Foulkes formally redesignated the Special Sections as Z Company in 1917 (PRO/WO95/486).

23. PRO/WO95/122, War Diary, Special Sections, 25 September 1916.

24. LHCMA, Foulkes Papers, Box 1, J-4, J. W. Bansall to Ken Crawford, 12 October 1969; Foulkes, *Gas!* p. 112.

25. LHCMA, Foulkes Papers, J-4, Foulkes to War Office, 7 October 1921.

26. PRO/WO95/486, War Diary, Z Company, 27–30 October 1917. Livens later filed a claim with the Inventions Commission for an award for inventing the flame-thrower, but it was rejected.

CHAPTER 12. SOMME STRANGE GUNS

1. Original author mercifully unknown, found copied in the 1917 diary of Arthur H. Betteridge (Liddle Collection, Leeds), and attributed to "Tennyson in Flanders." Betteridge, a runner, was wounded and gassed near Delville Wood in mid-July 1916.

2. Foulkes recalled that as early as August 1915, before Loos, Capt. Percy-Smith had suggested "firing a gas cylinder into the German trenches with a British equivalent of the German *Flammenwerfer*," but Livens maintained that Percy-Smith had gotten the idea from him (PRO/T173/702, Pt. 2, pp. 39–40 and 72–73).

3. PRO/T173/702, Pt. 1, p. 15.

4. Lieutenant Stewart, PRO/T173/702, Pt. 2, p. 34.

5. LHCMA, Foulkes Papers, J-32, J. B. K. Crawford to Tom Foulkes, 17 October 1975.

6. LHCMA, Foulkes Papers, J-4, J. W. Bansall to Ken Crawford, 12 October 1969; PRO/T173/702, Pt. 2, pp. 32–33; *SBNL* 36 (July 1975): 14.

7. J. B. Ventham, "Z Special Company R.E.," *SBNL* 36 (July 1975): 15.

8. The War Diary of the Special Sections shows experiments of this type as early as 14 July (PRO/WO95/122).

9. LC, "Recollections of Professor Leonard E. S. Eastham of his service as a corporal with J Company, Special Brigade."

10. *SBNL* 37 (November 1975): 9.

11. REM, 6106-06, c2, Frank Winn Papers, Drawings, and Maps.

12. LHCMA, Foulkes Papers, Box 1, J-4, J. W. Bansall to Ken Crawford, 12 October 1969; LHCMA, Foulkes Papers, J-32, Col. J. K. B. Crawford to Tom Foulkes, 6 February 1968. Interestingly, Foulkes was later to give express orders forbidding any Special Brigade officer to advise the artillery on use of the gas shell (PRO/WO95/120, War Diary, HQ, Special Brigade, 10 December 1916).

13. PRO/T173/702, Pt. 1, p. 16.

14. PRO/T173/702, Pt. 2, p. 13, Livens to his father, 10 August 1916.

15. PRO/T173/702, pt. 2, pp. 51–52.

16. Ibid., pp. 52 and 58.

17. Ibid., pp. 17–19.

18. Ibid., pp. 70–71.

19. Ibid., pt. 2, p. 38.

20. LHCMA, Foulkes Papers, Box 1, J-4, J. W. Bansall to Ken Crawford, 12 October 1969.

21. Foulkes calculated that although the Livens projector contained thirty pounds of gas compared to only seven for the Stokes mortar, the latter was capable of firing at a rate of twenty to twenty-five rounds per minute for up to seven minutes, while the projector could fire only once (PRO/T173/702, Pt. 2, p. 75).

22. LHCMA, Foulkes Papers, J-4, Foulkes to War Office, 7 October 1921.

23. PRO/WO95/122, War Diary, Special Sections, 3 September 1916.

24. PRO/WO95/121, War Diary, 2d Battalion, Special Brigade, 3 September 1916.

25. Ludwig F. Haber, *The Poisonous Cloud: Chemical Warfare in the First World War* (Oxford, 1986), p. 120.

CHAPTER 13. ANOTHER BRIGADE REORGANIZATION

1. LHCMA, John Oakey Diary, p. 91.

2. PRO/WO95/486, War Diary, D Company, March 1917.

3. Charles Howard Foulkes, *Gas! The Story of the Special Brigade* (Edinburgh and London, 1934), p. 183; LHCMA, Foulkes Diary, 5 January 1917.

4. The strength of Z Company in April 1917 was 363: 18 officers, 276 Royal Engineers, 28 transport workers, and 41 infantry (PRO/WO/95/486, 24 April 1917).

5. Ludwig F. Haber estimates the greatest strength in 1917 at 7,000 [*The Poisonous Cloud: Chemical Warfare in the First World War* (Oxford, 1986), p. 219].

6. For example, I Corps provided C Company with three three-ton lorries during operations in March 1917.

7. PRO/WO95/120, War Diary, HQ, Special Brigade, Circular Memorandum no. S/1/505, 12 February 1917.

8. The administration of gas companies returning to Reserve areas not under the command of an army reverted to Special Brigade HQ at Helfaut.

9. REM, John Thomas Diary, 6 July 1917.

10. LHCMA, Foulkes Papers, J-1, manuscript for chapter 20 of vol. 5 of "History of the Royal Engineers."

11. LHCMA, John Oakey Papers, War Diary, No. 1 Special Company, 5 December 1916. The War Diary of this company is missing from the PRO archives. The diary at King's College London appears to be the original.

12. REM, Thomas Diary, 25 February 1917. But Thomas was not too busy to observe and record that the coltsfoot and daisies were coming into bloom and that the larks were singing.

13. Typescript account of L. W. White, in author's possession, p. 3. Cotton also believed that the brigade was abandoning "that unreliable weapon chlorine gas supplied from gas cylinders." (H. Cotton, "Memoirs of an Army Meteorologist," Pt. 4, *Meteorological Magazine* 109 (February 1980): 22–23].

14. PRO/WO32/5174, Haig to War Office, 3 December 1916.

15. See Haber, *Poisonous Cloud*, pp. 132–133.

16. LHCMA, Foulkes Papers, J-21, speech to Fifth Army, 7 April 1917.

17. LHCMA, Foulkes Papers, J-21, speech to Second Army, 28 April 1917.

18. LHCMA, Foulkes Papers, J-21, speech to Fifth Army, 7 April 1917.

19. REM, Thomas Diary, 8 September 1917.

CHAPTER 14. "G" IS FOR GAS

1. *B.E.F. Times* (incorporating *Wipers Times, New Church Times, Somme Times*, etc.) 4:1 (Monday, 5 March 1917), "A B.E.F. Alphabet."

2. Berridge was later promoted to second in command of J Company in May 1918, the same month in which he was killed in action (PRO/WO142/338).

3. REM, 6106-06 S.4(h), "Q Special Company, R.E., 1916–1918," by "Anguish" (Angove), p. 3.

4. PRO/WO95/401, War Diary, J Company, February and March 1917.

5. Charles Howard Foulkes, *Gas! The Story of the Special Brigade* (Edinburgh and London, 1934), p. 196.

6. The story of the Canadians at Vimy has been vividly recounted in Pierre Berton's excellent book, *Vimy* (Toronto, 1986).

7. All reports cited in connection with this incident are from PRO/WO158/270. As of February the reorganization of the gas units had not yet come into force, and this unit still operated under the structure of 4a Battalion. Its commander, Captain Garden, however, was sick in the hospital, and taking his place temporarily was Lieutenant Davies, C Company.

8. They achieved a typical discharge rate of 92 percent, the unused percentage largely due to locally unfavorable conditions on the extreme right flank. On the 12th Brigade front, Lt. D. West's sections 71 and 72 achieved a discharge of 97 percent.

9. Foulkes, *Gas!* p. 247.

10. PRO/WO95/242, War Diary, E Company, March 1917.

11. PRO/WO95/401, War Diary, J Company, 3–4 April 1917.

12. "Gas Warfare," in Institute of Royal Engineers, *History of the Corps of Royal Engineers*, vol. 5, *The Home Front, France, Flanders, and Italy in the Great War* (London, 1952), pp. 520–523.

13. George Pollitt claimed that a solitary gas section ought to be capable of carrying out an "eight-mortar shoot" at 48 hours' notice [REM, 6106-06, Special Brigade, R.E., s.i.e, Walter Campbell-Smith Papers, "Attack Notes, Opera-

tions under Major Pollitt, O.C., Special Companies, R.E., 5th Army," by W. Campbell-Smith, O.C., P Company (written up in 1919), p. 2].

14. J. A. Cochrane, "The Special Brigade, Royal Engineers," *Chambers's Journal* (January 1920): 253.

15. PRO/WO95/486, War Diary, Z Company, Report No. Z/632 Lieutenant J. W. Bansall, 10 May 1917.

16. For some Yellow Star discharges, see PRO/WO95/549, War Diary, C Company, October and November 1917.

17. Martin Sidney Fox, "Corporals All" (typescript, 1965), p. 78; Foulkes, *Gas!* p. 193. When tested at Helfaut in battle simulation, Green Star was too easily ignited by incendiary bombs, throwing parapet pipes back into the trenches.

18. LHCMA, Foulkes Diary, 5 and 7 July 1917.

19. PRO/WO95/120, War Diary, HQ, Special Brigade, 5 and 7 July 1917.

20. PRO/WO95/401, War Diary, K Company, June 1917. An exhaustive list of the chemical compounds employed in World War I, dates of first use, employing countries, harassing concentration, lethal dosage, code names, and their physiological effects may be found in Stockholm International Peace Research Institute (SIPRI), vol. 1 (Stockholm and New York, 1971), pp. 31–52.

21. REL, Guy Crowden Papers, Report, 21 March 1916.

22. Mrs. Norman P. Campbell, *N. P. Campbell, Scientist, Missionary, Soldier* (Cambridge, 1921), p. 32.

23. PRO/WO95/549, War Diary, C Company, 5 March 1917.

24. LC, A. L. Robins, Memo, "Gas."

25. Foulkes, *Gas!* p. 87n1.

26. LC, taped interview by Peter Liddle.

27. PRO/WO95/549, War Diary, C Company, 9 July 1917. When C Company finally discharged them on 9 July, Davies could identify no German casualties positively, but he reported to Foulkes a "great success" based on subsequent reduced rifle fire and machine-gun fire from the sector and observation of 40 to 50 ambulances.

28. Martin Sidney Fox, "With the Special Brigade" (typescript, 1957), p. 68.

29. Foulkes, *Gas!* pp. 196–197.

30. PRO/WO95/549, War Diary, C Company, 17 April 1917.

31. LC, reminiscence of Capt. G. B. Riddell, 13th Battalion, Northumberland Fusiliers, who was working with the 21st Division at the time of this incident in July 1917.

32. PRO/WO32/5174, Douglas Haig to War Office, 2 April 1917.

33. REM, John Thomas Diary, 14 August 1917.

34. Memo of Lieutenant Platnauer, O Company, *SBNL* 14 (February 1966): 16.

35. Fox, "Corporals All," pp. 103–104.

36. PRO/WO95/334, War Diary, H Company, 29 May 1917.

37. PRO/WO95/120, Memo circulated by Foulkes, 7 June 1917.

38. *SBNL* 49 (April 1981): 11.

39. REM, Thomas Diary, 9 June 1916.

40. For a typical joint operation (with G Company in mid-May), see PRO/WO95/486, "Operation Order #6."

41. PRO/WO95/486, War Diary, Z Company, 24 April 1917.

42. PRO/WO95/242, War Diary, E Company, 14 May 1917.

43. PRO/WO95/402, Appendix 15, War Diary, N Company, 28 April 1917.

44. PRO/WO95/402, War Diary, N Company, 12 May 1917.

45. REL, Crowden Papers, 940.3:623.459:355, 486 (R.E.) A. 23287 Folder 1.

46. Fox, "Corporals All," p. 132.
47. S.S. 184. A complete run of these pamphlets may be found in the NAM.
48. PRO/WO95/334, War Diary, H Company, July 1917; PRO/WO95/401, War Diary, K Company, July 1917.
49. Fox, "Corporals All," pp. 81–82.
50. LC, Eden Papers, Summer 1917.
51. In October 1917, a delegation of Russians arrived to witness a demonstration at Helfaut, after which Foulkes delivered a lecture in French, a language which Hodgkin thought few of them understood (IMW, Adrian Hodgkin Diary, 2 October 1917). In February 1918, a delegation of ten Serbian officers enrolled in the Helfaut Gas School. The Italians asked for but did not always take the advice of the British in both defensive and offensive gas use. The Italian gas companies, Compagnia Lanciagas, preferred the flame-thrower to other gas delivery systems, which they bravely ignited with a rag soaked in oil, itself lit with hand-held matches (PRO/WO142/184, file AGD/15 "Report on Italian Gas Organization," p. 14).
52. PRO/WO142/9.
53. *SBNL* 46 (November 1979): 18.
54. Foulkes, *Gas!* p. 191.
55. Ibid., p. 233.

CHAPTER 15. THE LAST SEASON: 1918

1. CAC, Harold Hartley Papers, Box 31. The title of this wonderfully cadenced marching song is "There Was Mary." The delicious irony of this last verse must date this to the period around the armistice when many companies had been sent to aid the Yanks.
2. IWM, Robert Wilson Diary, January–March 1918.
3. PRO/WO95/241, War Diary, A Company, November 1917 to January 1918.
4. PRO/WO95/402, War Diary, N Company, January 1918.
5. IWM, Wilson Diary, January–March 1918.
6. LC, T. Eden Papers.
7. Charles Howard Foulkes, *Gas! The Story of the Special Brigade* (Edinburgh and London, 1934), p. 278.
8. PRO/WO95/242, War Diary, E Company, 23 December 1917.
9. PRO/WO95/241, War Diary, A Company, January 1918.
10. In March 1918, three regiments were authorized; this was later increased to nine regiments (54 companies), but only the six companies of the First Gas Regiment saw service in France [Ludwig F. Haber, *The Poisonous Cloud, Chemical Warfare in the First World War* (Oxford, 1986), p. 219].
11. *SBNL* 34 (November 1974): 7.
12. REM, S-1.c(iv) 6106, Walter Campbell-Smith Papers, "Report on Special Brigade Operations from March to November 1918" (report written by Foulkes, 19 November 1918); Foulkes, *Gas!* p. 277.
13. LC, W. T. Stirling, a reminiscence, "I Fell Back from St. Quentin," p. 2.
14. PRO WO95/120, War Diary, Depot, 1 March 1918.
15. PRO/WO95/240, War Diary, HQ, Special Companies with First Army, 1 March 1918.
16. D. M. Wilson, "March, 1918, and the U.S. Gas Companies," *SBNL* 42 (November 1977): 12; *SBNL* 44 (November 1978): pp. 3–5.
17. IWM, Wilson Diary, January–March 1918.

18. LHCMA, John Oakey Papers, War Diary, No. 1 Special Company, 25 March 1918.

19. PRO/WO95/242, War Diary, E Company, March 1918.

20. PRO/WO95/241, War Diary, A Company, 31 March 1918.

21. PRO/WO95/549, War Diary, C Company, March 1918; WO95/120, War Diary, Depot, March 1918.

22. REM, 6106-06, S.4(h), "Q Special Company, R.E., 1916–1918," by "Anguish" (Angove), p. 7.

23. REM, Campbell-Smith Papers, "Report on Special Brigade Operations."

24. Foulkes, Gas! p. 281.

25. "Collecting Projectors," SBNL 39 (November 1976): 9.

26. SBNL 34 (November 1974): 7.

27. PRO/WO95/240, War Diary, HQ Special Companies with First Army, April 1918.

28. PRO/WO95/120, War Diary, HQ, Special Brigade, 13 April 1918.

29. REM, Donald Grantham Diary, April 1918.

30. PRO/WO95/120, War Diary, Depot, 13 April 1918.

31. Martin Sidney Fox, "Corporals All" (typescript, 1965), p. 102.

32. LHCMA, Oakey Papers, War Diary, No. 1 Special Company, 13 and 14 June 1918.

33. Amos Fries and C. West, Chemical Warfare (New York, 1921), pp. 34–35.

34. Haber, Poisonous Cloud, p. 135.

35. William Moore, Gas Attack! Chemical Warfare, 1915 to the Present Day (London and New York, 1987), p. 184; Foulkes, Gas!, p. 140.

36. Haber, Poisonous Cloud, pp. 269 and 286.

37. Several photos of these petrol-tractors appear in "Light Railways of the BEF," Stand To! 6 (December 1982): 10–11.

38. P. N. Dawes, O Company, SBNL 33 (July 1974): 16.

39. Foulkes claimed that at first each company improvised its own means of electrical blowing of the cylinders (LHCMA, Foulkes Papers, J-4, Letter, Foulkes to War Office, 7 October 1921). D. M. Wilson of M Company claimed that Foulkes had originally planned for cylinder opening by hand, and that he, Wilson, had suggested a sealed outlet tube (SOT) by which the outlets might be opened more safely by simultaneous remote electrical detonators. Wilson claimed Foulkes "turned the idea down completely," but Wilson nevertheless obtained a War Office patent for the device. Foulkes reluctantly allowed Wilson to try his device at Robecq on 13 May, but when its success attracted some attention at GHQ, he was "promptly removed" from M Company command. When the two met after the war, Wilson claimed that Foulkes admitted he had sent Wilson off "because I [Wilson] was the 'inventive' type!" (CAC, Hartley Papers, Wilson to Hartley, 24 May 1971).

40. PRO/WO95/241, War Diary, B Company, 24–25 May 1918.

41. PRO/WO95/240, War Diary, HQ, Special Companies with First Army, 25 May 1918.

42. SBNL 32 (November 1973): 12.

43. PRO/WO95/241, War Diary, A Company, 4–12 July 1918.

44. Fox, "Corporals All," p. 108.

45. REM, Grantham Diary, 13 July 1918.

46. PRO/WO95/241, War Diary, B Company, July 1918.

47. PRO/WO95/242, War Diary, O Company, 12 and 13 July 1918.

48. REM, John Thomas Diary, 21 July 1918.

49. IWM, Adrian Hodgkin Diary, 22 July 1918.

50. REM, Thomas Diary, 7 August 1918.

51. IWM, Robert Wilson Diary, 27 August 1918; Foulkes, *Gas!* p. 297.

52. REM, Campbell-Smith Papers, "Report on Special Brigade Operations."

53. Haber, *Poisonous Cloud,* pp. 222–223.

54. CAC, Hartley Papers, Box 31, File A1, Miscellaneous Letters, Hartley to Gale, no date.

55. PRO/WO95/241, War Diary, A Company, 2 September 1918.

56. LHCMA, John Oakey Papers, War Diary, No. 1 Special Company, 4 September 1918.

57. PRO/WO95/241, War Diary, A Company, 4 and 5 October 1918.

58. IWM, Hodgkin Diary, 26–28 September 1918.

59. Ibid., 2 August 1918.

60. Foulkes, *Gas!* pp. 274–275.

61. PRO/WO95/549, War Diary, HQ, Special Companies with Fifth Army, Memo, 27 October 1918.

62. IWM, Wilson Diary, 15 October 1918.

63. REM, Thomas Diary, 19 October 1918.

64. *SBNL* 18 (July 1967): 16.

65. *SBNL* 20 (July 1968): 14–15. The Mons Star was an award that commemorated the famous "Retreat from Mons" of 1914.

66. REM, Campbell-Smith Papers, "Report on Special Brigade Operations."

67. PRO/WO95/242, War Diary, E Company, 8 April 1918.

68. PRO/WO95/549, War Diary, C Company, 13 July 1918.

69. IWM, Hodgkin Diary, 29 October 1918.

70. *SBNL* 32 (November 1973): 9–10 (copied from *Chemical and Engineering News,* 19 March 1973).

71. REM, Wilson Diary, 11 November 1918.

72. IWM, Hodgkin Diary, 12 November 1918.

73. REM, Thomas Diary, December 1918.

74. PRO/WO95/549, War Diary, C Company, December 1918; LHCMA, Oakey Papers, War Diary, No. 3 Company, January 1919.

75. IWM, Hodgkin Diary, 14 November 1918.

76. PRO/WO95/401, War Diary, N Company, November 1918.

77. LHCMA, Oakey Papers, War Diary, No. 1 Special Company, January 1919.

78. *SBNL* 21 (January 1969): 11–12. See also PRO/WO142/253, "A Historical Record of H.M. Cylinder Depot, Hamley, Staffs."

79. REM, Grantham Diary, 27 September 1919.

80. F. J. Scrase, "Porton Revisited," *SBNL* 24 (July 1970): 7–8.

CHAPTER 16. NO HUMANITARIAN SCRUPLES

1. PRO/WO188/213, Major Galwery, lecture to Staff College, Camberly, 18 February 1928.

2. For a popular summary of chemical weapons in antiquity, see B. W. Richardson, "Greek Fire: Its Ancient and Modern History" *Popular Science Review* 3 (January 1964), 164–177.

3. For a thoughtful discussion of the emotional reaction to gas warfare and its obstruction of objective analysis, see Ludwig F. Haber, "Gas Warfare, 1915–1945: Legend and the Facts" (Stevenson Lecture, 1975), pp. 3ff.

4. Martin Sidney Fox, "With the Special Brigade" (typescript, 1957), p. 6.

5. Victor Lefebure, *The Riddle of the Rhine: Chemical Strategy in Peace and War* (London, 1921), p. 28.

6. IWM, Dept. of Sound Recordings, Tape of James Davidson Pratt, #000495/06.

7. Letter to the editor from Conway Knapp of Graybill, Indiana, veteran of the 1st American Gas Regiment, *Chemical and Engineering News* 51 (March 1973): 48.

8. IWM, Charles Allen Ashley Diary, 19 July 1915.

9. Mrs. Norman P. Campbell, *N. P. Campbell: Scientist, Missionary, Soldier* (Cambridge, 1921), pp. 35–36.

10. The British raw data on gas casualties is found in literally hundreds of bulging boxes in the PRO under the general classification WO142. See also T. J. Mitchell and G. M. Smith, *Medical Services: Casualties and Medical Statistics of the Great War* (London, 1931). The most recent distillation of the medical data contained in the above-mentioned work, which is the official medical history of the war, is again Ludwig F. Haber, *The Poisonous Cloud: Chemical Warfare in the First World War* (Oxford, 1986), pp. 239–258. Haber analyzes in detail the figures of experts such as Douglas, Gilchrist, Prentiss, and Hanslian, all participants in chemical warfare in the First World War. For a simplified distillation, see also J. F. C. Fuller, *Thunderbolts* (London, 1946), pp. 70–71.

11. CAC, Harold Hartley Papers, Box 43, undated letter, Claude Douglas to Hartley.

12. J. B. S. Haldane, *Callinicus, A Defence of Chemical Warfare* (London, 1925). The author was the son of Lord Haldane, the great physiologist who had advised on gas defense in 1915.

13. Lefebure, *Riddle of the Rhine*, p. 237.

14. LC, A. L. Robins Papers.

15. LC, H. A. Siepman Papers, Letter to his mother, 16 September 1918.

16. LHCMA, Foulkes Papers, J-1. The date on the notation is December 1980.

17. CAC, Hartley Papers, Box 44, "Notes on a Conversation with Sir Harold Hartley [and Thuillier]," 14 August 1945.

18. Quoted in Foulkes Papers, J-17.

19. Lefebure, *Riddle of the Rhine*, p. 170.

20. Brian Bond, *Liddell Hart: A Study of His Military Thought* (London, 1977), p. 50; Sir Basil Liddell Hart, *A History of the First World War, 1914–1918* (London, 1972), p. 145. In his *Thoughts on War* (London, 1944), p. 174, Liddell Hart characterized gas as "ten to twelve times as humane a weapon" as the bullet or high explosive shell. See also his article "The Napoleonic Fallacy: the Moral Objective in War," *Empire Review* (May, 1925).

21. Gary Thatcher, "In War, Is One Type of Killing More Immoral Than Another?" *Poison on the Wind, Christian Science Monitor* Special Report, 1988.

22. LHCMA, Foulkes Papers, J-21.

23. *Daily Graphic*, 13 October 1921.

24. IWM, Richard Gale Diary, 22 September 1915.

25. CAC, Hartley Papers, George Pollitt to Hartley, 30 October 1960.

26. LC, Walter Campbell-Smith Papers.

27. LC, J. C. Hill Papers, Lecture, November 1919, p. 12.

28. IWM, Adrian Hodgkin Diary, 6 November 1917.

29. CAC, Hartley Papers, Box 44, William Pope to Hartley, 20 August 1917.

30. A. J. Flintham, "Gas Warfare in World War I," *Education in Chemistry* 15: 6 (November 1978): 175–177. The Smithells Papers are in the archives of the Brotherton Library at the University of Leeds.

31. LHCMA, Foulkes Papers, J-56, Foulkes to C. E. Brigham, Chief of Chemical Warfare Service, U. S. War Department, 3 November 1935.

32. Martin Sidney Fox, "Corporals All" (typescript, 1965), p. 38. The verse is the third stanza of the popular song "Corporals All."

33. Charles Howard Foulkes, Gas! The Story of the Special Brigade (Edinburgh and London, 1934), p. 209.

34. Ibid., p. 184

35. CAC, Hartley Papers, Box 44, "Fritz Haber," p. 6.

36. PRO/CAB45/120, C. D. Bruce to J. E. Edmonds, 23 May 1927.

37. IWM, Dept. of Sound Recordings, Tape of Victor Fagence, 000327/08/RO3.

38. LC, George Grossmith Papers.

39. The "live and let live" system is thoroughly analyzed by Tony Ashworth in Trench Warfare, 1914–1918: The Live and Let Live System (New York, 1980).

40. LHCMA, John Oakey Papers, War Diary, No. 1 Special Company, 29 June–25 July and 10 August 1918.

41. IWM, Dept. of Documents, F18.3, W. J. N. Howell Papers.

42. Shelford Bidwell and Dominick Graham, Fire-Power: British Army Weapons and Theories of War, 1904–1945 (Boston, 1985). See especially chap. 2, "The Tactics of Separate Tables."

43. Guy Hartcup, The War of Invention (London, 1988) p. 114.

44. CAC, Hartley Papers, Wilson to Hartley, 24 May 1971.

45. Lefebure, Riddle of the Rhine, p. 42.

46. Haber, Poisonous Cloud, p. 267.

47. Charles Howard Foulkes, "Chemical Warfare Now and in 1915," REJ 76 (March–December 1962): 183.

48. In 1917, E Company concocted a harmless discharge of forty-five cylinders filled with a mixture containing bone oil, an evil-smelling viscid substance; and seventy-five cylinders filled with water and two ounces of benzyl bromide dissolved in a pint of petrol to delude the enemy into thinking the gas was lethal (PRO/WO95/242, War Diary, E Company, 5 November 1917).

49. LC, taped interview by Peter Liddle.

50. LHCMA, Oakey Papers, War Diary, No. 3 Company, 26 June 1918.

51. LHCMA, Foulkes Papers, J-21, Speech to the Second Army, 28 April 1917.

52. REM, S-1.c(iv) 6106, Walter Campbell-Smith Papers, "Report on Special Brigade Operations from March to November, 1918" (written by Foulkes, 19 November 1918).

53. LHCMA, Foulkes Papers, J-45, Lt. Col. W. Twiss to F. R. Bingham, 26 February 1920.

54. LHCMA, Foulkes Papers, J-5, speech at Imperial College, 1922.

55. CAC, Hartley Papers, Box 31, Hartley to Douglas, 11 June 1958. Capt. T. H. Adams was Foulkes's intelligence officer.

56. PRO/T173/702, Pt. 2, p. 25.

57. H. Cotton, "Memoirs of an Army Meteorologist," Pt. 1, Meteorological Magazine 108 (August 1979): 243. Cotton's full memoirs are in IWM, 79/17/1T.

58. IWM, Dept. of Sound Recordings, Tape of James Davidson Pratt, 000495/06, RO4.

59. J. B. S. Haldane, "Science and Future Warfare," RUSIJ 82 (November 1937): 722–723.

60. CAC, Hartley Papers, Box 31, Hartley to Douglas, 26 March 1958.

61. Quoted in Edwin M. Spiers, Chemical Warfare (Urbana and Chicago, 1986), p. 33.

62. CAC, Hartley Papers, Box 43, Hartley to Pollitt, 28 August 1960. See Haber, *Poisonous Cloud*, p. 347n66.

63. CAC, Hartley Papers, Box 31, Hartley to Zucherman, 22 February 1966.

64. Haber, *Poisonous Cloud*, p. 259.

65. Ibid., p. 90.

66. The question may have taken him somewhat by surprise, for Campbell-Smith, also an Engineer, had in writing complimented Foulkes for his paternal consideration of his officers.

67. Haber, *Poisonous Cloud*, p. 90.

68. Foulkes, *Gas!* p. 86.

69. LHCMA, Foulkes Papers, J-1, speech at reunion dinner, 31 March 1922.

70. LC, T. Eden Papers, Diary, 1917.

71. Fox, "Corporals All," p. 105.

72. Ibid., pp. 102-103.

73. Ashworth, *Trench Warfare, 1914-1918*, pp. 157ff.

74. LHCMA, Foulkes Papers, J-1. Foulkes's manuscript draft for chap. 20, vol. 5, of "History of the Royal Engineers."

75. Winston Churchill, long a proponent of gas warfare, as colonial secretary after the war repeatedly urged the use of mustard gas during British gas "police bombings" of Kurds and other rebel groups in Iraq and elsewhere. See David Omissi, "British Bombing When the Natives Were Restless," *Manchester Guardian Weekly* 1 (March 1991), p. 21.

76. LHCMA, Foulkes Papers, Diary, June or July 1919.

77. LHCMA, Foulkes Papers, J-60. The following year, 1920, Foulkes's brother was murdered in Kohat.

EPILOGUE

1. LHCMA, Foulkes Papers, J-56, E. A. Berrisford to Foulkes, 11 August 1933.

2. LHCMA, Foulkes Papers, J-58.

3. LHCMA, Foulkes Papers, J-9.

4. REM, 7810-08.

APPENDIX B

1. LHCMA, Foulkes Papers, J-1, speech to reunion dinner, 4 February, 1933.

2. LHCMA, Foulkes Papers, J-56, Churchill to Foulkes, 31 October 1933.

3. Lord Cavan, at the time a field marshall and CIGS, had had paractically nothing to do with gas warfare and seems an oddly inappropriate choice. It was Cavan who had commanded the guards at Loos, and whose troops had entered the battle on the 26th, relieving the 21st and the 24th divisions, but gas played no part in the action. LHCMA, Foulkes Papers, J-56, Foulkes to Blackwood, 24 June 1934.

4. LHCMA, Foulkes Papers, J-56, Wigram to Foulkes, 27 October 1933.

5. LHCMA, Foulkes Papers, J-56, Wigram to Foulkes, 30 October 1933.

6. LHCMA, Foulkes Papers, J-56, Cavan to Foulkes, 17 November 1933: "If you connect them with 'Frightfulness,' it will be misinterpreted in many quarters."

7. LHCMA, Foulkes Papers, J-56, Wigram to Cavan, 18 November 1933.

8. LHCMA, Foulkes Papers, J-56, Foulkes to Cavan, 19 November 1933.

9. LHCMA, Foulkes Papers, J-56, Cavan to Foulkes, 20 November 1933.

10. Photo in Charles Howard Foulkes, *Gas! The Story of the Special Brigade* (Edinburgh and London, 1934), opposite page 238.

11. LHCMA, Foulkes Papers, J-56, Foulkes to Blackwood, 27 March 1934. The price of the book was a hefty 30/.

12. Foulkes Papers, J-56, Raymond Savage Ltd. to Foulkes, 7 March 1935.

13. LHCMA, Foulkes Papers, J-56, C. E. Brigham to Foulkes and H. L. Stafford to Foulkes, 16 November 1937.

Selected Bibliography

PAPERS AND UNPUBLISHED DIARIES

Ashley, Charles Allen. Imperial War Museum.
Campbell-Smith, Walter. Liddle Collection, Leeds, and Royal Engineers Museum.
Dawson, Robert. Liddle Collection, Leeds.
Eastham, Leonard E. S. Liddle Collection, Leeds.
Edwards-Ker, Douglas R. Liddle Collection, Leeds.
Foulkes, Charles Howard. Liddell Hart Centre for Military Archives. King's College London.
French, Sir John. Imperial War Museum.
Gale, Richard C. Imperial War Museum.
Gilliat, William. Imperial War Museum.
Grantham, Donald. Royal Engineers Museum.
Hartley, Sir Harold. Churchill College, Cambridge.
Heaseman, B. R. Royal Engineers Museum.
Hodgkin, Adrian Eliot. Imperial War Museum.
Kitchener Papers. Public Record Office.
Mitchell, G. O. Imperial War Museum.
Mitchell, Luther G. Imperial War Museum.
Oakey, John ("Jack") Martin. Liddell Hart Centre for Military Archives.
Parkes, Thomas. Liddell Hart Centre for Military Archives, King's College London.
Powell, Garfield. Imperial War Museum.
Purves, R. B. Royal Engineers Museum.
Rawlinson, Henry S. Churchill College, Cambridge, and National Army Museum.
Stirling, W. T. Liddle Collection, Leeds.
Thomas, John Miles. Royal Engineers Museum.
Thomas, Meiron. Liddle Collection, Leeds.
Wilson, Robert W. Imperial War Museum.
Winn, Frank. Royal Engineers Museum.

ARTICLES AND LECTURES

Auld, S. J. M. "Chemical Warfare" *REJ* (February 1921): 58–71.
Bernstein, Barton J. "Why We Didn't Use Poison Gas in World War II." *American Heritage* (August–September 1985): 40–45.

Cave, Terry. "The Indian Army Corps." Pt. 2. *Stand To!* 14 (September 1985): 24–29.

Cochrane, J. A. "The Special Brigade, Royal Engineers." *Chambers's Journal.* Pt. 112 (1 April 1920): 251–256.

Cotton, H. "Memoirs of an Army Meteorologist." *Meteorological Magazine* 108 (August 1979): 241–247; (September 1979): 276–285; (November 1979): 341–347; (January 1980): 22–26; (February, 1980): 58–63.

"The First British Gas Attack." *Chemistry and Industry* 46 (November 1960): 1395.

"The First Gas Attack: A German Expert's View." *Army Quarterly* 30 (July 1935): 302–305.

Flintham, A. J. "Gas Warfare in World War I." *Education in Chemistry* 15:6 (November 1978): 175–177.

Foulkes, Charles Howard. "Chemical Warfare Now and in 1915." *REJ* 76 (March–December 1962): 177–184.

———. "Fire, Smoke and Gas." *Journal for the Society for Army Historical Research* 19 (1940): 144–148.

Fox, Leon A. "Bacteriological Warfare." *RUSIJ* 78 (August 1933): 523–538.

Haber, Ludwig F. "Gas Warfare, 1915–1945: The Legend and the Facts." Stevenson Lecture, 1975. Presented at Bedford College, University of London, 1976 (copy at IWM).

Haldane, J. B. S. "Science and Future Warfare." *RUSIJ* 82 (November 1937): 711–728.

Hartley, Harold. "A General Comparison of British and German Methods of Gas Warfare." *RUSIJ* 46 (December 1920): 492–509.

Jones, Simon. "Gas Warfare: The British Defensive Measures. Part 1: The Second Battle of Ypres." *Stand To!* 14 (September 1985): 15–23.

———. "Under a Green Sea: The British Responses to Gas Warfare." *The Great War, 1914–1918* 1:4 (August 1989): 126–132 and 2:1 (November 1989): 14–21.

Lefebure, Victor. "Chemical Warfare." *RUSIJ* 73 (August 1928): 492–507.

Messenger, Charles. "Second Ypres." *War Monthly* 10 (July 1987): 328–335.

Poole, J. B. "A Sword Undrawn: Chemical Warfare and the Victorian Age." *Army Quarterly* 106 (October 1976): 463–469 and 107 (January 1977): 87–92.

Pope, Sir William. "The Case for Chemical Warfare." *Chemical Age* 4 (May 1921): 523–527.

Richardson, B. W. "Greek Fire: Its Ancient and Modern History." *Popular Science Review* 3 (January 1964): 164–177.

Scott, Peter. "Mr Stokes and His Educated Drainpipe." *The Great War, 1914–1918* 2:3 (May 1990): 80–95.

Thatcher, Gary. "In War, Is One Type of Killing More Immoral Than Another?" *Poison on the Wind, Christian Science Monitor* Special Report, 1988.

BOOKS

Ashworth, Tony. *Trench Warfare, 1914–1918*: The Live and Let Live System. New York, 1980.

Auld, S. J. M. *Gas and Flame*. New York, 1918.

Berton, Pierre. *Vimy*. Toronto, 1986.

Bidwell, Shelford, and Dominick Graham. *Fire-Power: British Army Weapons and Theories of War, 1904–1945*. Boston and London, 1985.

Blake, Robert, ed. *The Private Papers of Douglas Haig, 1914–1919*. London, 1952.

Bond, Brian. *Liddell Hart: A Study of His Military Thought*. London, 1977.

Browne, F. J. *Chemical Warfare: A Study in Restraints*. Princeton, N.J., 1968.

Callwell, C. E. *Field Marshall Sir Henry Wilson: His Life and Diaries*. 2 vols. London, 1927.

Campbell, Mrs. Norman P. *N. P. Campbell: Scientist, Missionary, Soldier*. Cambridge, 1921.

Carver, R. B., and J. M. Fenwick. *A History of the 10th (Service) Battalion, the East Yorkshire Regiment (Hull Commercials), 1914–1919*. London, 1937.

Charteris, John. *At GHQ*. London, 1931.

Collier, Basil. *Brasshat: A Biography of Field Marshall Sir Henry Wilson*. London, 1961.

Douglas, Sir George, and Sir George Dalhousie Ramsey, eds. *The Panmure Papers: Being a Selection from the Correspondence of Fox Maule, 2nd Baron Panmure, Afterwards 11th Earl of Dalhousie*. 2 vols. London, 1908.

Dunn, J. C. *The War the Infantry Knew*. London, 1987.

Edmonds, Sir J. E. *Military Operations: France and Belgium*. 14 vols. London, 1922–1949.

Ellis, J. *Eye Deep in Hell*. London, 1977

Farrar-Hockley, Anthony. *Goughie: The Life of Gen. Sir Hubert Gough*. London, 1975.

Foulkes, Charles Howard. *Gas! The Story of the Special Brigade*. Edinburgh and London, 1934.

Fox, Martin Sidney. "Corporals All" 1965. Typescript.

———. "With the Special Brigade, R.E.: A Brief History of 186 Company, R.E., and C Special Company, R.E., 1915–1919. 1957. Typescript.

Fries, Amos, and C. J. West. *Chemical Warfare*. New York, 1921.

Fuller, J. F. C. *Thunderbolts*. London, 1946.

Fussel, Paul. *The Great War and Modern Memory*. Oxford, 1975.

Gilchrist, H. L. *A Comparative Study of World War Casualties from Gas and Other Weapons*. Washington, D.C., 1931.

Gough, Sir Hubert. *The Fifth Army*. London, 1931.

Graves, Robert. *Good-bye to All That*. London, 1929.

Haber, Ludwig F. *The Poisonous Cloud: Chemical Warfare in the First World War*. Oxford, 1986.

Haldane, J. B. S. *Callinicus: A Defence of Chemical Warfare*. London, 1925.

Hallengren, Anders. *Operation Hades*. London, 1981.

Hanslian, Rudolph, ed. *Der chemische Krieg*. Berlin, 1925.

Harris, Robert, and Jeremy Paxman. *A Higher Form of Killing: The Secret Story of Gas and Germ Warfare*. London, 1982.

Hartcup, Guy. *The War of Invention*. London, 1988.

Inglefield, V. E. *The History of the Twentieth (Light) Division*. London, 1921.

Langer, William. *Gas and Flame in World War I*. New York, 1965.

Lefebure, Victor. *The Riddle of the Rhine: Chemical Strategy in Peace and War*. London, 1921.

Liddell Hart, Sir Basil. *A History of the First World War, 1914–1918*. London, 1934; reprinted 1972.

———. *Thoughts on War*. London, 1944.

———. *Through the Fog of War*. London 1938.

Lloyd, C. *Lord Cochrane*. London, 1947.

Ludendorff, Erich. *My War Memories*. London, 1920.

Macpherson, W. G. *History of the Great War Based on Official Documents:*

Medical Services, General History, Vol. 2, *The Medical Services on the Western Front and during the Operations in France and Belgium in 1914 and 1915*. London, 1923.

McWilliams, James L., and R. James Steel. *Gas! The Battle for Ypres, 1915*. St. Catharines, Ontario, 1985.

Maude, Alan H. *The 47th (London) Division, 1914–1919*. London, 1922.

Maurice, Sir Frederick. *The History of the London Rifle Brigade, 1859–1919*. London, 1921.

_____. *The Life of General Lord Rawlinson of Trent from His Journals and Letters*. London, 1928.

Meyer, Philip Julius. *Der Gaskampf und die chemischen Kampfstoffe*. Leipzig, 1938.

Mitchell, T. J., and G. M. Smith. *Medical Services: Casualties and Medical Statistics of the Great War*. London, 1931.

Moore, William. *Gas Attack! Chemical Warfare, 1915 to the Present Day*. London and New York, 1987.

Pershing, John J. *My Experiences in the World War*. 2 vols. New York, 1931.

Peterson, H. C. *Propaganda for War*. Norman, Okla., 1968.

Popham, Hugh. *The Dorset Regiment*. London, 1970.

Prentiss, A. M. *Chemicals in War*. New York and London, 1937.

Robertson, William. *Soldiers and Statesmen, 1914–1918*. 2 vols. London, 1926.

Sartori, M. *The War Gases*. London, 1940.

Sassoon, Siegfried. *Diaries, 1915–1918*. London, 1983.

_____. *Memoirs of a Fox-Hunting Man*. London, 1965.

_____. *Memoirs of an Infantry Officer*. London, 1931.

Schwarte, M., ed. *Die Technik im Weltkriege*. Berlin, 1920.

Slowe, Peter, and Richard Woods. *Fields of Death: Battle Scenes of the First World War*. London, 1986.

Spiers, Edward M. *Chemical Warfare*. Urbana and Chicago, 1986.

Stallings, Lawrence. *The Doughboys: The Story of the AEF, 1917–1918*. New York, 1963.

Stewart, John, and John Buchan. *The Fifteenth (Scottish) Division, 1914–1919*. London, 1926.

Stockholm International Peace Research Institute (SIPRI). *The Problems of Chemical and Biological Warfare*, Vol. 1, *The Rise of CB Weapons*. Stockholm and New York, 1971.

Terraine, John. *The First World War, 1914–1918*. 2d ed. London, 1985.

_____. *The Smoke and the Fire: Myths and Anti-Myths of War, 1861–1945*. London, 1981.

_____. *White Heat: The New Warfare, 1914–1918*. London 1982.

Thuillier, Sir Henry. *Gas in the Next War*. London, 1939.

Travers, Tim. *The Killing Ground: The British Army, the Western Front, and the Emergence of Modern Warfare, 1900–1918*. London, 1987.

Waitt, Alden H. *Gas Warfare*. New York, 1942.

Warner, Philip. *The Battle of Loos*. London 1976.

Watkin, T. F. *Chemical Warfare*. New York, 1968.

Williamson, Henry. *A Fox under My Cloak*. London, 1955.

Wilson, Trevor. *The Myriad Faces of War*. Oxford, 1986.

Winter, Denis. *Death's Men*. London, 1978.
———. *Haig's Command: A Reassessment*. London, 1991.
Woodward, David R. *Military Correspondence of F. M. Sir William Robertson CIGS*. London, 1989.
Wyrall, E. *The History of the 19th Division, 1914–1918*. London, 1932.

Index